# TRANSNATIONAL SOCIAL POLICIES

# TRANSNATIONAL SOCIAL POLICIES

## The New Development Challenges of Globalization

Edited by
Daniel Morales-Gómez

INTERNATIONAL DEVELOPMENT RESEARCH CENTRE
Ottawa • Cairo • Dakar • Johannesburg • Montevideo • Nairobi • New Delhi • Singapore

Earthscan Publications Ltd, London

© International Development Research Centre 1999

**Published in North America by the International Development Research Centre**
**PO Box 8500, Ottawa, ON, Canada K1G 3H9**

Canadian Cataloguing in Publication Data

Main entry under title :
Transnational social policies : the new development challenges of globalization

Includes bibliographical references.

ISBN 0-88936-854-6

1. Developing countries — Social policy.
2. Income distribution — Developing countries.
3. Developing countries — Economic conditions.
4. Africa — Social policy.
5. Asia — Social policy.
6. Latin America — Social policy.
I. Morales-Gomez, Daniel A. (Daniel Antonio), 1946–   .
II. International Development Research Centre (Canada).

HC60.M67 1998      338.9'009172'4      C99-980007-8


**Published in Europe by Earthscan Publications Ltd**
**120 Pentonville Road, London, N1 9JN, UK**

UK Cataloguing in Publication Data

A catalogue record for this book is available from the British Library.

ISBN 1 85383 633 8

For a full list of publications, please contact:
Earthscan Publications Ltd
120 Pentonville Road, London, N1 9JN, UK
Tel: +44 (0)171 278 0433
Fax: +44 (0)171 278 1142
Email: earthinfo@earthscan.co.uk
http://www.earthscan.co.uk

Earthscan is an editorially independent subsidiary of Kogan Page Ltd and publishes in association with WWF-UK and the International Institute for Environment and Development.

# CONTENTS

# FOREWORD

When concepts become slogans, intelligent debate is extinguished. The term "globalization" is now on that slippery slope. After a decade of researchers' breast-beating about its evil impacts, a growing body of opinion (backed up by trade figures) asserts that economies were just as open at the end of the 19th century as they are today. It is reassuring then that a number of essays in this book secure their analyses firmly within historical and geographical boundaries. So let us just say that globalization is a fact and get down to the task of understanding how, by whom, and for whom social policy is made and how it is financed. After all, Canada, with one of the world's most open economies, has built a reasonably equitable society and, for years, has been ranked number one in the league tables of the *Human Development Report* of the United Nations Development Programme.

An important contribution of the essays in this book is to remind us that it is impossible to divorce social policy from political institutions. The concept of social policy itself is linked to the specific historical evolution of modern Western societies. It is appropriate then that in 1998, the 150th anniversary of the 1848 revolutions in Europe, we review how societies are tackling issues of social inequality.

The political evolution that one century later gave us the welfare state gathered speed during a time that was remarkably like our own. The "champions of progress" were as enthusiastic then as their counterparts in business associations are today, with their confidence that the free forces of commerce will lead us to a happier, wiser, and peaceful civilization.

At the national level, the political changes in response to the dark side of this progress were muted but satisfactory for the middle classes, resulting in constitutions that may have been antidemocratic but were definitely antiaristocratic. They put paid to feudalism. However, in international politics, Europe (and particularly the United Kingdom) was dominant. Institutional change at the national level was nourished by the injection of political consciousness and permanent political activity among the masses, which was the great legacy of the French Revolution. Today, international mechanisms to achieve a global social balance persistently elude us, as they likely will for some time. Just as in the last century, when trade and capital flowed across geographic boundaries, the political developments of nation-states determine the nature of their social policies, although given the structures of colonial economies some of that trade may have closely resembled the intrafirm transfers of today.

The essays in this book address the challenge of designing transnational policies to achieve social balance in different countries with quite different political and economic histories. The search for transnational social policies will only bear fruit if democratic nation-states with a concern for social balance invest in the construction of international institutions. The example of Canada suggests that a country with a significantly open economy and a democratic political system can also build a fair society.

**Maureen O'Neil**
President
International Development Research Centre
Ottawa, Canada

# Introduction

## From National to Transnational Social Policies

*Daniel Morales-Gómez*

At the close of the 20th century, new expectations for a better society — prompted by forces of economic, political, and cultural globalization, changing demographics and new communication and information technologies — accelerate demands for comprehensive and effective public-policy reforms. This is happening at a time when governments are preoccupied with making more efficient and effective allocation of scarce resources and the international community realizes that existing development paradigms are inadequate to respond to the needs of the world's poor.

Developing countries in particular continue to struggle to identify developmental options, implement feasible growth strategies, and overcome persistent poverty and domestic social inequality. Industrialized countries, in turn, are beginning to realize that current consumption patters are a liability in maintaining basic domestic standards of social equity, social security, and human development. Internationally, there is an increasing lack of control over future market directions, global trade, the capacity of countries and regions to sustain achieved levels of economic growth, and the rapid social impacts of science and information technologies.

To compete in an increasingly interconnected world, developing countries are improving their international competitiveness, adapting to rapid technological change, and accommodating their production systems to external rather than domestic demands. In the process, social safety nets are weakened, and, as the research in this book indicates, social-sector reforms have been insufficient to strengthen these systems. In the attempt to find feasible solutions, available resources have been shifted away from costly social programs, and responsibility for the social well-being of people is being transferred from the state to the private sector. The effect of these changes is that greater responsibility for survival is placed on the shoulders of the poor and the communities in which they participate. Troubling, under these circumstances, is the growing transnational character of the factors influencing public-policy reforms in the area of basic needs, which have been dealt with until recently almost exclusively within the national domain.

The issue of transnational influences over national policies is not per se a new phenomenon. Traditionally, however, what has been understood as the "transnational dimension" of national development has been mostly limited to the fields of politics and economics. In this context, the notion has referred to a complex set of factors and influences determining decisions across established geopolitical boundaries. In economic terms, for example, it has been instrumental in understanding North–South relationships in regard to monetary issues, trade, and capital flows and accumulation. In political terms, it has been an explanatory factor in the role of national development in the larger scheme of power relations between developed and developing countries.

Today, the transnational dimension is acquiring an even more complex meaning. In a world geopolitically and economically more unidimensional, the transnational dimension of development is more than ever before an effect of globalization (Morales-Gómez and Torres 1995). Although the notion of globalization itself is controversial, central to its transnational character is the scope and magnitude of its intended and unintended impacts. In the past, the influence of capital flows, information and communication technologies, consumption, cultural products, trade, and transfers of science and technology had more limited influences on national decisions. Today, these factors affect national-policy boundaries and are necessary ingredients in national public policies and their reforms. In this sense, transnational influences are no longer single variables affecting only economic and foreign-policy relations between countries but complex sets of factors acting on a wide range of national public-policy decisions that are key to the management of national affairs. How this new scenario ultimately affects national policies linked to human and social development is a question not yet fully addressed.

Public-policy reforms in key social sectors are being promoted by a growing number of governments from industrialized and developing countries, as well as, international organizations, and, in particular, international financial institutions (IFIs). The underlying justification for action has several aspects. It is asserted that such reforms will improve efficiency of public-policy systems; that they are required to implement plans to reduce public deficits; that they will deliver more effective social programs and services; and, that they will ultimately help to improve the capacities of national economies. In this context, economic growth continues to be a dominant goal of public-policy reforms in order to reduce deficits, generate employment, and expand trade. Social development is then simply seen as a byproduct of these reform schemes. The chief schemes. The chief focus remains market liberalization, privatization, smaller and more financially accountable governments, targeting, and less state intervention in service provision. In this framework, the challenges for social development and poverty reduction are seen as those of the availability rather than the redistribution of resources. Policy reforms are thus expected to maximize the use of resources — "doing more with less."

In all these concerns, an overarching issue is not being addressed: the character of the new social ethos guiding policy reforms, an ethos which is increasingly determined by transnational cultural values. Policy changes at the macro- and microlevels are promoted as good and desirable without anyone's questioning the nature of the society pursued through these processes.

## Social-policy reform: a shift in the social-policy paradigm

The current emphasis on social development is reflected in actions by international organizations and governments to bring issues related to social and human development to the forefront of the international development agenda. Events such as the 1990 World summit for Children, the 1990 World Conference on Education for All, the 1992 UN Conference on Environment and Development, the 1993 UN Conference on Population and Development, the 1995 Fourth World Conference on Women, and the 1995 World Summit for Social Development are prominent indicators of this emphasis. Following the economic downturns of the 1970s and 1980s, which deeply affected the developing world, social development has become a priority in the mid-1990s. Development trends during this period made the state, evolution, and health of macroeconomic policies the main developmental concerns of governments and international organizations. John Ralston Saul (1995, pp. 122–123) argued that

> in imitation of the nineteenth century and the 1920's, we are deregulating everything in sight and even restructuring government and education along industry lines. We have fallen back in love with an old ideology that has never paid off in the past.
>
> Now, there are those who will mistake what I say for an anti-market tirade. They will be wrong. I love the market. I like trade, money markets, global economic patterns, all of it. It's like a game. It's fun for those who can afford to have a sense of humour. But I'm not fool enough to mistake these necessary and important narrow mechanisms for a broad, solid, conscious force that can lead society. The history of the marketplace has been repeatedly written by its actions. To ignore that history is to withdraw into severe unconsciousness.

Only the recent signs of the relative failure of a development model based on capital accumulation has made evident that macroeconomic equilibrium alone is not a development solution. Despite this evidence, "we keep hoping that we will rediscover prosperity through this mechanism called market forces" (Saul 1995, p. 122), and with such a goal in mind public policies are being changed on a massive scale.

Reaching macroeconomic equilibrium by itself is not likely to render the type of longer-terms results expected in terms of increased social well-being, better social welfare, and less poverty. This is particularly true if social- and human-development inequalities remain untouched by the reform processes. In this context, a trend is emerging to focus increasingly on social policy in a framework of public-policy reform. The aim is to achieve social-development objectives with more equity, effectiveness, and efficiency. This is the case in most of Latin American and Organisation for Economic Co-operation and Development (OECD) countries (Altimir 1997; Bonvin 1997). In a number of cases, this emphasis is leading to social-policy reforms in key social sectors. However, the emphases, results, and impacts of the experiences are very different, largely unknown, and not critically analyzed.

In some cases, governments and development agencies are stressing the need to put "people first" as a public-policy goal and to give development a "human face" to affirm ways to address social-development needs (Preston 1993; World Bank 1991). In other cases, emphasis is primarily on efficiency, cost-cutting, and balancing fiscal deficits and only secondarily on the needs of human development (Bardhan 1995). What is important here is that the overall tendency to reform public policies is not an isolated phenomenon; rather, it is part of a global trend to change the parameters and role of the welfare state in its various versions in developed and developing countries. The catalyst for this process in the 1970s and 1980s was a set of economic-stabilization measures and structural-adjustment policies to overcome inflation, fiscal deficits, foreign indebtedness, and trade imbalances.

From a broader developmental perspective, the policy-reform approach also reflects a deeper shift in the concept of what is a modern, efficient, and just society. At one level, this is the expression of the forces of economic globalization. In this regard, the OECD Development Centre argued that "an increasing number of developing countries have been pursuing policy reform to promote their integration into the global economy" (Bonvin 1997. p. 40). At another level, it manifests a series of profound social, demographic, and political changes shaping the profile of today's modern industrialized societies and those of many developing countries. Among these changes are rapid rural–urban migration, demographic growth, and democratization. They are added pressures that help to make current social policies unsustainable, inefficient, or ineffective. Perhaps more deeply still, the evolving change in the concept of a modern, efficient, and just society is a reflection of slow but profound changes in the ethics of modernization and development occurring in the second half of this century.

The combination of these factors explains a series of features of social development in developed and developing societies both as they appear today and as they are likely to unfold well into the first decade of the next century. These include persistently unsatisfied basic needs, evident as chronic, even deepening, poverty in some regions; a widening spectrum of altering social needs and increasing social and economic expectations that widen the gap with the growing frustration of vast sectors of the population, especially youth, who are unable to find productive work or access to new social opportunities; and a growing demand for alternative public and private, profit and nonprofit mechanisms to better handle the fiscal deficit and debt crisis while reducing the social costs of reforms. Beyond these most visible features are the continuing impacts of transnational private business, development organizations, and IFIs as they continue to alter the global social-development landscape; the deterioration of the role of traditional and family support systems; and, the emergence of pervasive social destitution, expressed in the phrase "social exclusion" (Rodgers et al. 1995).

Although policy reforms take different forms depending on the specific social, economic, and cultural environments in which they are implemented in Africa, Asia, Latin America, and the industrialized North, they also share common trends. First, they often have short-term objectives but long-term economic, social, and institutional effects. Second, the assessment of the available options to reform social-policy systems under various forms of welfare state is, at best, constrained by financial considerations and is in most cases nonexistent. Third, because in developing countries, national wealth is still distributed unequally and international development assistance, on which many rely to implement human-development programs, is unlikely to increase, government investments in social development are limited, despite international protocols, such as the various United Nations declarations. Measured in constant United States dollars (USD), total net flows of official development assistance to developing countries have remained stable between 55 billion USD and 60 billion USD since 1986. Other development finance has declined slightly, but this has been more than offset by substantial growth in private flows. Private flows now account for about 60% of net resource transfers, and overseas development assistance has fallen to about 33% of the total (OECD 1996). Fourth, despite changes in the international discourse about the debt burden, the size of external debt continues to constrain countries' freedom to redirect their investments into social-sector policies (Giddens 1995). Fifth, because of the obvious financial constraints of reforms everywhere, the OECD argued that earnings, savings, and tax revenues should be the main sources of investment in economic and social progress (OECD 1996). Sixth, at the recommendation of organizations like the OECD and the IFIs, participation in the global economy and the opening up of competitive business opportunities, rather than relying on international aid funds or state investments, is the emerging policy approach for overcoming poverty and for sustaining social-policy reforms (World Bank 1994; Bonvin 1997; Oman 1997).

Given the likely persistence of these trends, the need to examine the challenges posed by current policy reforms is even more urgent. Yet, it is safe to say that the international social-policy agenda is being "reformed" and implemented with almost a total absence of systematic assessment of the outcomes. In most cases, reforms are implemented not only without a reliable knowledge base but also with little input from recipient countries (Taylor et al. 1995).

Although, as some of the chapters in this book will show, the cases are very diverse, most countries in Latin America are better prepared to face the challenges of public-policy reforms, given their history of state and civil-society organizations, than most countries in Africa (Amin 1990; Gruat 1990; Gayi 1995). Some Southeast Asian countries have been able to adapt more quickly to the short-term objectives of policy reform than the majority of countries in Latin America (Osteria 1996). In other cases, such as in West and Central Africa, the notions of public- and social-policy reform have only recently entered the vocabulary of policymakers and social-sector practitioners. This is partly because the state is weak and its social-protection role is limited or almost nonexistent or because there are no consolidated policies to forward change. Yet, in other cases, the policy agenda for reform is more reflective of global, Western trends than the local necessity for change (UNRISD 1995; OECD 1997). Across the globe, and particularly in developing countries, policy reform often becomes almost exclusively a strategy to overcome poverty in the face of the constraints of external debt, the scarcity of international aid, the depletion of national development funds, and the lack of sustainable solutions to these problems through social policies developed on the basis of the welfare-state model.

Accordingly, a series of questions should be asked by anyone looking at particular national experiences: How is one to better understand the current process of social-policy reform? What does today's notion of social-policy reform mean in the context of social development? Is the policy-reform approach important in societies with a weak public-policy base to reform? What are the longer-term implications of social-policy reform for social and economic development? Are the current approaches to policy reform the most appropriate? Are there other options for public-policy change in the social sectors? The chapters that follow address some of these questions and open a discussion on the meaning, risks, and potentialities of the reform process for developing societies.

## Poverty alleviation or human development?

A key issue in the current social-policy reforms is the extent to which public-policy reforms should be guided by poverty-alleviation goals or aim at broader human concerns. Experience to date indicates that this issue is not yet resolved.

Since the early 1980s the approach to the reform of economic policies has been to open societies to the market and, in the process, break down barriers impeding the free flow of capital, consumer goods, and information (Thurow 1996; Altimir 1997). The opening of markets has been aided by a number of powerful forces: the revolution in communications and information technologies that allows the overnight transfer of capital that is equivalent to the economies of several poor countries; changes in the international geopolitical landscape; a growing emphasis on knowledge-based production systems; the formation of new trading blocks; and increasing flows of labour between countries. This is evident among countries of the European Union, the Southeast Asian Tigers (Osteria 1996; Mittelman 1995), other countries in the Association of Southeast Asian Nations, as well as those in the North American Free-Trade Area and MERCOSUR (Argentina, Brazil, Paraguay, and Uraguay). In several cases, developing countries have been active in adopting economic reforms — and their attached public-policy packages — for diverse reasons, including loan conditions set by the IFIs, the search for new market opportunities in the global economy, and changes in national political structures that reflect moves to the political right.

From the point of view of economic-growth indicators, the results are mixed and, in most cases, questionable, especially in Africa, where structural-adjustment programs form the core of the policy-reform debate (World Bank 1993b; Mosley 1994; Ponte 1994), and in Latin America, where poverty and extreme poverty have increased (Beneria and Mendoza 1995; Helwege 1995; Altimir 1997). The most recent troubles of the Asian economies, which have served as models for the rest of the world, cast further doubts.

There have been, however, important social advances (UNDP 1996). Large sectors of the population in some developing countries have greater access to social services, including basic education, literacy, basic health care, and drinking water; greater exposure to mass media and information in terms of access to radios, televisions, and newspapers; and, better and more democratic conditions for political participation. Still, however, across the developing world, social problems have increased in magnitude, despite advances in global development. Latin America is a very telling example. With the exception of a handful of countries, the region exhibits the greatest inequality in the world. In 1990, global social welfare in the region, measured in terms of real per capita income, was 15% lower than in 1980. Today, more households are living in poverty than 20 years ago. In 1990, the number of people living in poverty in the region reached 115.5 million (Altimir 1997).

Much of the progress witnessed today in countries in Latin America and Africa only brings the gains in social and human development back to the levels some of these countries had reached before the debt crisis. In this sense, the gains in social and human development are relative. In many instances, poverty has actually increased, and new forms of poverty have appeared, particularly in middle-class sectors (Helwege 1995; Stahl 1996). The compound effects of poverty, unemployment, lack of political participation, inequality, and various forms of discrimination have greater exclusionary effects on larger sectors of the population today than before. This has obvious implications for basic-needs satisfaction, social-service provision, and prevention of the social disintegration expressed in violence, extreme poverty, and urban crowding.

The reform of social policies is perceived as a practical response to these problems. At least two reasons are given as a rationale for this view. First, persistent social- and human-development problems are perceived to be linked to the inequity caused by the poor effectiveness and efficiency of welfare-state policies and state mechanisms. Second, the advocates of the reform approach assume that there is a positive correlation between reformed policies, better policies, higher growth, and higher human development (Ponte 1994). This, however, is rarely the case. The assumption that reform processes help to put the "right" policies in place to improve the role of the state, to correct economic distortions, or to better deliver social-sector services raises at least two basic questions: Why is a reform approach the most feasible solution? What concept of social development inspires these policy reforms?

The various cases presented in this book show that the notion of social development is differently interpreted in different settings, ranging from an emphasis on poverty alleviation and eradication, to human-resources development, to social integration and capacity development. In principle, these emphases complement each other. In practice, however, they imply very different points of departure for understanding why, how, and when a policy-reform approach may be an appropriate strategy to meet basic needs as well as different points of departure for identifying the policy-reform options that take into account financial considerations without excluding social, cultural, and environmental variables.

The reasoning behind current policy reforms follows a recognizable pattern (Meier 1993). In 1991, after considerable international debate, the World Bank acknowledged that investing in people provides the firmest foundation for lasting development (World Bank 1991). For the World Bank and for other international organizations, this meant in principle better education, higher standards of health and nutrition, less poverty, a cleaner environment, more equality of opportunity, greater individual freedom, and a richer cultural life. However, reaching these ends requires economic growth, which, under current global economic conditions, depends heavily on productivity, technological progress, and human capital. To increase productivity, countries must therefore compete effectively in the global market and make optimum use of new technologies. Accordingly, governments have to favour the factors that positively influence the achievement of these ends, such as investment in human capital, liberalization of the economy, and improvement in the efficiency of governance systems, including democratization. At the same time, they are to avoid negative factors, especially those that distort the market (World Bank 1991). Concretely, this means reforming the state and its social and economic policies.

According to the World Bank, governments need to spend fewer resources more efficiently in social services, shift spending priorities, target expenditures, and increase resource mobilization. However, the challenge is not to expand the role of the state but to exploit the complementarities between the state and the market (World Bank 1991), particularly between government, nongovernment, and profit-oriented private organizations. In this view, social development is both a prerequisite and a consequence of economic growth and the setting for collaboration between state and market institutions. The reform of social policies is needed because, as the argument implies, current policy models are inadequate.

However, interpretations of these issues vary. The Canadian International Development Agency's (CIDA's) definition of social development, for example, focused in 1987 on the concept of human-resource development. *Sharing Our Future* identified four principles of social development: poverty alleviation must be put first; people must be helped to help themselves; development priorities must prevail; and partnership must be the key (CIDA 1987). This interpretation was shared by the World Bank: it recognized that adjustment must be complemented by poverty alleviation, its "refound" goal (World Bank 1990). However, in 1991, CIDA modified these principles. CIDA's new mission statement was to support sustainable development in developing countries. Social development became an element of a much larger objective. Still, in the broader picture, in 1995, Canada set as a target to invest 25% of its official development assistance in basic human needs: basic education, primary health, safe water and sanitation, and family planning (GOC 1995; Van Rooy 1995). The total CIDA envelop for basic human needs is 21% of Canadian official development assistance, which falls short of the 25% target announced by Canada in 1995. The distribution of funds in Asia, Africa, and the Americas represented 16.4, 12.8, and 9.7%, respectively, of total disbursements (Van Rooy 1995). In terms of programs, CIDA's approach emphasizes poverty alleviation and self-help through its focus on basic human needs.

The Economic Commission for Latin America and the Caribbean (ECLAC) promotes an approach driven by technological and economic considerations as outlined in its proposal, *Transformación Productiva con Equidad* (productive transformation with equity; ECLAC 1990). In this proposal, development is characterized as the increase in the level of well-being of the population resulting from multiple factors: the prevalence of human rights; democratic political regimes; a minimum of equity, social solidarity, and growth; and the availability of goods and services to all sectors of the population. Growth and the availability of goods and services may come only through economic growth, which in turn is fostered by competitiveness.

This proposal is not, on the whole, new to the region. Its novelty is in its emphasis on competitiveness through the introduction of technological innovation, rather than depressing salary levels, overexploiting natural resources, or implementing successive devaluations — mechanisms that proved ineffective in the past. The rationale for this view of development in general and of social development in particular is as follows: to be economically competitive, countries need, for example, to offer more or better products or offer the same products for less. Because an increase in productive capacity is essential to development, technological change is a condition *sine qua non* of development, being the only means to increase productivity. However, technological change is a systemic process and requires human resources capable of understanding, learning, managing information, and adapting innovations to local conditions. ECLAC's assumption is that a growth strategy based on the introduction of technological change has a "proequity" bias, as it improves flexibility and competitiveness of the labour force between and within sectors. ECLAC also indicates that equity cannot be left exclusively to the care of a production strategy, but it should be pursued in a complementary and coherent way through other public policies, including education and other social policies (CELADE 1996; IADB 1996).

In the case of Africa, the human- and social-development situation is far more complex; accordingly, the ways to approach it are different, as the chapters by Aina and by Osei-Hwedie and Arnon Bar-on show. At one level, it is urgent to address basic human needs. Key social indicators for the region are worse than in most low-income countries. A comparison between sub-Saharan Africa and low-income countries as defined by the World Bank, shows that sub-Saharan Africa has 11 years less in average life expectancy (52 compared with 63 years), 9% higher adult illiteracy, 34% higher infant mortality, 2.6% higher fertility, and 34% lower primary-school enrolment for girls (OECD 1997). Between 1980 and 1987, for example, gross national product per capita in sub-Saharan Africa declined by an average 2.8% annually. This situation is even more critical for countries in the Sahel. Countries in the Sahel show an average of 48 years life expectancy, compared with 52 years in sub-Saharan Africa and

63 years in low-income countries; 71% adult illiteracy, compared with 43 and 34%; 112‰ (per thousand) infant mortality, compared with 92 and 58‰; 6.6% fertility, compared with 5.9 and 3.3%; and 35% primary-school enrolment for girls, compared with 64 and 98% (OECD 1997).

Yet, despite this critical situation, social development is, in practice, held as secondary to other development issues deemed more critical as a foundation for sustainable human and social development (Herbold Green 1996). The World Bank's *Adjustment in Africa: Reforms, Results and the Road Ahead* is one of a series of documents outlining the issue of adjustment in Africa (World Bank 1994). The premise of the World Bank's approach is that growth is an outcome of having the right policies (World Bank 1994). Structural-adjustment measures are needed to ensure this. Once corrective measures are implemented, basic education and basic health care become intervening factors that help to raise the income of the poor and thus social and human development. In this view, the main social- and human-development challenges are those posed by the factors affecting economic growth. These include lack of peace and social stability, poor governance, an inefficient public service, political corruption, lack of macroeconomic viability and market liberalization, absence of a skilled labour force, and unreliable infrastructure.

OECD puts people up front, proposing a social-development concept in terms of capacity development at all levels — national, regional, local, and individual. This view applies across the spectrum of public-sector and civil-society organizations. In the OECD's perspective, this framework not only reflects a major shift in the dominant paradigm of development thinking but also parallels a more general paradigm shift in economic thinking under the rubric of the "new growth theory." This theory emphasizes human and social capital as the capacities of individuals, groups, and whole societies to learn, adapt, and cooperate (Paye 1996). Social capital is the whole web of norms and networks of social engagement. It is an asset that grows out of the relationships between and among people and their organizations. Whereas human capital relates to the capacity of individuals to make efficient decisions, social capital relates to the capacity of a collective entity to make competent decisions (OECD 1996). The broad concept of capacity development embraces human and social capital and the "new institutional economics" (that is, the study of the economic impact of constitutional rules and norms at the macrolevel and the behaviour and performance of individual institutions at the microlevel; OECD 1996). Social development is much more than just poverty alleviation because it involves the idea of capacity development across the board, involving both the poor and the nonpoor.

One of the most comprehensive approaches to social development to date came from the World Summit for Social Development (WSSD). The United Nations (995, pp. 41–42) summarized WSSD's understanding of social

Nations (995, pp. 41–42) summarized WSSD's understanding of social development, arguing that it

> is inseparable from the cultural, ecological, economic, political and spiritual environment in which it takes place. It cannot be pursued as a sectoral initiative. Social development is also linked to the development of peace, freedom, stability and security, both nationally and internationally. Promoting social development requires an orientation of values, objectives and priorities towards the well-being of all and the strengthening and promotion of conducive institutions and policies. ... The ultimate goal of social development is to improve and enhance the quality of life of all people.

Two social-policy implications of this view of social development should be highlighted. First, the perception is more or less explicit that social policies developed on the basis of the welfare-state model are inappropriate in most countries to meet current social needs and their levels of demand. Second, independently of the point of departure in understanding social development, poverty alleviation is only part of the problem, despite the fact that poverty is what often attracts the most political attention.

Social development is a multiple and interrelated undertaking that involves all levels of a society, not just the poor. In a broad developmental context, poverty is a systemic problem and not one affecting only a particular fraction of the population. To see the factors causing poverty and impeding social development as set of problems constrained by demographic, age, gender, or geographic boundaries is to see only a partial picture of the conditions affecting developing countries. In most instances, countries suffer poverty in Africa, Asia, and Latin America because wealth is concentrated and unequally distributed, productivity is low, learning opportunities are disparate or entirely unavailable, and access to power is uneven. Behind each one of these causes are ingrained social structures and institutions, political agendas, values, and practices of specific actors and social groups, whose choices make them reinforce inequality while protecting their class interests.

Because of this, from a policy-analysis perspective (Boothroyd 1995; Burdge and Vanclay 1995), the social-development agenda in developing countries cannot be reduced to a number of single goals: to adjust the economy, correct corrupt forms of governance, provide more education, or deliver more health care. Social development should include a wide range of actions across policies, sectors, and institutions and especially across a wider spectrum of social groups. The actual social-development challenge that most countries face is to design policies that can realistically and sustainably address the needs of the traditional poor and those in mid-socioeconomic sectors now excluded from the benefits of progress and modernization — the "new poor" (Bradford 1993) — and that involve the elites key to the policy- and decision-making processes affecting the distribution of the benefits of development.

Social development is thus a fundamental premise and not a linear outcome of economic growth or a follow-up effect of economic restructuring. This is why it is so important to take society as a whole into account, rather than individual sectors. This is also why it is important to consider the wide range of development policies and not only those aimed at poverty reduction or alleviation. And this is why taking action implies more than overcoming poverty. Without doubt, the alleviation of extreme poverty is a priority (Chambers 1994; Helwege 1995). However, it must be recognized that in isolation, poverty alleviation is a short-term concern. The critical issue is how to address poverty in the broader framework of public policies and how, in so doing, to lay the base for sustainable development over the long term.

A good example is education. Without question, we need to provide basic education. Empirical evidence indicates a positive correlation between years of primary schooling and basic income, particularly among women. However, from a social- and human-development perspective, the most critical issue is to provide education of high enough quality and relevance across the complete educational system. Educational reforms intended to improve basic education alone, without a broader, longer-term aim, ignore the need to mobilize the entire spectrum of social groups to build countries' capacities to understand, use, and create knowledge. Educational reforms that only addresses the needs of a society to read or to write, although essential, do not address the broader issue of building the relevant knowledge and skills to understand and contribute to the production process. The educational field is littered with examples of educational reforms that addressed short-term political objectives and ended by creating internal conditions for more inequity and even stronger external dependencies, reinforcing the state of some countries as consumers and users of knowledge and technologies produced elsewhere.

Within this perspective social development can be part and parcel of human development understood as the process of acquiring values and learning skills and participation capacities that individuals and communities must have to benefit from progress. From this perspective, social development is more than the satisfaction of basic needs — shelter, basic education, primary health care, and a minimum wage. Ultimately, social development is an issue of the values that lead a society to allocate equitably material resources and redistribute opportunities.

This view of social development, that is, as a comprehensive process centred in the creation of learning and participation capacities, is not really new. The traditional notion of capacity-building in international development has this idea at its core. What is new about this outlook in the context of policy reform is its insistence that social development should be reconsidered in systemic and not exclusively targeted terms. In the context of social policies, this indicates that social-policy changes should be the cutting edge of a broader strategy to deal with increased inequities in income distribution, unemployment, low productivity, and the lack of competitive capacity and opportunities for vast population sectors. This is the point of view with which policy reform is examined in this book.

## The purpose of this book

The purpose of this book is to examine, using a comparative approach, some of the theoretical and practical challenges developing countries face in bringing social-policy reform to the forefront of their development agendas. This book identifies and critically analyzes the dilemmas developing countries must overcome while they are attempting to reach higher levels of social and human development.

Each chapter assesses the options countries face to enhance social development in the context of policy reforms. Each discusses issues such as changing state–civil-society relations, the impact of transnational influences brought about by international development agendas that promote public-policy reforms, internal conflicts eroding an already weakened political consensus supporting the nation-state, and the crisis of resources exacerbated by, among other things, patterns of unequal distribution of wealth.

Collectively, these chapters address some of the following questions: What are the assumptions in the current understanding of development that developing countries are expected to accommodate in reforming their social-policy systems? What are the implications of international agendas for nations attempting to implement social-policy reforms within a framework of local values and cultures? What are the obstacles developing countries face in implementing feasible approaches and institutional structures to reflect more closely the integration of the principles of social equality, equity, and participation? How are these countries responding to the demands for greater efficiency and effectiveness in formulating, implementing, and delivering their social policies and programs while maintaining acceptable levels of social justice? What consideration is given local attempts to identify innovative solutions to respond to evolving social demands? What types of policy options are available to developing countries in implementing effective social-policy changes with their limited resources? What are the new risks these countries will face in the years to come if adequate solutions are not found to prevailing social-policy demands?

This book is divided into two parts. Part 1 identifies and analyzes from a political-economic perspective the factors influencing the focus, values, direction, and feasibility of policy-reform options available to developing countries. It examines the global framework of assumptions and challenges faced by developing countries in their efforts to strengthen their social safety nets through social-policy reforms. The chapters in part 1 argue that although globalization is not a new phenomenon, it drastically affects the quality of life, the security of people, and their established sets of values. Globalization is resulting in local changes not only in the quality and composition of the labour force and production patterns but also in the social-security, protection, and value systems that depend on a stable economy. Health care, training, education, and key social programs for the poor are affected by a transnational paradigm of social and human well-being, based on a market ideology. This part of the book discusses the growing transnational character of the premises underlying social policies in a context of global social-development interdependencies and their effects on countries' capacities to provide social services to meet minimum standards of well-being.

Part 2 examines the impacts of the economically driven model of public-policy reform on social-sector policies in selected countries. Owing to changes in the global economy and international trade, the competitive capacities of many countries determine the types of social-security and social-protection systems they put in place. They also determine the types of social-sector services they are able to make available. These chapters examine how countries in Africa, Asia, and Latin America are reforming social-delivery systems and mechanisms. Some questions these chapters address are the following: How do these changes affect the steps countries in these regions take to prepare new generations to enter a changing labour market? What efforts are these countries making to incorporate the sectors most affected by these changes (youth and women) into the design of short- and medium-term policies and programs to increase competitive economic and technological capacities. What kinds of appropriate social-security mechanisms are being put in place to compensate for rapid changes in labour-market structures, employment patterns, and social safety nets to maintain acceptable standards of social equity. These chapters discuss these issues from the perspective of selected social-policy reforms, showing the interplay between growing internal demands for more effective social policies, the constraints faced by governments in their strategies to respond to these demands, and the role of global factors in facilitating or impeding their ability to improve social and human development.

The book's concluding chapter reflects on the reform dynamics affecting national policy decisions and reviews the basis for the belief that measures such as privatization, decentralization, free-market determination of wages, and budget readjustments facilitate a rapid transition from costly social-welfare systems to more effective and just systems of social protection. This final essay confronts some of the questions for which answers are still only rudimentary, including the longer-term equity effects of such measures on the social fabric of nations, on their basic cultures and value systems, and on basic social institutions. In doing so. it calls attention to the need to identify research entry points to help respond to the central question, What kind of social-policy reform is required for what kind of society?

# PART I

# NEW CHALLENGES

# CHAPTER I

# SOCIAL POLICY AND SOCIAL ORDER IN TRANSNATIONAL SOCIETIES

*Andrés Pérez Baltodano*

Social theory provides "the constitutive understanding necessary for continuing, reformed, or purified practice" (Taylor 1983, p. 16). Such understanding shapes social practice, and through it, the very institutions it tries to elucidate. "If theory is about practice," Charles Taylor points out, "then what makes a theory right is that it brings the practice out in the clear. And what this leads to is that the practice can be more effective" (Taylor 1983, p. 78).

Concepts are the building blocks of social theories and explanations. Concepts are "data containers" (Sartori 1977, pp. 24–49). They "slice" and interpret different aspects and dimensions of a social reality (Sartori 1984). When a social reality changes, concepts have to change to grasp the new significance and constitution of social life and social phenomena. Modern social sciences show a tendency to use concepts in an ahistorical manner. The result is the frequent use of concepts as simple names or labels. The concept of the state is an example. It represents the specific historical experience of the organization of the territorial, social, political, cultural, and economic life of the Western world over the last 400 years. Nevertheless, the term is widely used to describe national structures of power around the world — in Asia, Africa, and Latin America — regardless of the different and unique historical foundations these structures may have.

The ahistorical use of concepts has several implications. It affects the capacity of both social scientists and policymakers to define the nature of the problems they address and, consequently, the options they have in articulating solutions to those problems. This is especially true at times of radical social transformation, such as the world is undergoing today, that lead to new historical circumstances, unrepresented in the prevailing conceptual vocabulary. One of the results of this process is that many of the current social-science concepts are unsuitable for grasping and fully representing the nature of today's challenges and the choices that need to be made in dealing with them.

This chapter argues that the concept of social policy is intimately linked to the specific historical evolution of modern Western societies. More specifically, this concept is linked to the evolution of the social strategies used by the modern state to achieve social order. However, the conventional notion of social policy, as a practice that is historically rooted in the formation and evolution of sovereign states, has been made inadequate by the forces of globalization. Today, the causes and consequences of the social issues and problems that the notion of social policy addresses transcend the physical, legal, and political boundaries of national states. This new historical situation needs to be reconceptualized to design new and more effective ways to confront the challenges of the future and meet the need for new forms of social intervention.

The shortcomings of the conventional notion of social policy in a time of transnational influence are more serious in societies that have long used the conventional notion to explain social realities significantly different from those of Western developed societies. The state in Latin America, for example, never achieved the levels of sovereignty and the regulatory capacity of the European state. Moreover, the historical evolution of Latin America has never produced the civil societies needed to condition the roles and the functions of the state. As this chapter argues, the historical specificity of Latin American societies severely limits the capacity of the concept of social policy to grasp some of the fundamental dimensions of the relations between state and society in this part of the world. Under such circumstances, globalization often widens, rather than closes, the gap between the conventional concept of social policy and the given social reality.

This chapter examines the phenomenon of globalization as a historical process that reduces both modern societies' capacity to overcome contingencies (Luhmann 1982) and the capacity of the state to provide citizens with a sense of "ontological security"; that is, it reduces confidence "in the continuity of their self-identity and in the constancy of their surrounding social and material environments of action" (Giddens 1990, p. 92). States such as those controlled by the Nazis or Pinochet in Chile provided this form of security to some sectors of their populations while instilling others with the utmost terror and uncertainty. States ruled by the elites of Guatemala or Peru deny to large segments of their populations some of the most basic forms of human security. A modern state, in a general, ideal sense, is nevertheless a political structure designed to provide people with a sense of ontological security, and different historical manifestations of the modern state represent different degrees of the realization of the ideal. The capacity of the modern state to fulfil this ideal depends largely on its capacity to compartmentalize history and thus contain and control, within legally defined territorial boundaries, the causes of a community's social, economic, and political evolution. By doing so, the modern state enables national histories to differ from world history (Luhmann 1982). As Reinhard Kosseleck (1985, p. 275) pointed out, "it is the tension between experience and expectation which, in ever-changing patterns, brings about new resolutions and through this generates historical time." The state is thus an active participant in the management of the tensions between social experiences and social expectations. One of its most important functions is to synchronize these two dimensions of history to create a sense of social order and continuity. Over the past 400 years, the development of the state's political and administrative capacity to perform this function made possible the formation of territorially based "communities of aspirations and memories" (Visscher 1957, p. 206). Central to the development of this administrative and political capacity was the emergence of social policy in the 20th century, as a mechanism to reduce contingencies and secure social order. Globalization, however, has reduced the capacity of the state to synchronize social experiences and expectations, thus creating a state of affairs in which ontological insecurity is more likely to occur — a state of affairs in which "the ordinary circumstances of everyday life constitute a continual threat" (Laing 1971, p. 171).

The social and political consequences of ontological insecurity can be disastrous. This is especially so for countries that never developed the capacity to truly compartmentalize their national histories and thus create their own national communities of aspirations and memories. In some regions of the world, this means nothing less than what Robert Kaplan (1994, p. 73) described as the "re-primitivization of man."

To address these issues, this chapter discusses the relationship between territorial space, historical time, and ontological security and examines the emergence and development of the sovereign state as the modern expression of this relationship. Globalization undermines this relationship and the capacity of the modern state to provide ontological security. Accordingly, this chapter explores the prospects for developing transnational social policies that recreate the relationship between territorial space, historical time, and ontological security.

## Territory, history, and ontological security

One of the constant dimensions in the evolution of history is the tendency for human beings to find their identity and security in the territorial organizations of social life. In "primitive cultures," the relationship of territory, historical identity, and security was expressed in the reverence that people had for their land.

In modern political societies, this is expressed, for example, in the territorial aspirations of nationalist movements.

Answers to the fundamental question about the roots of the territorial dimension of social organization are found in at least three theoretical perspectives. A biological explanation of the territorial dimension of social phenomena states that the "territorial imperative" is the product of an animal instinct to control property and power (Ardrey 1966). In the same tradition, Randolph Bourne (1946, p. 100) argued that "the State is the organization of the herd to act offensively or defensively against another herd similarly organized." From a political theoretical perspective, Robert Sack (1986, p. 19) expressed the view that "territoriality" represents "the attempt by an individual or group to affect, influence, or control people, phenomena, and relationships, by delimiting and asserting control over a geographical area." Sack's position is an important departure from the biological explanation. For Sack (1986, p. 2), territoriality is not "biologically motivated, but rather … socially and geographically rooted." Territoriality, in this perspective, involves the use of politics to organize the control of people over people and transcends individuals' basic instincts for survival. Marxist scholars have also explored the territorial dimension of social organizations. Henri Lefebvre, for example, viewed states as spaces created by violence. This violence (Lefebvre 1991, pp. 280–281),

> must not be viewed in isolation: it cannot be separated either from the accumulation of capital or from the rational and political principle of unification, which subordinates and totalises the various aspects of social practice — legislation, culture, knowledge, education — within a determinate space; namely the space of the ruling class's hegemony over its people and over the nationhood that it has arrogated.

Both fundamental and common to the biological, political, and economic explanations is the relationship they establish between territory, social order, and security. What separates them is their different emphases on the factors determining this relationship. According to the biological explanation, the territorial dimension of social life is the result of human instinct; for Sack, the relationship between territory and social order is the result of a political impulse; and for Marxist researchers, this relationship is explained by the economic imperative of capitalism.

## The evolution of the notion of territory

From the beginning of organized human life, territory has functioned as a container of "social time", understood as the passage of time collectively experienced by the members of the community. Territory naturally limits human experiences and therefore expectations as well. But by doing so, it also limits uncertainty and reduces contingencies. This even applies to nomadic societies who usually migrate through relatively similar terrain. The human tendency to use territory as the foundation for social organizations may be rooted in inductive thinking. At some point in our evolution, humans saw that territory limits human experiences. Once this is a given, it is easy to conclude that by controlling territory, one also controls the events taking place within it, and by controlling events, contingencies are reduced and security is achieved. Thus, the idea of territory as a container of time and experience may have originally been a mere observation, later transformed by experience into a fact that, today, is taken for granted. The suggestion that inductive thinking and common sense could be at the root of the relationship between territory, history, and security is supported by the theoretical development of the relationship between time and space in physics. Inductive reasoning and common sense were, according to Alfred North Whitehead (1925), the foundations of Newton's conceptualization of this relationship, especially as rudimentary instruments of scientific analysis and observation did not allow scientists to go far beyond the use of their own senses.

The tendency to think of territorial spaces as containers of historical time was pronounced in agricultural societies, with "the formation of density," or the grouping of small villages into complete communities, which brought about "communal life and hence the need for law and authority to enforce it" (Gottmann 1973, p. 124). These communities developed the ability to manage internal conflict and to overcome contingencies by establishing rules and regulations. The development of these communities represents the emergence of what Sheldon Wolin called "political spaces," geographical areas "where the plans, ambitions, and actions of individuals and groups incessantly jar against each other — colliding, blocking, coalescing, separating" (Wolin 1960, p. 17).

Another stage in the evolution of the relationship between history, territorial space, and security was that of universal imperium (Gottmann 1973, p. 124). Alexander the Great expanded the territorial foundation of social organizations previously contained in city-states. The imperial experiment of the Hellenistic age was later repeated in the Roman Empire, which controlled the Mediterranean and western Europe through a system of administrative planning, law, and economic relations. Its eventual collapse opened the doors for the expansion of the Christian Church and the consequent Christianization of the Roman world. Thereafter, the social organization of the West would be based on both a universal structure of religious belief and a fragmented structure of political power. The medieval Europeans derived a precarious sense of security from both. Feudal relations determined everyday life while religion gave meaning to that life and provided answers to the larger questions about human existence.

Within the local territories that constituted the foundations of medieval social life, the future resembled the past in a world that moved through cyclical time regulated by the seasons. "In all Christendom," as Manchester (1993, pp. 22–23) remarked,

> there was not such a thing as a watch, a clock, or, apart from a copy of the Easter tables in the nearest church or monastery, anything resembling a calendar. Generations succeeded one another in a meaningless, timeless blur.

The short collective memories of medieval people limited their expectations (Koselleck 1985). Dealing with uncertainty and achieving security in this world of limited experiences and expectations was ultimately founded on religious faith and resignation (Le Goff 1988). The distant past and the distant future stood beyond the control of human intervention and "tended to fuse together in the darkness of mythic time" (Luhmann 1982, p. 271). Medieval society, as Poulantzas (1978, p. 109) observed, "does not make history, it bathes in a continuous and homogeneous historicity."

In the mid-1500s, Europe faced a great crisis produced by profound social, religious, technological, political, and economic changes that would eventually transform the medieval relationship between territory, history, and security. These changes created a gap between the experience of medieval society and previously unimagined historical possibilities. The crisis was not only institutional but also psychosociological. It was a crisis of both social order and of human security that required a rethinking of the most basic foundations of social and spiritual life. At the social level, it centred "on the location of authority," and questions such as "what is authentic authority?" and "where does authority come from?" At the human level, the questions were even more fundamental: "are there solid and stable certainties?" "what is order and how certain is it?", "what is truth and how is it achieved?", and, ultimately, "can one rely on anything?" (Rabb 1975, p. 33). These questions presupposed that the distant past and the distant future were no longer under the control of God and the Church. This created both a sense of liberation from the "theological dogma and animistic superstition" of medieval societies and a sense of alienation from a world that no longer offered "a redeeming context within which could be understood the larger issues of human existence" (Tarnas 1991, p. 326). Ontological security could now only be achieved through human and, more specifically, political intervention. Therefore, the belief expressed in the idea "no salvation outside the Church" would be replaced by "the defining maxim of modern politics: no security outside the state" (Dillon 1995, p. 156). In these new circumstances, the role of state policy would become crucial to the creation and re-creation of social order within the new political spaces of the modern era.

# The state and the spatial delimitation of history

History is seen here both as a social interpretation of a community's past and as a reference point for anticipating the future. From this perspective, history consists of experience and expectation (Koselleck 1985). Increasing expectations for social order and ontological security expanded the scope of state policies and the state's regulatory capacity from the 17th to the 20th century, until the concept social policy emerged to make explicit the role played by the state in shaping the social conditions of its citizens. This expansion can be divided into two phases: the era of Hobbe's Leviathan and absolute monarchy and that of civil society (Barry et al. 1996).

The first phase corresponds roughly to the era of absolutism in the 17th and 18th centuries. Within this context, "police science" emerged to articulate instrumental theory for the purpose of social engineering. The main objective of this science was the organization of social order. To achieve this objective, it looked into a wide range of issues, including moral and welfare issues, such as food and housing. It is important to note that the form of social order that the state tried to articulate during this period relied solely on what it considered feasible and desirable. No form of popular participation or consultation was used or even deemed necessary by the state to organize the lives of its citizens (Fraile 1994).

The new social conditions of the first phase were launched by the crisis in the mid-1500s that expanded social life beyond the boundaries of the territorial units of medieval Europe. Increasing trade, the emergence of a bourgeois class, and the increasing mobility of labour weakened the medieval powers controlling social relations at that time (Anderson 1974).

With the expansion of the scope of territories as containers of historical times, the construction of social order required the institutionalization of expectations (Luhmann 1990). This in turn required the centralization of power and the creation of a new foundation for authority. The historical answer to these requirements was the emergence and consolidation of monarchical absolutism, which recreated the territorial scope of social life by forming a centralized structure of political power that overran the microsocieties of the Middle Ages.

The foundation of authority for this new structure of power was the idea of sovereignty, best expressed by Hobbes in 1651. Hobbes' argument in favour of the formation of a "collective will for the establishment of peace at home and cooperation against enemies abroad" demonstrated the continuing importance of territory as the physical foundation of social order and security. Sovereignty involved a radical reconceptualization of the medieval relationship between territory, history, and security, creating the foundation for the development of a society's capacity to generate "a strictly political history of chains of events, which replaced the archaic fusion of mythical and genealogical time" (Luhmann 1982, p. 333). With this new sense of history, philosophy would gradually replace theology, and "the omnipotent God" would become "the omnipotent lawgiver" (Schmitt 1985, p. 36). Moreover, with the emergence of the great Leviathan, ontological security would be not only politically created but also planned and delivered by the state in a process guided by the doctrine of *raison d'etat*, that is, by the subordination of public morality to state power, where the rational calculation of all possible consequences became the first political commandment (Koselleck 1988).

Otto Hintze (1975, p. 175) argued that in this period,

> the idea of a general citizenship began to penetrate into the political sphere, by virtue of the regime's absolutist nature and the unitary character of the state; to this idea the notion of general citizen rights was soon added. The population accustomed itself to fixed duties laid down by the state, to taxation and military service, to daily contacts with the civil servants of a centralized state, and, in consequence, acquired a sense of political cohesion, the rudiments of a common political interest. The idea of a unified political order — for which absolutism had created the needed external forms, became now an innermost concern of the population itself. A latent consciousness of nation and state originated, and it needed only special occasion to emerge in all its strength.

The principle of rational calculation in the decisions and actions of the absolutist monarch required the development of administrative mechanisms to synchronize social experiences with social expectations and to create national communities with a common history.

The role of the state, as a synchronizer of social expectations and social experiences underwent significant change with the Enlightenment idea of progress, and political practice in this era created the conditions for democratic theory and the principles of popular sovereignty and representative government. Social and economic progress created a gap between society's historical experience and its expectations. It created "an open future that was not constrained by the past" (Luhmann 1982, p. 281). This made social relations and historical identities more difficult to sustain, as the past could no longer be used as a "means of orientation" (Elias 1992, p. 38). This shift represented a formidable challenge to a society's ability to achieve security and overcome contingencies. However, the ideas of popular sovereignty and representative democracy expressed a new faith in human ability to control destiny, despite the uncertainties of the future. Democracy placed sovereignty in neither the king nor the state but in people. It conceived of the state as a social mechanism to act in accordance with the dictates of the people. Increasingly, the need for the state to maintain social order and the need for society to achieve security would be expressed in the form of state policies designed to create adequate social conditions for the people living within the territorial boundaries of a nation.

Popular sovereignty and representative governments thus resolved the challenge that progress posed to society's needs for security. Through a combination of political fiction and reality, the democratic state guaranteed a response to people's needs and demands. This guarantee would reduce the risks faced by a society. In practice, the democratic state did respond to people's needs and demands, but not simply as a result of the passive reading of the people's will. The state, through its administrative machinery, became an active organizer of that will by creating and enforcing historical identities with separate notions of "the public interest." As R.M. MacIver (1964, p. 126) put it,

the very fact that administration and law have determinate boundaries knits together those who live within them and separates them from those who are subject to other administration and law. The evolution of a common order proceeds separately and therefore diversely within each state, and so the sense of likeness within and difference without is fostered.

Thus, in this period, the state actively participated in the creation of "imagined communities" (Anderson 1991) tied together by administrative structures. These structures made the development of nationalistic values possible (Nisbet 1981), and this, in turn, helped to synchronize society's historical experience with its expectations.

The theory of popular sovereignty and representative government was not therefore simply the expression of secular faith. It was also the result of having an administrative system whereby faith in human beings' capacity to control history could be realized. This is why the principle of sovereignty, as articulated by Hobbes, was later developed "to perfect the state and to realize the opportunities presented by its accumulation of power" (Hume 1981, p. 20). Through this, it became increasingly clear that institutionalizing abstract social relations required the use of efficient administrative machinery. This was best expressed in Jeremy Bentham's concern for "the idea of rational rules as paramount standards of administrative behavior" (Bahmueller 1981, p. 186). The ultimate objective of these rules would be to contribute to "the maximization of the Benthamite's values of security, predictability, stability, and physical comfort" (Long 1977, p. 118).

Thus, the establishment of the modern state as an institution was accompanied by the development of its capacity to regulate social relations. By operating at both domestic and international levels, the administrative apparatus of the state facilitated the spacial delimitation of history; in other words, the development of the state's administrative capacity to regulate social relations across territorial space made it possible to regulate social relations across historical time. This is because continuous regulation of social relations across territorial space tends to institutionalize "behaviourial expectations" (Luhmann 1990). At the domestic level, the administrative apparatus of the state responds to domestic demands and limits the range of acceptable (and consequently legal) economic, political, and social behaviour. At the international level, it resists external pressures — by means of war, diplomacy, and international law — to protect domestic markets and political self-determination. By regulating domestic conditions and filtering external pressures, the state makes the conformation of national histories possible.

The second phase in the development of the state's capacity to regulate social relations corresponds to what Foucault called "the discovery of society" (Barry et al. 1996, p. 9). This period roughly corresponds to the 19th and 20th centuries. The main characteristic of this period is the emergence of civil society as a network of social relations with not only a considerable degree of independence vis-à-vis the state but also the capacity to condition the power of the state. The emergence of society as a complex network of social relations with a dynamic of its own made the police science obsolete as a mechanism for social order. As Rose (1996a, p. 43) points out, "government now confronts itself with realities — market, civil society, citizens — that have their own internal logics and densities, their own intrinsic mechanisms of self-regulation." To create and maintain conditions of social order, the state had to consider the growing capacity of society to articulate its demands and had to rely on the institutions of society to respond to the demands of its citizens. According to T.S. Marshall (1965), citizenship rights in the United Kingdom evolved from civil rights (liberty of the person, freedom of speech, the right to own property, etc.) in the 18th century, to political rights (political participation and the right to vote) in the 19th century, to social rights (economic welfare and security) in the 20th century. Citizenship rights evolved throughout Europe, and social policy emerged as a mechanism to help create and preserve social order by counterbalancing the negative effects of the market on the working class, including unemployment and dangerous working conditions. From this perspective, the creation of social-insurance programs should be seen as an instrument designed by the state to overcome contingencies and provide a minimum of security to its people. Social insurance, according to Rose (1996, pp. 48–49),

> incarnates social solidarity in collectivizing the management of the individual and collective dangers posed by the economic riskiness of a capricious system of wage labour, and the corporeal riskiness of a body subject to sickness and injury, under the stewardship of a "social state."

The emergence of "a social state" and of social policy resulted from the interaction of national societies, national economies, and national states operating within the legal and territorial boundaries of sovereign national territories. The evolution of citizenship rights from the 18th to the 20th century provided societies with the capacity to condition the functions and priorities of the state. In turn, the state had the capacity to redistribute the benefits generated by economic systems. From this perspective, a basic assumption of democratic theory is that the participation of the state in the formation of national histories is determined by the people. David Held pointed out that democratic theory assumes the existence of "a 'symmetrical' and 'congruent' relationship between political decision makers and the recipients of political decisions." According to Held (1991, p. 198), this symmetry and this congruence are supposed to hold at two levels:

> first, between citizen–voters and the decision-makers whom they are, in principle, able to hold to account; and secondly, between the "output" (decisions, policies, etc.) of decision-makers and their constituents — ultimately "the people" in a delimited territory.

The democratic principles of popular sovereignty and representative government are realized through the relationship between decision-makers, along with their decisions, and the population affected by political decisions (Held 1991). By controlling the state apparatus, people in democratic societies control the processes through which the state synchronizes their collective historical experience with their expectations for the future. Through these processes, states create collective identities and national histories institutionalized in their organizational values, structures, and processes. Therefore, synchronizing collective expectations and experiences is, in a democratic society, a reflexive process, whereby social demands influence public policies, which, in turn, constitute part of the social structure for political decisions (Giddens 1991).

In sum, social policies are the result of a set of particular circumstances in the history of the modern state. They are the result of the development of civil societies' capacity to condition the functions of national states that, in turn, can condition the functioning of the economy and the distributions of wealth and opportunity in society. Three historical conditions led to this complex relationship between society, the market, and the state: first, the consolidation of the principle of sovereignty, allowing national territories to contain the main determinants of their political evolution within legal, territorial, and political boundaries; second, the development of the capacity of the state to regulate and condition social relations; and third, the evolution of citizenship rights.

These three historical conditions enabled European societies to create national histories, with national actors and institutions. A central factor in the formation of these national histories was the generation of social order and security through national social policies. Therefore, the concept of social policy expresses a national reality. A national territorial state and a national population should be the main points of reference used to identify both the problems in social policy and the means to confront them. New historical problems, such as those produced by capital mobility and global migration, significantly reduce the capacity for social policy to generate conditions of order and security.

To illustrate and to gain a broader comparative understanding of the processes of state formation and social policy, the following subsection contrasts the Latin American experience with that of Europe.

## The Latin American experience

The historical evolution of the political societies of Latin America differs significantly from that of the European state in at least three important interrelated respects. First, the legal principle of sovereignty that is formally attached to Latin American states by international law lacks the historical, social, and political significance that it had for European political societies. The Latin American states were never able to contain or territorially delimit their history. They never developed the capacity that European states achieved to contain within their boundaries the basic causes of their internal political, economic, and social evolution. Instead, their historical development has depended on external cultural, political, and economic factors.

Second, the Latin American state never achieved the social regulatory capacity of the European state. It never developed the capacity to synchronize social memories and aspirations through the formulation and implementation of state policies. Inefficient administration of justice, poor delivery of educational and health services, incompetent and corrupt police organizations are only some of the manifestations of the very limited capacity of the Latin American states to organize social relations within their territories.

Third, the social evolution of Latin America has not produced civil societies with the capacity to condition the role and function of the state. It has not produced a structure of citizenship rights capable of creating conditions for the kind of symmetric and congruent relationship between the state and society central to democratic systems. Even in today's democratic experiments in the region, the main challenge of prodemocratic forces is the creation and consolidation of independent public spaces for the articulation of social strategies to influence the role of the state (O'Donnell 1992).

Social policy in Latin America is the outcome of (1) clientelist relationships between the state and those sectors of the population with the capacity to be recognized by an externally dependent and highly exclusionary state with limited capacity for social regulation; and (2) external influences and pressures, such as from international organizations, development agencies, and financial institutions (IFIs). Clientelism and external pressures have produced two models of social policy in Latin America: state corporatist social policies and social policies offered as an alternative to citizenship. In his classic analysis of corporatism, Schmitter (1974, pp. 102–103) defined state corporatism as a system in which "corporations" are "created by and kept as auxiliary and dependent organs of the state which founded its legitimacy and effective functioning on other bases." The idea of social policy as an alternative to citizenship is taken from Marshall. In his classic analysis of the evolution of citizenship, Marshall (1965, p. 88) argued that the *Poor Law* in England "treated the claims of the poor, not as an integral part of the rights of the citizen, but as an alternative to them." His analysis suggests the possibility of treating social policy as a form of state intervention "divorced" from citizenship.

State corporatist social policies are more visible in the most socially advanced societies of the region, such as Argentina and Brazil. Social policies offered as an alternative to citizenship prevail in countries such as Guatemala, Mexico, Nicaragua, and Peru. State corporatist social policies respond to corporatist interests, rather than to broad social or class demands. As Malloy pointed out, pressure groups in these corporatist societies do not "bargain for general rights of citizens, nor even for right of classes." Rather, pressure groups in these societies bargain for "group-specific rights" (Malloy 1993, p. 235):

> The pattern of coverage in all cases formed a kind of power map of each country. The first and best coverage went to groups like civil servants and the military who controlled parts of the state apparatus itself; coverage of high quality next went to groups in strategic economic activities in export products such as railroads, docks, maritime, etc; these were followed by groups in critical urban services such as banks, electricity, transport, etc; the last to receive coverage, and of a lower order, were manufacturing workers ... the rural sector as well as the urban informal sector were excluded.

Social policies offered as an alternative to citizenship are designed to benefit segments of the population that suffer systematic forms of social, political, and economic exclusion. The people in this category are citizens only in a formal manner. They are recognized as recipients of social policy by the same states that deny their rights and sustain their exclusion. The most visible groups in this category are the indigenous populations across the region.

Understanding the differences in the nature of the state, citizenship rights, and social policy in Europe and Latin America is essential to understanding the impact of globalization on the nature of state–society relations in these two parts of the world. The next section addresses the issue of globalization and its impact on social policies.

## Globalization and the changing nature of social policy

Globalization refers to "the intensification of worldwide social relations which link distant localities in such a way that local happenings are shaped by events occurring many miles away and vice versa" (Giddens 1990, p. 64). Although the origins of globalization can be traced to the emergence of the United Kingdom as the world leader in finance and trade during the second half of the

19th century, the first institutional expression and the mechanisms of the glob-
alized economy were set in place only after the end of World War II, with the
birth of an international monetary system at the Bretton Woods conference in
July 1944 (Mitchell 1992). On the basis of this agreement, the International
Monetary Fund (IMF) and the International Bank for Reconstruction and
Development (IBRD) were created.

Since World War II globalization has continued to evolve, manifesting
itself in areas other than the economy. At present, it is possible to distinguish
several macroscopic trends of this phenomenon, including

- The internationalization of trade, finance, and corporate organization;

- The internationalization of the world's security system;

- The rapid transformation of technology;

- The spread of ecological problems; and

- The emergence of new social movements with both a local and transnational consciousness (Camilleri and Falk 1992).

These expressions of globalization reduce the capacity of the state to spatially
delimit history. They "'lift out' social relations from local contexts of interaction" and restructure those relations "across indefinite spans of time–space"
(Giddens 1990, p. 21).

The internationalization of trade, finance, and corporate organization has
produced a growing disharmony between the national scope of the political
authority of the state and the transnational reach of the market. Thus, multinational corporations operate within a corporate, rather than a geographic,
view of the world's space (Clarke 1985; Heilbroner 1992, 1995).

The disharmony between the state and the market created by this situation is reflected in the changing nature of social policy in both Europe and
North America. The welfare state in these societies was founded on relatively
harmonious relationships between politics and economics at the national level.
It was the political ability of the state to redistribute the benefits of economic
growth that made the development of social rights and of national networks of
social services possible. Today, however, "domestic" economic and social relations are increasingly shaped by global-market forces, rather than by domestic
ones (Reich 1991; Heilbroner 1992). This makes it increasingly difficult for governments to "domesticate" economic forces (Falk 1993, p. 636) to maintain
social policies and with them, a sense of ontological security.

Moreover, the transnational character of economic relations and the
increasing "irrelevance of corporate nationality" create conditions for what
Christopher Lash (1994) called "the revolt of the elites." According to Lash, the
globalization of economic relations enables elites to severe their loyalty from

their own national societies. They can withdraw their economic and political support and their contribution to their countries' attempts to sustain national identity and history.

However, in addition to economic relations, technology also contributes to the globalization of social relations. In his article "Jihad vs. McWorld," Benjamin Barber (1992) argued that

> the information arm of international commerce's sprawling body reaches out and touches distinct nations and parochial cultures, and gives them a common face chiseled in Hollywood, on Madison Avenue, and in Silicon Valley. ... What is the power of the Pentagon compared with Disneyland? Can the Sixth Fleet keep up with CNN?

Barber (1992, p. 58) further remarked that "McDonald's in Moscow and Coke in China will do more to create a global culture than military colonization ever could."

Whereas communication technology tends to diffuse values from North to South, global migration "moves" values from South to North. Global migration is motivated by the search for better living conditions by the inhabitants of countries in the deprived regions of the South. Whereas television carries the values that define the national histories and identities of the North into the living rooms of the South, migrants carry the frustrations of their own history, as well as their aspirations to the North. In 1993, the United Nations High Commissioner for Refugees estimated that every year "150,000–300,000 people are accepted for resettlement on humanitarian grounds, and more than 2 million seek asylum in a foreign country." According to the same source (UNHCR 1993, p. 24), "the immediate cause of flight is usually an imminent threat to life, liberty or security."

Because of the transnational character of economic forces, information technology, and migration, they reduce the state's ability to contain the causes of its social, political, and economic evolution within its own boundaries. Furthermore, the administrative machinery of the modern state is quickly being transformed into a "spreading network" of "subtle and direct interconnections and interdependencies that enmesh public administrators from one part of the planet to another" (Luke 1992, p. 15). This has serious implications for the management of social policy. The transnational and international transformation of the state apparatus surely creates tensions and contradictions between the liberal concept of the modern state, with its emphasis on domestic responsiveness and accountability, particularly in areas of social provision, and the economic imperatives of the global market. The result is a crisis of authority arising from the state's increasing inability to respond to its domestic social needs and demands (Rosenau 1992).

In many ways the magnitude and implications of this crisis are similar to those faced by medieval institutions when the main social issues were the redefinition of authority and the identification of its legitimate sources. As has been pointed out, democracy implies a congruent relationship between policymakers and the recipients of policies. Citizens are supposed to maintain a considerable degree of control over the administrative functions of the state. Through this control, people actively participate in the spatial delimitation of historical time. The result is a lessening of uncertainty about the future and therefore greater security. However, the development of the modern state's role in "engendering social conditions" (Luhmann 1993, p. 67) has been accompanied by a decline in the political capacity of people to influence the public policy-making process. This is becoming increasingly evident in social-sector policies, including employment and education. Therefore, a person affected by policy decisions "sees himself as endangered by decisions that he neither makes himself nor controls" (Luhmann 1993, p. 107). Globalization tends to promote a rupture in the congruent relationship between decision-makers and the populous that eliminates the *raison d'etre* of political participation as traditionally conceived. To win a national election today, for example, is not to achieve the capacity to govern vis-à-vis social needs and priorities but to assume the role of intermediary between increasingly powerful global forces and active but increasingly ineffective domestic pressures (Ventriss 1989; Simeon 1991).

However, globalization does not create homogeneous social conditions around the world. Far from it. Globalization is a force to be reckoned with, but it is a force that confronts the resilient variety and heterogeneity of the human condition (Migdal 1988). Therefore, the impact of globalization on the capacity of states to spatially delimit history and generate conditions for security will vary according to a state's capacity to filter external pressures and to respond to domestic needs and demands. To understand this, the traditional notions of developed and developing societies remain useful because they are not simply categories for differentiating levels of economic advancement, but, more importantly, they represent levels of institutional capacity to reconcile people's social experiences with their expectations. More specifically, these categories represent different levels of state capacity to create conditions of social order and security through public policies (Johnson 1977).

These important differences are not properly captured by the concept of social policy that is used ahistorically to represent state actions in both developed and developing societies, regardless of their different histories and different social conditions. The specificity of the impact of globalization on social policy in the two types of society is lost if these fundamentally different historical experiences are represented by a concept of social policy that claims universal applicability and value.

The historical evolution of the political societies of Latin America shows weaknesses and deficiencies in terms of external sovereignty, social regulatory capacity, and civil society. Consequently, globalization can have devastating social effects in states like those in Latin America that are without the capacity to organize social interventions to respond to domestic needs and demands. The effects of globalization in Latin America became increasingly evident during the stabilization and adjustment crisis of the 1980s, particularly through the conditions and restrictions imposed by multilateral credit organizations on the governments of the region. According to Rosenthal (1990, p. 63), the crisis was prompted by

> high levels of indebtedness combined with a dramatic rise in real interest rates, deteriorating terms of trade, an abrupt decline in fresh sources of external financing, and the increasing uncertainties and instabilities of the rules that governed world trade and financial flows.

These unfavourable conditions were aggravated by a loss of dynamism in the two main engines of growth in Latin American economies in the post-World War II period: the export of primary products and industrialization based on the expansion of domestic demand. The increasing obsolescence of these traditional economic engines is reflected in the fact that the total value of exports in 11 of the 19 economically most important countries of the region remained unchanged or declined during the 1980s. Moreover, the participation of Latin America in the world exports went from 7.7% in 1960 to 3.9% in 1988 (ECLAC 1990). These changes are not a cyclical phenomenon but result from a profound transformation of the international demand structure, which includes changes in consumer preferences and technological changes. They are, in other words, the result of a discrepancy between "the composition of the Latin American exports and the structure of demand, production and technology of the international economy" (ECLAC 1990, p. 24).

During the 1980s, Latin American governments negotiated with the IMF and the World Bank to obtain new credits to restore external balance. In securing new credits, these countries agreed to introduce a number of economic, political, and institutional reforms along neoliberal lines (Sunkel and Zuleta 1990). The implementation of these reforms involved opening national economies to international competition, reducing the size of the state, reducing government services (for example, in health and education), and privatization. Unfortunately, the social costs of these reforms have been dramatic.

In terms of the medium- and longer-term effects on social policy and social-security systems, the stabilization and adjustment crisis of Latin American societies and the introduction of neoliberal economic policies during the 1980s and 1990s should not be treated as a temporary phenomenon. They have triggered a historical transition to a new model of both social and economic development, in which the market determines the organization of economic and social affairs. The market-centred model of development tends to replace the different versions of the Keynesian development model that prevailed in Latin America after the 1930s. The Keynesian model is based on a combination of international economic *laissez faire* and state interventionism (Schamis 1993). In the Keynesian model, the role of the state includes the responsibility for providing workers and marginal sectors of society with a network of social services that, at least in theory, guarantees their social rights. In fact, the idea of the welfare state in Latin America has found extremely diverse expressions: from the sophisticated, universal, Uruguayan social-security system introduced by José Batlle y Ordõnez between 1903 and 1915, to the highly exclusive systems of countries like Guatemala and Peru. Regardless of the wide range of national variations, the Keynesian model expresses the notion that state intervention is needed to bring about economic development, to safeguard the social rights of the population, and to create social order. The introduction in the 1980s of structural-adjustment programs and stabilization programs signaled a radical reconceptualization of the role of the state and state–society relations, particularly insofar as they pertain to social provisioning. This emerging model is part of a global trend that is reconfiguring state–society relations on the basis of market considerations. Needless to say, the sociopolitical implications of this model are profound.

The Inter-American Development Bank (IADB) and the United Nations Development Programme (UNDP) have pointed out that in absolute numbers and as a percentage of the total population, there was more poverty in the region in the early 1990s than at the beginning of the 1980s (IADB and UNDP 1993).

*The Social Panorama of Latin America, 1995* reports "moderate progress" in the alleviation of poverty. However, these efforts have not been enough to recover the social conditions that prevailed at the end of the 1970s (ECLAC 1995). Moreover, the rate of economic growth for this decade is insufficient to absorb the growing labour force. According to ECLAC (1995, p. 23),

> this situation was initially interpreted as a specific consequence of the early stages of the reform process, but it now appears to have become permanent, even in cases where the process is at an advanced stage and growth rates are high.

Finally, ECLAC (1995, p. 27) reported that

> the economies of most Latin American countries during the 1990s have been characterized by an unequal distribution of the costs of adjustment and by a notable rigidity of income distribution during expansionary phases.

With more than 200 million people in the region living under the poverty line (ECLAC 1997), it is possible to argue that politics in Latin America is to a considerable extent about social policy (Faria and Guimaraes Castro 1990). People's participation in the promotion and consolidation of political institutions is guided not only by ideals of political freedom and democracy but also by a practical concern for survival and security.

The intimate relationship between social policy and politics in Latin America is conditioned by economic policy. In Latin America, the current processes of economic and political development involve profound tensions and contradictions between the institutional establishment of democracy as an inclusive political system and of exclusive neoliberal economies (Calderón and Dos Santos 1991). Awareness of these tensions and contradictions prompted observers of Latin American affairs to argue that the introduction of liberal-market economic policies has produced "regressive social effects and severe political conflicts, with unpredictable consequences for the recently restored democracies [of the region]" (Sunkel and Zuleta 1990, p. 35). IADB and UNDP (1993, pp. 3–4) indicated that

> excluding large sectors of the population from the tangible and intangible benefits of progress is incompatible with the consolidation of increasingly open, pluralistic and stable democratic systems. Sustained economic exclusion reflects in political exclusion which undermines governance.

More recently, the final report of the 24th Conference of the Food and Agriculture Organization of the United Nations, celebrated in Asuncion, Paraguay, in July 1996, warned governments in Latin America and the Caribbean of the grave social consequences of hunger and malnutrition in the region. According to this report, 13% of the population of Latin America and the Caribbean suffer from hunger today. At this conference, representatives of workers' organizations also warned participants about the dangers of large-scale social insurrections produced by the intensification of poverty in the region (La Prensa 1996).

The inability of the Latin American states to respond to the social needs and demands of their populations has not been offset by the market. The market has the potential to empower people through self-employment and wage employment. However, under present and future conditions of many Latin American countries, this potential is unlikely to be realized. Projections for 2000 show the development of a widening gap between the rates of growth of the labour force and those of employment. This trend is a central characteristic of the phenomenon of "jobless growth" affecting the world today (UNDP 1993). Moreover, the problem of labour today is not only expressed in a quantitative discrepancy between demand and supply. Job security is also deteriorating. In both industrial and developing societies "enterprises have been reducing their reliance on a permanent job labour force, engaging instead a highly skilled group of workers surrounded by a periphery of temporary workers" (UNDP 1993, p. 37). In 1993, the Program to Promote Educational Reform in Latin America and the Caribbean reported that although overall economic growth in Latin America was producing more jobs, 8 out of 10 new jobs since 1980 were concentrated in the informal sector, which includes small business, self-employment, and domestic service. Needless to say, most of these jobs were of very poor quality.

The inability of the state to provide people with social security, compounded with the inability of the market to provide people with employment and job security, creates the proper conditions for ontological insecurity, a situation, recall, in which "the ordinary circumstances of everyday life constitute a continual threat" (Laing 1971, p. 171).

ECLAC suggests possible linkages between socioeconomic conditions and increasing violence and insecurity in Latin America. Based on a survey of the regional press carried out between January and August 1995, ECLAC (1995, p. 123) reported that in Uruguay "85% of the population believes that violence has increased in the last 10 years and there is little confidence in the police." In Honduras,

> police functions have been transferred from the military to the civil authorities, but the police have proved incapable, through lack of resources, of curbing the violence which led to 3,600 deaths in 1994 and 835 up to June 1995, according to police statistics.

In Venezuela, "lynching of criminals in working-class areas demonstrates the degree of dissatisfaction with the policy and processes of justice." In Guatemala,

> the electoral platforms of several political parties agree on the need to combat crime, give more power to the police, increase their wages and provide more equipment, and to increase awareness of civic responsibilities and punish corruption in the forces of law and order.

The proliferation of ontological insecurity can result in the delegitimation of the state and political institutions, whose existence can only be justified in the first place by their contribution to social conditions under which "the ordinary circumstances of life do not afford a perpetual threat to one's own existence" (Laing 1971, p. 42). Therefore, the delegitimation of the state and political institutions can easily result in the depoliticization of social conflict: that is, a condition in which the struggle for status, power, and scarce resources takes place outside established political processes and institutions (Coser 1956).

The consequences of the deinstitutionalization of Latin American politics can be dramatic. The elimination of the state as the object of political conflict and competition can create conditions in many of the countries of the region for a war of all against all. This is because the withering away of state power does not eliminate the tensions and contradictions that plague Latin American societies; rather, it eliminates the possibility of using state power as an effective instrument for the promotion of social justice.

# Conclusion: too close for comfort — social life in the global village

In a world of transnational societies, the causes of — and, presumably, the solutions to — the problems of social order and security are not confined to national territories and national social structures and institutions (Faist 1995; Huysmans 1995; Rodriguez 1995; Jordan 1996). These problems need to be reconceptualized to account for the impact of globalization on the capacity of the state to recreate national histories within the boundaries of national territories. This is especially the case for societies like those of Latin America that never developed the capacity to contain the main determinants of their historical evolution within territorial boundaries.

The study of social policy can no longer take nation-states as sole referents; rather, it has to be studied from both national and transnational perspectives. Abram de Swaan wrote an interesting speculative article exploring the question of transnational social policies. He argued (de Swaan 1992, pp. 33–34) that transnational social policies per se do not exist today:

> What exists at present is development aid: transfers from the richer to the poorer states, generally aimed at promoting productive activities rather than supporting citizens in times of need. In fact, for many years now, the net capital flow has been in the opposite direction. Humanitarian — non-governmental — organizations operate to support the hungry, the sick and the homeless in the poor nations with private donations collected in the richer countries, but these transfers do not entail legal obligations or enforceable claims, they constitute charity, on a global scale but marginal and incidental at best. A transnational welfare scheme would imply that some nations would contribute to payments made to the citizens of other nations in a systematic manner and under binding arrangements.

Although it is true that a transnational welfare system as defined by de Swaan (1992) does not exist and may never be in place, it is also true that the transformation of the spatial foundations of international systems of modern states brought about by globalization has forced national and international organizations to move in the direction of transnational social policies. This tendency can be seen not only in Europe but also in the framework of relations between developed and developing countries, in which the globalization of key social problems has blurred the differences that used to clearly separate the theoretical and practical fields of development aid, humanitarian aid, and social policy. This is most clearly manifest in the emergence of a global social-policy agenda and in the more incipient discussion on the institutional requirements for its implementation.

Fernando Filgueira (1995[1]) identifies three conditions that have to be fulfilled for a policy issue to become global. First, the issue has to be analytically

---

[1] Filgueira, F. 1995. Los inicios de una agenda global en políticas sociales: el caso de América Latina. Paper prepared for the Globalization and Social Policy in Latin America project, International Development Research Centre, Ottawa, ON, Canada, Jul.

identified as a treatable social problem with transnational manifestations. Second, the issue has to be perceived as a problem whose causes, consequences, and potential solutions transcend the boundaries of national states. Third, an institutional transnational capacity has to be articulated to confront the issue. Based on these criteria, there is very little doubt that some key social issues are becoming global. This is expressed, for example, in the conceptualization of the causes of poverty and in the design and implementation of potential solutions to this problem by the IFIs that are part of the so-called Washington consensus. The globalization of social policy is also expressed, although mainly symbolically, in the general agreements reached by participants in international forums such as the World Summit for Social Development and the Fourth World Conference on Women.

Several potential motivating factors in the emergence of transnational social policies can be identified. De Swaan (1992) pointed out two: ecological factors that create global interdependence and give poor countries some bargaining power to improve distribution of wealth around the world; and global South–North migration that can have the capacity to motivate developed countries to promote better social conditions in the poor countries of the world. To these two, one can add the social requirements of the global market; that is, the requirements for global social order and stability required by the increasing interdependence of national markets, the intensification of trade, and capital mobility.

However, the interdependence created by ecological problems, global migration, and the global economy are only manifestations of the fundamental problem (and challenge) posed by globalization. More than anything else, globalization represents a fundamental change in the relationship between people, territory, and ontological security that developed for 400 years. Globalization has penetrated the walls of sovereign states, thus linking national histories with world history. The result of this penetration is the end of national politics as a domestic activity capable of determining a society's future. The consequences of this fundamental change can be dramatic (Richmond 1994; CGG 1995; Wallerstein 1995). Even the most optimistic observers of the current process of global interpenetration agree that globalization will probably create significant levels of insecurity around the world long before a new national, regional or global institutional capacity to overcome contingencies is developed (Kennedy 1993; Singer and Wildavsky 1993; Thurow 1996). This is why, as Robert Heilbroner observed, the dominant mood of humanity at the end of the 20th century is apprehension. According to Heilbroner (1995, p. 89),

> in four respects Today stands in contrast to Yesterday. First, the Future has regained some of the inscrutability it possessed during the Distant Past. Second, the marriage of science and technology has revealed dangerous and dehumanizing consequences that were only intuitively glimpsed, not yet experienced, by our forbears of Yesterday.

Third, the new socioeconomic order proved to be less trustworthy than when it appeared during the late eighteenth and early nineteenth centuries. And last, the political spirit of liberation and self-determination has gradually lost its inspirational innocence.

For the wealthy societies of the world, the challenge posed by globalization has not only a national but also a transnational dimension, as their responses to the social problems of the South will not only determine the fate of people in developing countries but also the developed countries' identity as nations. Identities, Charles Taylor (1991, p. 48) remarked, depend on "our dialogical relations with others." The way societies deal with the "others" also defines their own identity. To put it bluntly a country cannot, for example, close the door of its hospitals to "illegal aliens" and continue to celebrate its democratic traditions and humanitarian principles.

The comfortable territorial and mental spaces created by the modern state are falling apart. The unhistorical sovereign territory is being quickly replaced by multihistorical and open spaces. To administer the new forms of social conflict and turmoil generated by this emerging historical ahistorical condition, societies around the world must develop new capacities to generate conditions for human security. With global interpenetration, transnational social policies are slowly emerging as a new social reality. However, the forms they are taking suggest that they can only be used to protect the rich against the effects of the poverty created by national and transnational socioeconomic structures. Moreover, the transnational institutional system that is in charge of articulating these transnational-policy measures is immune to social pressures and social demands.

One should not assume, however, that politics is dead and countries must resign themselves to the dictates of the global market. Any solution to the serious problems that globalization presents will inevitably require the revitalization of politics at both national and transnational levels (Heilbroner 1992; CGG 1995). This revitalization should not be based on a voluntaristic view of history, according to which governments and decision-makers can decide whether or not to participate in the process of global interpenetration in which modern societies operate today. Voluntaristic views of globalization reduce social phenomena to a problem of human will and political decisions. To transcend the inadequacies of this perspective, history should be seen as "the permanent result of a tension between objective possibilities and human choice" (Guerreiro-Ramos 1970, p. 32). From this perspective, the challenge for social scientists and policymakers is to devise ways of assessing the framework of limitations and possibilities within which morally significant policy decisions have to be made. The challenge is also to expand the scope of political and moral opportunities to confront the negative consequences of globalization and to realize the opportunities of the new millennium.

# CHAPTER 2

# SOCIAL-POLICY ISSUES AT THE END OF THE 20TH CENTURY

*Luis Ratinoff*

Many people believe that the world is experiencing a "Copernican Revolution" in social-policy formulation. Globalization has expanded the parameters of social policy from a domestic to an international frame of reference and from sectoral to societal processes. Awareness of the society-wide implications of specific social-policy issues comes with the realization that global interconnections tend to limit social-policy options to a narrow range of new but restricted solutions. It is becoming increasingly transparent that this range is conditioned by the interplay of two sets of rules: those allocating general benefits among groups, sectors, and regions and those providing special protection and inducements to foster specific goals or to compensate for the negative consequences of resource-allocation processes.

This chapter argues that the emerging global scenario restricts local capacities to protect and compensate people for social inequities and discrimination. The following sections will show that the new social-policy issues are not so much related to program inefficiency as to the systemic bias of resource-allocation processes. If these processes sustain or increase existing regressive conditions, improved social-program efficiency will be insufficient to turn the tide. Compensatory interventions only succeed if they can prevent further inequalities and if allocation norms are not biased by inequities and segregation. However, in developed and developing countries, political elites are now slowly learning that they cannot develop social policy in domestic isolation. Although their constituencies remain local, their actions in one place and in one public-policy area have forward and backward effects and multiple and complex linkages beyond national borders and sectoral concerns.

# Global concerns and local constraints

Global interconnectedness has resulted in a mosaic of new domestic situations in which everyone is exposed to global trends. However, this vulnerability to external influences is not everywhere the same. The degree of consolidation of existing social-policy systems seems to be a factor determining the extent of the impact of global forces. Thus, for example, local constituencies firmly committed to social policies and to social objectives in developed countries often interfere both in the range of the adjustments taking place and in the overall fluidity of the global network of influences. Such local constituencies marginally regulate changes in existing systems and provide political support for a diversity of ethical concerns central to current social-policy changes. Thus, cultural traditions and the elite's ideologies and interests often become the main limiting factors once economic isolation is broken.

Globalizing reform processes, particularly in social policy, can easily change social-policy objectives and institutional makeups; however, the destruction of the fabric of society implies human sacrifices and political prices that deter local elites from radicalizing or speeding reforms to globalize economic and social policies. Open opposition, negotiated settlements between domestically and internationally oriented political groups and interests, and expressions of passive resistance and frustration become formidable and sometimes hidden barriers to the legitimacy of elite interests. Widespread cynicism, apathy, youth alienation, corruption, and a surge in crime tend to contribute to a climate of social impotence in dealing with the human side of globalization. Authoritarian responses seem to deepen these trends, and piecemeal concessions are often insufficient. To preserve their legitimacy, therefore, local elites must build and renew social consensus.

Other sources of opposition reduce the autonomy of globalizing elites. In advanced industrial countries, where constituencies count, there are also strong civic groups capable of mobilizing public opinion in favour of environmental concerns, human rights, and social issues. In many instances, global activism has increased, parallel to the consolidation of international markets. It is not yet known whether this is a systemic trend or a momentary reaction to a few extreme and undesirable consequences of global-reform processes. However, the rise of civic organizations seems to be a significant phenomenon in globalizing scenarios, especially when disengaged constituencies search for civic values outside political parties.

## Utopian and ideological arguments

The proponents of the current rhetoric of economic globalization use two types of argument. They appeal to both modernization utopia and free-market ideology. Utopia and ideology define the justification of social objectives in unprotected environments. Utopianism appears to expand the scope and depth of equity concerns with a host of complimentary public policies and programs while free-market ideology reduces social policies to a residual role.

The utopian argument emphasizes how progress in an environment of market continuity will have modernizing effects that spill over into social structures and political systems. This argument assumes that in the long run, free markets destabilize economically oppressive conditions. Whereas protectionist policies seem to consolidate distortions that perpetuate the privileged status of rent-seeking interests, open economies are thought to institutionalize more impersonal and efficient resource-allocation processes. However, the reduction of opportunities for profit has several noneconomic implications. Standard modernization theory suggests that the struggle for control of assets and rents is replaced by the control over markets through competition. Class-conflict issues that find a fertile ground in protected constituencies are thought to be replaced by economic-efficiency concerns and enlarged consumption as the more real and effective political pacifiers. Once maintaining a protected field of assets and opportunities is no longer the overall condition for accommodating interest groups, it is postulated that the achievement of economic efficiency and growth will become the organizing principle of social integration.

The cornerstone of modernization utopia is the idea that improved competitiveness reduces the risks of an open economy and expands opportunities for material progress, regardless of initial inequalities. Utopian discourse emphasizes the role of a sequential evolution requiring an increasing supply of adequate human capital and the development of social and political capacities for decentralized coordination, based on trust and democratic decision-making. Within this framework, an open economic system is thought to become fully sustainable wherever the human and social capital reinforce the gains of prosperity and the expectations generated by enlarged consumption.

On this utopian model, social-policy interventions are justified only under exceptional conditions. This is particularly the case when the human-capital stock is inadequate to sustain economic growth or when the depth of inequities and discrimination prevent good governance. Both exceptions seem to be broad enough to include most social programs. However, their exceptional nature also opens the way for a more restricted and ideological view of public responsibility.

Although in general, public-policy goals reflect the utopian outlook, implementation strategies harbour, in fact, many of the ideological concerns of the proponents of market dominance. Universal provision that guarantees access to benefits, for example, is replaced by focused interventions to concentrate resources where needed so as to reduce the waste of undeserved subsidies. Consequently, the scope of social policies is defined in terms of over-

or under-concentrations of resources, and their effectiveness is measured primarily in terms of overhead costs.

This combination of utopianism and free-market ideology requires a great deal of tolerance for ambiguity. On the one hand, the priority of social goals is recognized, but as complementary to other goals. On the other, the "realism" of putting the engine of prosperity first emphasizes the ideal of a community committed to the utilitarian values of economic efficiency and competition. These ideological concerns call for the institutionalization of a unidimensional culture fully consonant with the complex workings of capital returns and optimization. They suggest the need to enforce a utilitarian value system and in the process dismiss any other cultural concerns. But the ethical abhorrence of human deprivation and the need to maintain and create solidarity express other dimensions of social interaction and imply different opportunity costs in the process of redesigning the fabric of a society. Although the utopian side of the globalization project helps to promote the notion that there are public social responsibilities, it does not help to determine whether these priorities are to have an ancillary or a residual role.

The ideal of communities operating as unregulated fields for open competition not only excludes the logic of solidarity and universalistic social policies but also influences their implementation strategies. A commonplace in many social-policy reforms stemming from the process of economic adjustment to globalization is the proposal that the effectiveness of social programs can be improved by making them imitate the market. However, such proposals often disregard the specific circumstances, factors, and challenges faced by public-policy reforms. Often, an organizing theme of such reform proposals is to blame inadequate public-sector policies, abusive bureaucracies, public-sector unions, and politicization. The underlying implication is that in competitive and prosperous environments, sanitizing the field through "efficient" technical interventions can achieve more with less.

The new model of social-policy implementation emphasizes the centrality of resource optimization over politically defined goals. The very strategy of focusing the provision of benefits helps to reduce political pressure from influential groups that do not need the subsidies. In such a context, the reformers offer a battery of "solutions" to reinforce resource optimization, including decentralization, diversifying the delivery of public services, privatization, downsizing, and subcontracting.

Although these approaches seem to be consistent with market ideology, the increasing use of civic organizations to diversify and decentralize involves a heterodox array of agents, with values of solidarity and sometimes political solutions as well. This presents another challenge requiring a great deal of tolerance for ideological ambiguities, as the effectiveness of using civic organizations depends on the ideals of human cooperation and the commitment to achieving social goals over those of resource management. The blending of issues, activism, and social mobilization with the bureaucratic market-oriented system of social-policy implementation is a Machiavellian concession to pragmatism, really incompatible with the ideal of a community of individuals devoted to capital-returns optimization. Efforts to improve the allocation of resources in the social sectors by changing command structures into incentive systems, for example, have had mixed results. It is likely that as a result of these reforms, subsidies have become more transparent, and profit-seeking interests have had less access to the benefits. In this context, the social sectors are more efficient, in the sense of lowering overhead and applying subsidies to the really needy. However, this does not mean that the programs are more effective; in many places, there are signs of a decline in the effectiveness of programs.

## Beyond delivery systems

The growing and dynamic role of activist civic groups in social-policy formulation and implementation fills, in part, the policy vacuum left in the wake of resource-optimization strategies and their strong emphasis on the technical rebureaucratization of social services. Although the goal of efficiency makes sense in delivery systems and is embedded in sectoral issues, most civic organizations work on the sectoral fringe or very much beyond. They deal with problems in those uncharted territories that bureaucracies and systems do not reach, such as family disorganization, depressed neighbourhoods, violence, and abandoned and abused children.

These issues transcend the limits of conventional social-sector policies and highlight the shortcomings of the resource-optimization strategies and the growing importance of nonsectoral challenges in public-policy debate. The relevance of this frontier is confirmed by the dynamic role of civic associations, social-mobilization experiences, and the incapacity of sectoral approaches to identify and tackle emerging substantive issues in a more interconnected world. Furthermore, it seems that the sector outcomes of policy delivery are becoming increasingly conditioned by this frontier of new social problems. Lessons are slowly coming together.

Good sector performance has marginal long-term progressive effects. This, however, is the case only if short-term segregation is not overwhelming and can be managed. But bad performance and inequities tend to sustain or even increase regressive conditions. Thus, for example, low-quality health or education reinforce segregation and poverty, rather than enabling individuals to break away from them. This raises a serious issue: the social environment surrounding sectoral interventions cannot be neglected any longer; otherwise, sectoral costs will increase while the effectiveness of social-sector policies diminishes.

It may be argued that the elites who emphasize the benefits of globalization are on the right track when they insist that favourable general economic conditions have the potential to smooth out the need for costly, piecemeal social engineering and when they emphasize the overall importance of a dynamic economy. But they take the wrong turn when they assume that unilateral economic parsimony is enough. The enabling environment for social-policy change depends on more than favourable economic prospects. Many of the conditions for such an environment are related to the structure of human interactions, involving economic, social, political, cultural, and ethical factors.

Civic organizations often try to deal with these issues. Their contributions to the social-policy agenda are anchored in specific issues (for example, human rights, women's roles, unemployment, civic participation, violence, and personal security) and substantive problems (for example, children at risk, youth, family violence, shelters, training, ethnic discrimination, old age, and disabled persons). However, despite their strong ethical message, they tend to shy away from radical proposals. They tend to bring into the forefront substantive policy concerns and have a significant influence on public opinion and political decisions, but these efforts represent only the tip of the iceberg.

## The role of civil society: social entrepreneurship

In today's context of social-policy change, civic organizations are bringing back the notion that social-policy effectiveness is a central parameter for assessing a policy's success. This pushes the often limited bureaucratic horizons of the sectoral delivery system beyond the range of single substantive issues and constraints. The relevance of the social environment surrounding the delivery systems in explaining costs and results reveals the shortcomings of sectoral resource allocation as the main tool to improve social-sector effectiveness. Thus, for example, health-system costs and results are conditioned by several external factors, such as lifestyles, family structure, physical and social environments, health cultures, and standards of life and nutrition. Selecting among alternative health-delivery priorities to allocate resources better may improve levels of health but only to the extent allowed by such environmental factors. Similarly, educational institutions perform poorly in adverse socioeconomic conditions. Special programs to compensate for this may be required, but they add to the costs, and in many cases expectations are lowered. The lesson to be learned is that schools and health-delivery institutions are not designed to deal with these issues, although they can be severely affected by them.

Although a less ideological social agenda seems to be slowly emerging, it too brings complex challenges. From the perspective of policy implementation, the contribution of civic organizations poses new problems. On the one hand, highly formalized and regulated systems designed to address nonsectoral challenges do not seem to respond to the existing heterogeneity of circumstances, resources, and opportunities. On the other hand, the many single-issue strategies to achieve social goals through decentralized agents and interventions may be easier to implement but require abundant local capacities and initiative, the enabling ingredients of a strong civic society. As these are not found everywhere, issues are raised with increasing frequency about the effectiveness of the civic-organizations approach. There is also a growing awareness that decentralized interventions tend to become remedial and restricted and that local success stories often have limited multiplying effects.

In practice, the civic-organizations approach could be both remedial and preventive. The relative significance of prevention depends to a large extent on the amount, intensity, and sustainability of the "disturbances" that civic associations generate in the existing systems in the process of influencing public opinion and decision-making. Successful disturbances, for example, have had profound consequences for the public ethical commitment to social well-being and to social and human development. Most civic associations respond to the lure of ideological incentives and many of them become vocal in their criticism of the existing order. These "noises" are disturbing because they emphasize ideological concerns to set ethical limits to unregulated interests, such as insisting on basic rights, environmental preservation, equity, political fairness, and fair distribution. In a public arena increasingly devoid of values and long-terms goals, civic associations fill a vacuum. Although most are critical, not all are equally vocal. They all share the endeavour to focus public opinion on the specific issues they promote. Today, their disturbances are as important as the other benefits and services they deliver. But, unfortunately, this ideological contribution sometimes comes with the paralyzing effects of the challenges posed by increasing social-policy complexity.

This less organized side of social policies often deals with strategic clusters of human interaction, and the success of a specific program is bound to have enabling consequences that improve sector performance and participation at the local level. Strategic clusters have such multiplying effects because they condition the outcomes of a gamut of sectors and interactions. Successful support programs for families, women, youth, children, and for neighbourhood and community reconstruction, for example, seem to have an overall enabling effect that improves sector performance and modifies individuals' behaviour. It is known that decentralized, nonbureaucratic agents achieve impressive results. The issue then is not the success but how sustainable these efforts are. Several instances of this appear in case studies in part 2 of this volume, illustrating how effective and cost-efficient decentralized intervention can be, but these studies also point out the difficulties in recreating these success stories. To identify and replicate success one needs a new type of capacity. Societies are slowly learning to train social managers to operate in bureaucratic environments requiring a great deal of coordination, resources, mobilization, and community cooperation. However, we are still a long way from knowing how to multiply the number of these "social entrepreneurs," for they are the decentralized, nonbureaucratic agents who can create or recreate specific social programs, including design, development, resource mobilization, implementation, personnel management, recruitment, motivation, and adaptation to changes and emerging opportunities.

Current trends in social entrepreneurship suggest that this approach involves a complex combination of philanthropy and activism and the relationship between individual motivations and social incentives. At one level, personal commitment highlights the overall importance of motivation in the recruitment of social entrepreneurs. Despite the contemporary cultural emphasis on power and material gains, some institutions and traditions continue to instill altruistic values and attempt to disseminate integrative cultural and political themes in social-policy discourse and action. Social incentives, in turn, reinforce the ideal that the real world still has room for nonutilitarian convictions and enable the transformation of generous concerns into actions and programs.

Social entrepreneurship is a critical issue for any decentralized social-development strategy based on private civic organizations. In this regard, the question is one of balance and resources, particularly in times of the retrenchment of public-sector programs that occurs with the assumption that local authorities will meet responsibilities through civic-society associations and initiatives. In this context, the success of charities as tools to reduce social inequities, for example, depends on a progressive economic and social environment. Often, however, such tools are not effective alternatives for the regressive systems in place, except for the ethical influence they have through their capacity to create disturbances.

## Social entrepreneurs and systems

The existence of civic associations as social-delivery agencies at the local level is often precarious. This is because the large scale of service-delivery operations and their need for continuity require an adequate and steady supply of private or public funds; in practice, donors tend to define standards and impose nonspecific conditions. One of the outcomes of this is that civic groups enter into asymmetric relationships of financial dependence.

Although this dependence may seem initially attractive to many civic organizations, when financing opportunities entail the expansion of their operations, at least three adverse consequences are difficult to avoid: constrained, self-regulated step-by-step programs become externally regulated by donors; less room is given for self-initiative and innovation; and more supervisory control becomes indispensable. One of the outcomes of this is that the relationship between those who grant the funds and those who provide the services tends to be one of implementation through subcontracting. In some cases, these arrangements may be more flexible than command structures and also more cost effective; however, it is reasonable to assume that increases in bureaucratization in the delivery systems may result in donor-induced rigidities and higher costs. Despite this, subcontracting with civic organizations may be an alternative that pays back in areas and in situations beyond the capabilities of hierarchical social-delivery systems.[1]

In the world of contemporary social-policy change, a lot has been said in favour of the participation of civic-society groups in social-policy implementation. However, we do not have enough information to know how much to expect from them. Unrealistic hopes may be a fertile ground for frustrations, and the truth is that no matter how successful they become, their interventions are designed to be limited in scope and number.

Without doubt, a better understanding of the limitations of these new arrangements may be helpful. In addition to the difficulties of finding social-entrepreneurship capacities and the hidden effects of such alternatives as subcontracting, the ability of these arrangements to deliver results with low costs is limited in scope, given the limitations in the design of the programs. In most cases, the maximum multiplying effects occur when new possibilities emerge as a consequence of the social-mobilization that civic organizations unleash. However, this requires a great deal of political tolerance and restraint on the donors' side. Civic organizations that generate social mobilization for specific issues often become gradually tolerated as a source of social "turbulence." The tolerance, however, depends on the subordination of their role to existing institutional frameworks. Civic associations can and do influence political opinion, but they are not political parties. The latter define their positions vis-à-vis specific issues from a relatively consonant ideological range of views. Civic associations are issue oriented, and up to now they have not tried to provide general economic and social cures. In fact, their very ability to influence across party lines enhances their power and ethical resonance. They are not radical groups with their minds set against the established order. Civic associations are indeed critical of the ways the established order performs with respect to specific issues, but they propose to improve it step by step, through programs, new rules, and persuasion.

---

[1] A new jargon has emerged in the last 10 years to distinguish the genuine nongovernmental organizations (NGOs) from government-induced or government-controlled NGOs (GONGOs) and from donor agency-induced or donor agency-controlled NGOs (DONGOs). Experience shows that GONGOs and DONGOs tend to duplicate NGOs in the same areas and sectors and are less adaptive and effective and therefore less cost effective. They experience some corruption as a result of the amount of the external financing they receive, often from a single source, and the bureaucratic influences and interests that shape their operations and their very survival.

Genuine expressions of local government and political autonomy in social-service delivery seem to step over an ambiguous threshold. From the point of view of the global interests promoting policy reform, the concept of civil society seems to loose its positive connotations when a broad political movement emerges articulating claims such as universal-equity goals beyond local and specific concerns or when civic associations reject their subordinate status. Thus, social policies designed to transfer responsibilities to private agents and to deprived groups, without simultaneously opening up opportunities or fostering capacities and more power-sharing, are bound to face some complex challenges. The notion of empowering people has made some conceptual and even a few practical inroads, but up to now such efforts seem to fall short of achieving their goals. Nobody knows how much empowering is enough or how to deal with the lack of initial powers. Furthermore, we have no clear consensus on how much power to transfer. Similarly, restricting equity to poverty issues, as is often done when social organizations become involved in service delivery, creates the danger of a significant political backlash. Although the idea of a nonrevolutionary political backlash is difficult to grasp, still it may have serious consequences.

In more protected societies, the threat of social upheaval has been the ghost that supports the political mechanisms in place; however, in the less protected global environment, with a nonpolitical but nevertheless implicit modernization agenda, macrosocial imbalances can generate "implosions" that undermine the effectiveness of specific countries' existing institutions. Some of the signs of this phenomenon are collective feelings of political withdrawal, youth alienation, deep cultural fractures, and increasing violence and crime. All of these point to the emergence of radical trends, anarchic individualism, and the weakening of social bonds and ethical commitments.

## Frictions and strategic social clusters

One of the main challenges in the current global scenario is to achieve social order in the context of rising social disintegration. This is no longer just a political issue — one of achieving formal institutional stability. Modern implosive environments affect, in practice, the fabric of human social interaction. Once the politics of hope, based on achieving a more equitable social order, is replaced by the politics of prosperity, based on reaching a higher rate of economic growth, little room is left either for the public expression of social tensions and aspirations or for articulating these frustrations in a comprehensive political project. Experiences indicate that although it is unrealistic to expect major social upheaval, if nobody proposes workable political alternatives, one can expect a number of specific challenges that tend to exceed institutional capacities for sustaining law and order. This is an implosive social horizon. In fact, drug consumption has increased in most places, as have crime rates in urban centres. The phenomena of alienated youth and an adversary youth culture have made significant inroads in the last 20 years. Furthermore, citizens' perceptions of personal insecurity and political corruption seem to contribute to a political culture of detached and uncommitted individuals. These trends suggest that a working social order cannot be taken for granted. In this context, the failure of the resource-optimization approach, either as a restricted, residual policy or as a broader ancillary strategy, stems from the assumption that a working social order is given and that the task at hand is to perfect it through technological progress and prosperity.

The simplicity in the design of this approach and the complexities of the issues suggest that persistent social issues are determining the extent to which sector efficiency can be translated into social-policy effectiveness. This is often described in terms of "friction" generated by the resistance from the field to program implementation. It is thought that the new social-policy challenge is to overcome the countercurrent and the turbulence. However, contemporary social-policy practitioners have identified a number of strategic interaction points. Many of these strategic interaction points reflect the impacts of modern technology on human society; the increasing exposure to global risks that in the last 20 years have helped to deepen those impacts; and the ongoing trends that seem to sustain them. The following sections discuss some of these strategic interaction points.

## The rediscovery of the family

At the end of the 20th century, the strategic importance of the family in sustaining the fabric of society has been rediscovered. Unfortunately, this is occurring in the context of a debate clouded with normative overtones. The issue of the family has become an area in which rhetoric converges with cultural diversity. This issue illustrates the inability of modernization utopianism to settle other ideological divides that are polarizing societies. The current debate helps to focus attention on the problems for the survival of family life under harsh urban conditions, but disagreements over issues and solutions have paralyzed the development of a better coordinated strategy.

The state of the family plays a crucial role in contemporary social-policy change. Most people agree, for example, that the state of the family has profound implications for social-policy implementation. Thus, the cost effectiveness of health and educational systems seems to be related to family integration and stability. Something similar can be said of welfare policies. Although this is not the place to elaborate on these complex linkages, it is relevant to emphasize that policies to help families at risk are difficult to design. In most cases, family groups are highly adaptive, but they cannot cope with some of the effects of globalization. As evidence shows, a great deal of family disorganization observed today is due to the indirect influence of transnational factors in the socioeconomic environment.

Not all of these can be controlled or eliminated, but the conditions for family life can be improved by reducing a significant number of them. Some of these obstacles are specific, simple to deal with, and have multiple implications for family-group stability, such as child-care services and access to recreational facilities and subsidized housing. However, not all these factors are so specific or respond so well to immediate treatment. The more diffuse the linkages are, the more complex is the challenge, such as unemployment, the negative influences of depressed neighbourhoods, some inherited lifestyles, or the magnetic values of contemporary commercial culture. By eliminating social-protection systems and mechanisms and by increasing the exposure of the individual and the family to risks, for example, globalization is helping to enhance the strategic importance of stabilizing values and rules. The influence of cultural factors is still diffuse, despite the fact that families are anchored in explicit normative frameworks. The erosion of traditions and the emphasis placed on returns to capital, even in areas of social development, has weakened legal frameworks for family protection. The law is no longer enough to protect the family when exposure to risk is on the rise, and in many cases, existing norms have become inadequate.

Today, families face problems that hinder their capacity to stay together and to produce services and allocate rewards. Finances for the special services that family groups provide are under severe strain. Experiments in substituting families for institutional alternatives have not been successful from the point of view of quality or cost. Supporting and strengthening families would be a much more cost-effective approach. The increasing participation of women in the labour force is a sign of the type of adjustments taking place, as well as being an expression of women's attempts to break away from their traditional entrapments in a world that undervalues the role they play in the family. The gap between the normative models and the realities of family life has gradually become wider. On the one hand, the increase in one-parent households, or "incomplete" family groups, is significant. On the other hand, adaptive practices are often legitimized in direct contradiction to local cultural patterns.

## Demographic trends are still a challenge

Despite contemporary cultural debate on reproductive rights, population issues have become an indispensable social-policy dimension. Demographic trends determine the human quantities, the crucial bottlenecks, and the relationship between the age structure and the allocation of risks. Furthermore, the new patterns of sexual behaviour generate health and educational costs along the way.

For modern residual social policies, population trends are increasingly becoming essential background information. It is assumed that economic prosperity will change human attitudes toward the meaning of life, disease, and death but, in the meanwhile, only restricted interventions make sense and have this effect, especially in the field of reproduction. The aging of the population, the new mortality and morbidity patterns, the increased length of schooling, the impact of a spreading culture of freedom, earlier sexual maturity, and the higher rate of female participation in the labour force cannot be easily dismissed as expressions of demographic transition, as they affect social and economic choices. A battery of social programs may be needed to deal with these complex issues.

## Adults come from children

Abandoned, exploited, and abused children are becoming a widespread problem in high-density areas in both developed and developing countries. Modern conditions are not only adverse to family integration and survival but also to the well-being of children. These problems are related, but they are not identical. The increasing number of dysfunctional families is probably a factor; however, from a social point of view, high birth rates among deprived social sectors and the high incidence of illegitimacy are also important contributing factors. A significant surplus of children and adults who shy away from parental responsibilities create opportunities for exploitation and abuse. For social-policy purposes, the recognition that high birth rates alone do not explain the exploitation and abuse of children in contemporary societies has opened the way to a reassessment of, for example, socialization processes and the role of legal-protection systems.

## Undernourishment has become urbanized

Hunger and malnutrition are still present. They have become urban problems in modern social settings. Enough evidence shows that these problems are closely related to poverty and that they have sequels of terrible consequences. Child undernourishment incapacitates children's development for a lifetime. It hinders the development of intelligence; it reduces attention and learning capacities; and it reduces the vitality of individuals, as well as making them more prone to disease. Good ethical arguments can be cited in favour of nutrition programs, and from an economic perspective the long-term costs and productivity losses from malnutrition are significant. Although nutrition programs and policies are easy to design, they are difficult to implement. Many target groups tend to misuse the general-purpose help they receive because they have other unsatisfied needs. But focused interventions produce limited results and must be provided in association with other social services and programs. The lifestyle of many of the groups affected is conditioned not only by poverty and deprivation but also by the lack of an adequate nutritional culture.

## Alcoholism and drugs

Alcohol and drug abuse are also commonly found in modern societies and have incapacitating and dangerous consequences. Both are often associated with poverty, discrimination, and other inequities that generate feelings of alienation. Although some room is left for prevention through education, rein-forced by group pressure, it is symptomatic that available resources are spent on rehabilitation programs and police interventions to reduce the supply of drugs. This occurs despite the fact that not enough is known about, for example, the cultural aspects and the specific circumstances of the abuse of psychoactive substances. The idea that these problems are not new is difficult to refute; nevertheless, the current social-policy challenges are to reduce the scale and curtail the spread of the problem.

For the most part, police interventions are expected to resolve the social concern about drug cultures and the entrapment of young people in addictions. However, in many industrial countries, not only is the illegal-drug market dynamic, but also the demand adapts to new products when the supply of others dwindles. Daily news of the drug situation reinforces the image of supply adaptability, but the factors that explain the demand side remain in the shadows. The control of the supply of drugs has produced limited results; a better understanding of demand is needed together with new social policies directed to dealing with these problems, particularly health and education policies.

# The syndrome of reduced teaching intensity and modern education

The current social-policy focus on sectoral-allocation issues, specifically in the case of education, obscures the consequences of the syndrome of reduced teaching intensity (RTI), or the teaching efficacy of schools. Teachers know that the school climate is a powerful component in the process of producing an educated mind. High teaching intensity results if the transmission of knowledge is associated with the transmission of values and habits. Emotional problems seem to block the process of learning, but values and habits contribute to emotional stability. In other words, classroom teaching efficacy is negatively affected if the school values clash with those of an adverse cultural environment. Educational institutions tend to adjust their expectations to the possibilities and opportunities of their cultural environments. Thus, in deprived and violent areas, school results are below average because they reflect not only the insufficient motivation of families, groups, and neighbourhoods for education but also the lower efficacy of the adjusted classroom standards. In modern societies, RTI syndrome is becoming one of the most serious challenges to social equity because it dulls the progressive edge of educational processes.

In the context of globalization, RTI syndrome originates in the conflict between a culture under pressure to modernize and introduce technology and school systems unable to respond to these new challenges. This discontinuity is raising costs while lowering the standards of the services delivered. Furthermore, the multiple attractions of modern societies, passive socialization through impersonal electronic media, and the processes of active emotional socialization through affiliation networks all seem to have advantages over the procedural teaching methods of school systems, but they fail as substitutes for formal education. Further, a less intense formal education cannot compete with these alternative ways of learning.

This situation seems to have some perverse consequences. Teaching intensity broadens the children's information horizons and nurtures the skills of abstract reasoning to deal with the challenges of complex modern societies. However, the abundant information flows associated with economic globalization and transnational influences produce negative reactions and feelings of insecurity if individuals do not have the capacities to deal with a simultaneous multiplicity of disturbing signals. A creative use of heavy information loads is incompatible with simplification and requires a great deal of mental discipline developed through systematic learning. We are slowly learning that information overload is not so much a function of the amount of information per se but of individuals' capacity to use information in discursive, symbolic, and interactive ways. When this capacity is low, individuals seem to close their minds and select whatever information reinforces their basic beliefs.

The social challenge posed by higher information density is to develop people's capacities to find the right balance of needed information and to avoid the negative consequences of information overload. The idea that abundant flows of information may slowly replace classrooms and be compatible with less intense formal education ignores the role played by the educated mind in structuring information; without this structure, signs, and messages generate mainly automatic reactions and images perpetuate passivity and imitation. To develop people's capacity to convert signs, messages, and images into discursive and active understanding requires both extending education to new social sectors and using more intense strategies to deepen the cultural influence of formal learning.

## The transition to adulthood

Youth problems are signs of modern times. Rapid technological change has helped to increase the cultural gap between generations. More than ever before, the continuous obsolescence of language, values, and expectations has emptied the common ground that used to link young people with the adult world. This trend is reinforced by the commercial marketing of youth products, by postponing the age of incorporation into the labour force, and by the uncertain opportunities offered to young people at the end of this latency period.

The problems are not necessarily new, but they have accumulated over time. The insufficiency of existing social systems to respond to young people's demands has established an area of public neglect that has a wide range of negative implications. The commercial exploitation of the images of youth has resulted in the gradual fading of the limits between fantasy and reality in terms of young people's expectations, and the emphasis on material consumption is helping to water down idealism. The lengthy educational period required by labour markets and the weakening of sustainable legal-protection systems for children and young people have institutionalized a latency period that raises expectations. The more uncertain the light at the end of this tunnel, the more difficult is the integration of young people into the mainstreams of adult life in global societies. The syndrome of youth alienation and young people's adoption of more radical lifestyles suggest that these problems are generating future costs both for society and for these young individuals. These developments also suggest the need for new types of social policy.

## Neighbourhood traps

Rapid urbanization and population growth are redefining the global social scenario. The provision of basic services and jobs continues to lag behind demands while a process of social deterioration is taking place, particularly in the urban areas. Increasingly, cities and neighbourhoods are becoming social territories, segregated by frontiers formed by different levels of productivity and investment and the availability of meaningful opportunities. For example, significant sectors of the urban population experience the benefits of the modern city only through the deprived territories they inhabit. These depressed human environments tend to sustain existing regressive conditions and represent tremendous obstacles to the effective implementation of social policies.

To develop linkages of neighbourhoods in depressed urban territories is a complex task that requires societies to create trust in the absence of the necessary reserves of social capital. This task has important institutional implications. The challenge is to decentralize responsibilities and powers while reestablishing the role of publicly elected authorities and central institutions. The development of a sense of neighbourhood requires the universal prevalence of law and order and provision for local needs. To have sustainable results, the economic bases of the neighbourhood must be rebuilt, and adequate social services must be provided.

## Simple designs, complex execution, and economic constraints

In the current public-policy environment, it is often difficult to execute, coordinate, and balance ancillary social-policies while achieving the global economic goals of improving system efficiency, using decentralized implementation strategies, and reducing the obstacles to more progressive conditions. Because the decentralized approach is disorganized, its success requires attaining indirect multiplier effects beyond the direct policy objectives. The nonbureaucratic coordination involved in this approach needs to build on the mutually supporting synergies that social policies are supposed to generate, and their multiplying effects have to exceed the inequities the current structures of society create. The participation of people in this social-policy compact is the only factor not directly conditioned by resource availability. All others are resource driven.

The globalization paradigm that lies behind the processes of economic-policy reform involves the assumption that the free flow of capital and technology will ultimately minimize the need for costly social-policy interventions. However, it is recognized that social policies have a role to play during the transition and that the resources and capacities invested in them should reflect their relevance — without, that is, jeopardizing material progress. Until now, utilitarian arguments have relied on utilitarian assumptions, but it is always difficult to consider the long-term effects of social interventions in dealing with immediate problems. Moreover, not everyone believes that the progress brought about by globalization is beyond the reach of politics and the interests of specific constituencies. It is also believed that despite visible global trends, social order remains grounded in local conditions. In fact, the globalization project contains no proposals to replace national authorities or to allow the free flow of people across borders to alleviate tensions resulting from structural adjustments and social-policy reforms.

Politics and values indeed play a role in this transition. Beyond ideology and utopianism, the progress of global integration requires a great deal of sustained political negotiation to accommodate the imperatives of internal order and to recognize the cultural traditions that make communication meaningful. People are slowly realizing the importance of cultural traditions. The costs of law and order are bearable if people share commitments and identities, but chaotic conditions seem to emerge with radical disengagement from the past. Some contemporary political experience suggests that people without history are unable to supply the bases for institutional stability or for civic culture. A discrete range of similar feelings of time and space provides people with a common identity and frames the meanings that facilitate interactive communication.

For those who think that nonutilitarian values and goals play a significant role in policy change, international market integration is also desirable from the viewpoint of the economy, and they argue that the social and cultural implications of globalization should involve political decisions about the distribution of the sacrifices and benefits — gains and loses. This line of thinking emphasizes that governments still have responsibilities to their constituencies, despite the complex and sometimes volatile workings of global markets. The exaggerated notion of an impersonal, self-regulating system is a political myth that serves to justify inaction and neglect. The proponents of an ethical political framework for globalization try to use the opportunity provided by the new policy scenario to maintain and develop a feasible order, applying the benefits to achieve a reasonable degree of social fairness, participation, cultural identity, and more effective legal protection. This requires, for example, formulating political projects — projects that sustain cultural diversity and the commitment to moral rights and obligations, open the political field to new participants, gradually reduce deprivation, and pursue equity through more competitive social processes.

## Social policy as a legitimation agenda

An alternative social-policy agenda, promoted by the policy-reform process, has gradually emerged from the contemporary experiences of many societies suffering basic-needs deprivation, violence, crime, alienated constituencies, cultural turmoil, feelings of widespread corruption, and growing personal and job insecurity. A heterogeneous coalition of moral conservatives, churches, civic-society activists, union leaders, and members of the disaffected middle classes supports the hypothesis that these implosive symptoms come from an unresolved macrosocial disequilibrium that increases the costs of maintaining a feasible order.

Although ancillary social policies in a global environment are mainly concerned with making economic prosperity a functional reality, ethical considerations do emerge in regard to achieving and maintaining a feasible order in the midst of the present chaos. The organizing themes are the legitimation of normative frameworks and procedures to provide minimum levels of stability and to fill the void created by the denial of the role of nonutilitarian values in generating social integration and development. These themes are often not components of a predetermined ideological set but simply make up an ad hoc list of concerns. However, they are more than just a loose enumeration. Behind their apparent randomness lies the contemporary experiences of out-of-control social trends working to undermine the fabric of society. A more detailed examination highlights some of the emerging concerns.

## Fairness

The notion of equity cannot be reduced simply to that of charity. It is charitable to eliminate destitution, either through direct assistance or expanding work opportunities for the less productive sector of the labour force, but justice relates more to the fair allocation of rewards and opportunities. The modern phenomenon of increased consumption, coupled with increased levels of personal dissatisfaction with the existing order, is indicative of prosperity but also of negative expectations in relation to the distribution of rewards and opportunities in society. Although material well-being is a powerful pacifier that may induce conformity, social justice is a much more complex social stabilizer. In fact, the concept of fair social protection is normative, interactive, and dynamic. A profile of existing invidious economic disparities and the ways rewards are allocated is useful in understanding people's expectations of overall social fairness.

Two structural dimensions can be used to gauge levels of equity generated by social policies: income distribution and vertical social mobility. Reducing poverty may simultaneously lead to increasing economic disparities, and this is incompatible with the expectation of participating in a fair social order. But high levels of income concentration suggest conditions that prevent or slow trickle-down processes, especially if regressive trends remain unchanged. Low social and economic mobility are signs that despite economic growth, opportunities remain concentrated and unequal.

Experience has shown a less than perfect relationship between economic and social competition. Although low wages, the accumulation of resources, and the monopolization of opportunities may foster economic competitiveness, they close rather than open social systems. A simple projection shows that with more regressive prevailing economic conditions, higher growth rates are required over longer periods of time to achieve better redistribution; this is because existing discrimination becomes deeply entrenched and slows down the expansion of economic participation.

## Legal protection: rights and obligations

Adequate legal protection is a critical social-policy issue. However, the more abstract the system of rights and obligations, the lower the chances for effective legal protection. Formal rules provide a regulatory framework. However, in most cases, they directly or indirectly assume that rights exist mainly for those who have the resources or affiliations to claim them.

Without widespread moral commitments, a mosaic of segmented legal expectations emerge: for some groups, the law is an oppressive framework; for others, it is a normative framework to facilitate interaction; for others still, it is an instrument to win additional advantages when an effective normative system in society is lacking. The erosion of the moral community helps to consolidate a situation in which a pragmatic legal culture progressively dominates the moral normative structure.

The main symptoms of a fading moral community are the declining cost effectiveness of the justice system and the gradual privatization of the little social protection that is still provided. In these cases, good arguments can be developed for implementing legal reforms and improving the administration of justice, but a moral community is grounded in observance of a system of rights and obligations rather than in imposing specific rules. And the rehabilitation of the moral community is essential to any social-policy system established to restore society.

## Social participation

Alienation is widespread in modern societies. Regulating competition among political elites does not seem to resolve the issues posed by today's complex societies for representative government. Political representatives quite often become self-serving and develop agendas and compromises to help them gain power. However, those agendas are insufficient to tighten their bonds and commitments to their constituencies. More and more, people feel that they are underrepresented and believe that neither their support nor their opposition to a political representative makes any difference to the ways decisions are made.

The growing politics of interest representation in the age of globalization has slowly eroded the role of values in public life and encouraged politicians to pay less attention to the problems affecting people's daily lives. The increasing use of highly divisive issues to mobilize minorities to break down the apathy of the majority is becoming a permanent component of representative democracy, but it seems to reinforce these negative trends. Constrained by a wide range of interests, modern political representatives at all levels are no longer keen on values. Visions of a better community have become dysfunctional empty illusions useful only for the opportunistic politics of market integration.

The power that political representatives enjoy today does not seem to expand their freedom to chose alternative options. They feel at ease negotiating interests but impotent to deal with value-loaded issues. In a world of political interests, structural reforms seem the only way out: a reorganization of the deadlocked space may open room for a new manoeuvre. What is lacking, however, is the realization that these reforms demand human sacrifices, have visible direct beneficiaries, and also require a considerable waiting period to achieve progressive results.

The reaction of modern constituencies is understandable: the numbers of "informal" systems of representation are rapidly increasing. Civic organizations have become self-appointed representatives of forgotten political values, and grassroots associations tend to reclaim that portion of popular sovereignty that formal systems took from people. Empowerment has become a loosely defined piece of contemporary political jargon. Systems for informal participation are central to solving social problems today. Under the rhetoric, the extension of citizenship beyond the boundaries of segregation and neglect requires the gradual transfer of power to grassroots civic associations.

## Cultural diversity and deprivation

Cultural deprivation is a complex syndrome of globalization. Initially, it was a problem for minorities and ethnic groups forced to abandon their values and traditions to become part of modern life. Shame and guilt were associated with the process of giving away their cultural identities. Anthropologists have analyzed how some of these groups and individuals became trapped in a void, feeling guilty for being themselves and feeling unable to become something else. Societies today understand very little about how cultural traditions work, perhaps because fantasies and emotions are involved. However, a great deal of information suggests that "continuity" solutions seem to produce the best results. People who keep their cultural identities face difficult dilemmas, but at least they tend to compromise themselves in more creative ways.

Cultural deprivation is becoming widespread. The global commercial culture is taking over and reducing local diversity to a fringe. Cultural expressions are no longer determined by time and space; they are fantasies without points of reference in reality. This gives people under their spell a sort of liberating experience, but they are unable to bridge the gap between their daily lives and the electronic sounds and imagery. Also, this pervasive commercial culture seems to provide no signs or avenues to higher levels of culture. Culturally, it is more important to entertain, and the subliminal effects are more important than the message.

The revolution in communications afforded by information and communication technologies, including the Internet, is opening as many new opportunities for cultural oppression as for cultural freedom. For those who can understand and add meaning, the Internet provides cultural freedom. But in many places, the symptoms of a cultural deprivation are beginning to emerge. The need to live according to uprooted fantasies produces a symbolic space devoid of meaning, together with an incapacity to create meaning. Audiences are growing, but this culture is either passive or reshaping the world in the image of its fantasies. Cultural traditions that remain on the borderline between reality and imagination are lost in this process, and they are no longer sustained. The issue of cultural diversity has come to the forefront because the countries that have been able to modernize their cultural identities seem to fare better, despite living in a world of high exposure to risks and uncertainties.

## Conclusion: resources optimization or goal achievement

Without sustainable prosperity, residual social policies will fail to make sense. The more the effectiveness of the ancillary approach depends on the reduction of friction, the more complex and wasteful this type of social-policy will become. Prosperity-driven social solutions for a globalizing world assume that increased consumption and the expanded opportunities created by economic success will be enough to gradually improve social equity. This, however, implies a slow but systemic expansion of more rewarding opportunities.

If the equity effect of prosperity is less than satisfactory, governments may require a more political and universalistic, not necessarily a more centralized, approach to social policy. Also, governments ought to replace resource-optimization criteria with goal-achievement criteria; otherwise, the political pressures might prove to be difficult to manage and policies may evolve toward a patchwork of unrelated programs.

The experience of the last 20 years illustrates how the incentives design of ancillary and residual policies requires a complex set of special programs to achieve results. Available information suggests that the cost-containment motive implicit in most resources-optimization social policies has three significant impacts. First, social-sector standards are kept low, for improvements in social service increase unit costs. Thus, for example, the aggregate cost of a larger student population tends to grow disproportionately. Second, some former public expenses are now transferred to families and to private groups. Third, there is need to provide additional public or private financing for special, nonsectoral programs. However, the indicators of social equity suggest very slow or no improvement. In fact, this type of policy approach fails to achieve progressive social goals.

The long-term feasibility of globalization trends may increasingly depend on more effective social policies to better distribute the high cost of adjustments. The emerging issues dwell on two sides: more effectiveness and coordination in social-policy programs and also regulatory frameworks to facilitate market integration through processes less wasteful of human lives and social capital. The development of noncommand structures of social-policy coordination is still a challenge. "Mimicking the market" makes sense to non-altruistic interests, but altruism and commitment to service require examples, models, and incentive structures to create, spread, and adopt innovations and build-in institutional learning processes. Experiences with trying to metaphorically frame social programs within "market-competitive" solutions have not shown the results expected by the institutional social engineers. New forms of bureaucratization and command have emerged, sometimes more orderly in their first stages but also more rigid. The lack of adaptability has been the doom of preceding command structures, and the prices that must be paid in these cases have been too high. Further, the diversity of needs in the age of globalization often exceeds the available capacities to provide for them.

# PART II

# REFORMING SOCIAL POLICIES FOR COMPETITIVENESS AND EQUITY

# CHAPTER 3

# WEST AND CENTRAL AFRICA

## SOCIAL POLICY FOR RECONSTRUCTION

## AND DEVELOPMENT

*Tade Akin Aina*

Any meaningful and relevant analysis of social policy in Africa today must start with an understanding of the twin processes of poverty and development. It must investigate both process and context in terms of the most recent experiences in countries of the region. Such an analysis must revisit the development process, its failures and, in particular, the recent epoch of persistent crisis and adjustment and recognize the significance of that crisis, not only for development in general, but also for policy-making. Such an analysis must include an understanding of "development consciousness," or the ways people perceive, think of, and are conscious of development as a process intended to transform their lives in a positive and beneficial direction and of its contribution to the improvement of material and other well-being.

These elements of the analysis are important because one of the major consequences of Africa's prolonged crisis has been, not only the delegitimization of the African state and its forced withdrawal from the provision of basic services and other forms of direct social provisioning, but also the emergence of a kind of consciousness that denies the validity and relevance of social policy in the development process. Quite often this denial is couched in a language of social-policy reform and restructuring that challenges both the basis and practice of conventional social policy.

This systematic denial and reorientation are the result of the recent appropriation of the responsibility for economic and social-policy management of several African countries by international financial institutions (IFIs). This appropriation, the product of the globalization process and a response to the protracted economic crisis experienced by these countries, has been defined mainly in terms of the dominance of a neoliberal market doctrine, emphasizing deregulation, liberalization, and privatization (Mkandawire and Olukoshi 1995; Founou-Tchuigoua 1996). Rather than improving the quality of life for the majority of people, this approach has only worsened it. Development should be seen as a process of systematic transformation of the conditions of existence of the majority of people in a beneficial manner to enhance their attainment of individual and collective well-being. More than ever before, Africa needs not only to reclaim development, but also to face the challenges of social reconstruction, that is, rebuilding social institutions and support systems eroded by years of neglect and the efforts of both internal and external forces to undermine them.

This chapter argues that reclaiming development and the reconstruction of society in a context of transnational influences can only be tackled effectively through a systematic and sustained initiative. This involves putting in place sustainable economic-development strategies that include frameworks of coherent and relevant social policies geared at building and rebuilding institutions in the region and recovering peoples' collective self-confidence, integrity, and social integration.

However, systematic, state-lead social provisioning was one of the earliest victims of the IFIs solutions to the economic crisis ravaging the nations of West and Central Africa. Conventional social policy was seen as wasteful and negative, contributing little or nothing to economic growth and national revenues, rather than as a major contribution to the development process.

This chapter challenges this negative view of social policy and attempts to show that social policy is an intrinsic dimension of the development process, particularly during stages of transition and reconstruction, such as in Africa today. Any systematic review of such policies must be popular and participatory, involving various social sectors and beneficiaries, including traditionally excluded groups such as poor women, rural dwellers, the elderly, youth, and children. More pressing today than ever before is the need to comprehensively reappraise and understand the role and significance of social policy. This is particularly relevant, given the dominance of the economic and so-called death-of-the-social paradigm (Rose 1996). The shift to this paradigm is creating an important gap in the development process. Allowing this gap to grow may lead to ad hoc, hastily designed, and ill-considered actions that do more harm than good, further dividing society, undermining social integration, and forestalling confrontation with the issue of poverty.

A concern with social policy and social development, however, is not a mere technocratic concern with "welfare" or with policy-making as a means to the "alleviation of poverty." A concern with social policy is at the heart of a deep preoccupation with the development process and its objectives of positively transforming the human condition. In other words, it is primarily a concern with human well-being, how it is conceived, organized, and facilitated, and how the burdens of achieving it are distributed over various sectors of society. This concern, of course, is not new and can be traced back to earlier debates on the nature of social inequality and how this should be tackled. These issues are still on the theoretical and policy agenda, as is evident from the worldwide concern of politicians and intellectuals with the social-policy debate (Torres 1995).

In the countries of West and Central Africa, however, current political and cultural conditions impose certain challenges regarding the direction of the development process and the role of social policy. We need to consider alternative visions of, and paths to, social and economic development that integrate the satisfaction of individual basic needs with the broader goals of society for collective security and social sustainability. Achieving these objectives implies creating living conditions and organizing society and politics in ways that differ from the oppressive and stifling precolonial structures and the exploitative and repressive colonial and postcolonial systems. It further implies the need, in Africa in particular and in the world's less privileged societies in general, to design alternative modes of organizing the economy and society to guarantee economic productivity and surplus while preserving and valuing social equity, justice, and democracy. Such alternative development requires the relevant human-centred social policies as key elements. Transforming the current inadequate conditions of human development requires the emergence of people who are not only liberated but socially responsible and people whose integrity, dignity, and rights are preserved and guaranteed. This, in turn, requires specific kinds of development and developed societies that preserve social and economic rights and guarantee respect for diversity and humanity, rather than subjection to a market determinism.

## Social policy in West and Central Africa

### The region

The West and Central African region is extremely diverse in ecology, history, politics, and language. Culturally and geographically, it brings together disparate areas called West Africa and Equatorial Africa. These include the Sahel, forests, coastlands, adjacent islands, lakes and river basins as diverse as those of the Niger and Congo, Lake Chad, and the Great Lakes. Comprising about 26 independent states, the region includes not only some of the most populous and well-endowed states in Africa but also some of the poorest, least-developed countries in the world. With Chad, Mali, and Niger at its extreme north, the countries in the world. With Chad, Mali, and Niger at its extreme north, the region stretches to the Republic of Congo and Zaire at its most southerly point and Burundi and Rwanda in the east.

Reflecting its colonial experience of Belgian, British, French, Portuguese, and Spanish domination, the region embraces linguistic groups with the colonial heritage of British West Africa, French and Belgian Africa, and the tiny Portuguese and Spanish enclaves. In many ways, the region expresses most of the core characteristics of sub-Saharan Africa, particularly its vulnerability to change in natural conditions, its political and economic fragility, and other structural weaknesses. The countries of the region are particularly vulnerable politically and economically. Politically, the small nation-states are fragmented. The majority of these countries are predominantly suppliers of primary products, which makes them highly vulnerable economically to fluctuating prices of commodities in international markets. The heavy reliance on monoproducts also renders these countries highly vulnerable to fluctuations in weather conditions. Heavy dependence on rain-fed agriculture entails that production, consumption, and export earnings are at the whimsical mercy of weather conditions. Over the past three decades, recurrent droughts have adversely affected desertification-prone areas, especially in the Sudano–Saharan countries. The resulting food crises and related problems have adversely affected living conditions (Adepoju 1996).

Despite the presence of countries with abundant natural resources — such as Cameroon, Gabon, Nigeria, and Zaire — West and Central Africa are still perhaps some of the most poverty-stricken regions in terms of both economic and human development. This is compounded by an extreme diversity and absence of cultural and even ecological coherence. Samir Amin grouped all of Africa into three broad regions, based on the pattern of their incorporation into the world capitalist system and the specific function and role of each entity within it (Amin 1972). Apart from one or two ambiguous elements, mainly those of Rwanda and Burundi, the region covered by this discussion embraces Amin's Africa of the colonial-trade economy and his Africa of the concession-owning companies. Amin's classification provides an analytical handle combining geography and history and the existence and pattern of exploitation of natural resources providing a basis for the region's political economy. Amin's classification also provides an analytical foundation for understanding the nature of the colonial experience of different parts of the region, their development experiences, the extent of their underdevelopment, and the pattern of the current experience of globalization (Amin 1992). In sum, it provides some useful linkages between the evolution of social policy from colonial times to today's situation.

## Broad patterns in social policy

Before examining the experiences of social policy in West and Central Africa, it is perhaps necessary to touch briefly on the definition of social policy, owing to the vague and ambiguous ways this concept is often used and the differences in theoretical traditions using this notion (Hill and Bramley 1986; Esping-Andersen 1990).

In addition to difficulties defining *social policy* in Western literature, a different set of problems is found in the review of the African literature. Rather than defining or focusing on social policy, African researchers have been more concerned with the broader notion of social development. This, in practice, represents some recognition of the specific conditions of African societies as least-developed or developing countries (Jinadu 1980; Sanda 1981; Osei-Hwedie, 1990; Chole 1991; Mohammed 1991). In other cases, the literature shows either the prevalence of a more professionally oriented and restricted notion of social policy, as social work and social welfare, or an emphasis on social services and their effectiveness (Fyle 1993; Semboja and Therkildsen 1995). It should be further noted, however, that except in a few cases (Kibuka 1990; Patel 1992; Kaseke 1994, 1995), the wider notion of social policy is rarely used in a way that captures the unique challenges of African human-development priorities and concerns.

In the African context, social policy can be conceived as the set of systematic and deliberate interventions in the social life of a country to ensure the satisfaction of the basic needs and the well-being of the majority of its citizens. Social policy is thus an expression of socially desirable goals through legislation, institutions, and administrative programs and practices in accordance with specific development objectives. It embodies both the policies and the areas of basic needs for interventions in the pursuit of human well-being. Understood in this way, social policy is thus a broader concept than the more technical or professional notion of social work and social welfare. Although this concept of social policy is often used as synonymous with social development, the later implies a larger structural transformation of cultures, social structures, productive systems, and the quality of life. Social policy nevertheless makes a major contribution to ensuring and maintaining social and human development.

In practice, conventional social policies are not neutral. Social policies in West and Central Africa are often the subject of manipulation and influence by diverse interests and riddled with inequalities of gender, race, class, region, and age. Certain inequalities, such as those of gender, for example, despite being highly negative, are rarely perceived as reproducing systematic social inequities in the predominantly patriarchal societies and sexist states of the region. Gender blindness and discrimination still constitute predominant characteristics of the economic and social policies formulated and implemented in the region, without any consideration of the unequal relations between the sexes either in the households or in terms of access to strategic resources, such as land and credit (Sow 1993), or in key areas of social life, such as education, health, employment, and politics. Gender inequality is therefore a persistent aspect of conventional social policy, with the result that, rather than empowering women, social policies contribute to reinforcing and expanding inequitable relations and structures (Williams 1989; Etta 1994).

However, social policy in West and Central Africa has not been static. It has changed in response to historical processes in the formation of countries in the region or in wider international and global systems. Thus, social policy in West and Central Africa has changed in response to the major events in the history of the region. Broadly speaking, the region's relevant history can be divided into the colonial and postcolonial periods. Neither represents a monolithic, undifferentiated development, and within each there are distinct phases with specific trends in various aspects of economic and social life. These notions are used here more as a mode of ordering experiences and events, rather than in the sense of the larger cultural definition that characterizes current trends in discourse on postcoloniality.

## The colonial period

The colonial period was very complex, with great variations across and within regions and societies. These variations resulted both from the ways societies were differentially incorporated into the global capitalist system and from the functions they fulfilled in it, either as labour reserves, areas of mining concession, or regions of the colonial-trade economy, which was based on peasant agricultural production for metropolitan markets. The cultural and political peculiarities of the Belgian, British, French, and Portuguese colonial powers and the ways they organized and managed their colonies also affected how specific states and political economies emerged. However, despite these differences, each was exploitative and had the metropolitan orientation of the colonial, "plunderer" state (Crowder 1968; Bathily 1994; Zeleza 1994).

Formal social policy in the region during this period emerged from these complex and often contradictory influences shaped by "the ideologies and structures of state provision," which "reflected a very narrow interpretation of social welfare" (Boyden 1990, p. 200). As a result, colonial social policy had certain major features.

First, it was largely determined by the colonial mission, the economic exploitation of the resources of the colonies. According to Fadayomi (1991, p. 137),

> economic growth was superseded only by economic exploitation, while the minimal degree of social development that existed had resulted entirely from colonial

provision of the basic social services and physical infrastructure necessary to facilitate the exploitation of natural resources. In other words, social development was merely incidental to the development of the metropolitan economy.

In other words, colonial social policy took a residualist approach. As pointed out by Vivian (1995, p. 21),

> during the colonial era, welfare ideas and policies were essentially residualist-holding that "social welfare institutions should come into play only when normal structures of supply, the family and the market, break down." ... That is, welfare services (including not only economic support but also other forms of social provisioning such as education and health services) were only to be provided to those who could not provide for themselves.

At the service of the colonial mission, dominant interest groups helped to change the interpretation and definition of that mission. Among these groups were the colonial officials (military and administrative); the business and commercial interests, in certain cases white settlers, who were present in West and Central Africa but not as strongly as they were in East and Southern Africa; missionaries; and officials of volunteer agencies. A major form of support provided by these vested interests, particularly the missionaries and volunteer agencies, was that of providing education for the production of people to service both the colonial administration and its economy (Fadayomi 1991; Endanda 1993).

Second, colonial social policy was restrictive both socially and spatially. In many cases across West and Central Africa, social services were located only in urban areas or neighbourhoods where colonizers were found in large numbers. As Boyden observed (1990, p. 180),

> the types of welfare services provided ... reflected the concerns of the rulers rather than the needs of the ruled. One of the explicit priorities of colonial governments was to provide protection for the expatriate community against a hostile physical environment. The Nigerian health service, for example, was established in the areas where expatriates lived primarily as a result of the great fire that consumed Lagos in 1877 and the outbreak of bubonic plague in 1924. ... The expatriate settlers and colonial administrators were also worried about the threat to themselves from youth crime, and made begging and vagrancy and public order concerns predominant.

Furthermore, the settlements were not only segregated but also classified according to the provision of social services, such as in the case of the *Town Planning Act* of 1917 in Nigeria (Mabogunje 1968; Onokerhoraye 1984; Aina 1990). An outcome of the concentration of social services and other forms of amenities in these colonial centres was the emergence of cities with origins in colonization and the growth of uneven and unequal spatial and socioeconomic development. This law classified Nigerian cities and towns into first-, second-, and third-class towns, on the one hand, and native towns, on the other. This classification then determined administrative structures and the provision of infrastructures, such as electricity and pipe-borne water. The social services and administration of these towns depended on this classification; the native towns suffered almost absolute neglect. Lagos, the colonial capital was the only first-class town.

Social policy was thus selective, discriminatory, and exclusionary, geared to protecting and advancing colonial interests and those of the white settlers (Patel 1992). Social policy included the local population only if it played important roles in the colonial structure or if continuous exclusion could fundamentally threaten colonial interests; for example, colonial powers only introduced environmental health services in coastal West Africa when malaria was rampant in that region.

The main social actors were the colonial officials, the agents of the foreign volunteer agencies, particularly the missionaries, and foreign economic interests, settlers, and various categories of local people. The latter included chiefs, particularly the "warrant chiefs," created by the British colonial administrators in the pursuit of indirect rule (Crowder 1968), the emerging educated elites, in some cases culturally defined as *evolués and assimiladoes*, and rich traders. In certain cases, racial groups such as mulattos and Levantine and Asian skilled workers and entrepreneurs were also included. These constituted the key beneficiaries of colonial social policy.

The benefits from colonial social policies for these groups differed. In most cases, the major preoccupation was with protecting the interest of colonial officials. Before World War II, for example, these benefits in most parts of West and Central Africa were restricted to the provision of social services, such as water supply, health services, educational facilities, and roads. The objectives were to maintain law and order and a local low-level administrative cadre to exploit effectively the natural and other resources of the colonies and to create colonial markets for metropolitan export. In practice, this entailed minimal provision of social services for the majority of people. However, an excessive concern was shown for the safety, health, and security of the colonial officials, traders, and settlers. This preoccupation also included colonial town planning and the functioning of official institutions, such as prisons, courts, and hospitals. Social security, pension plans, etc. were not provided universally but meant mainly for colonial officials and war veterans. Thus, social policy in colonial West and Central Africa was not only restrictive and exclusionist but also tied to the physical security of the colonial conquerors.

With the transition from the colonial to postcolonial administration, social policy took on completely different functions and objectives. It became a means of legitimizing the new regimes constructed by the African nationalist rulers of the weak and fragmented postcolonial states.

# The postcolonial period

The postcolonial period in the region included two distinct overlapping phases. The first is the early postcolonial period, or the constructionist phase. The second is the crisis phase, which began in the mid-1970s and became evident and protracted in the decade of the 1980s.

## The early postcolonial period

The early postcolonial period roughly corresponds to the first 10 years of independence for most countries in West and Central Africa, from the late 1950s to the mid-1970s. It coincides not only with the attainment of independence by most states in sub-Saharan Africa but also with a surge of nation-building, development projects, optimism, confidence, and some stable economic growth, albeit over a short period. It ended with the first global economic crisis, occasioned by the Organization of Petroleum Exporting Countries' increase in petroleum prices. Along with the oil crisis, which has been called the African Crisis, and its associated economic downturn, other phenomena began to take shape, including drought and famine resulting from the Sahelian ecological crises and a wave of persistent political crises. These political crises resulted in the virtual collapse of the state and social order in countries such as Burundi, Liberia, Rwanda, and Zaire.

This constructionist phase was one of consolidation and expansion of the neocolonial-accumulation model that characterized the development paths of many African political economies (Mbaya 1995). Coupled with this model was the legitimation strategy of the populist programs of the nationalist movements that came to power after independence (Mkandawire 1995). Central to the legitimation strategy was a strong social-policy initiative tied to an essentially constructionist ideal of economic development, that is, building physical, social, and human infrastructures. This was also a period of "constructing" major social programs in education, housing, health, urban planning, and elaborate social subsidies. This was matched by the construction of new physical signs of nationhood, such as airports, ports, military bases, five-star hotels, elite residential estates, parliament buildings and government offices, and the sites of the early import-substitution and export-processing industries.

Except in very impoverished economies, this was a phase of some distinctive postcolonial affluence for the more privileged strata and classes of postcolonial African societies, which were gradually transformed or incorporated into new elite positions and status. This was also a time of some stabilization in producer prices for some countries and an economic boom for others, such as Côte d'Ivoire, Ghana, Kenya, Nigeria, Zambia, and to some extent Senegal, Sierra Leone, and Uganda. At the same time, the demand was growing to create space within the economy for a framework of social-policy provisions, with the call coming from emergent vocal groups of urban workers, bureaucrats, traders, members of the armed forces, and urban-based professionals.

The early postcolonial period was thus predominantly geared to the expansion of social and economic structures to incorporate indigenous interests and groups barred from the colonial system. Addressing these demands was central to the nationalist legitimation model and constituted perhaps the core of an attempt to spread the fruits of independence to those groups with the greatest claim. According to Laakso and Olukoshi. writing on social policy in the nationalist project of the postcolonial regimes (1996, p. 15),

> the post-colonial economic boom experienced in the early post-independence years facilitated the steady expansion of social services and bureaucracies in a manner that enabled governments to accommodate the emerging elites-political, religious, economic, bureaucratic, and social of various ethnic groups and cater for the basic welfare and social needs of the populace as part of the post-colonial "social contract."

However, the accumulation and legitimation models ran into trouble, as they soon reached the real limits of their capacity to incorporate more and more new elements both socially and economically, given finite resources and rapid population growth. From the late 1960s to the early 1970s, the core elements of the nationalist project began to disintegrate politically. The struggle for legitimation and incorporation gave way to increasing authoritarianism and monolithism. The emergence and consolidation of one-party states came to be a common feature, as well as military regimes, run increasingly through clientelistic and personal-rule mechanisms. Simultaneously, an increasingly unfavourable global context began to appear (Laakso and Olukoshi 1996, pp. 16-17):

> Deep-seated economic problems in the context of a recessionary international economic environment meant that the post-colonial "social contract" and the various alliances and networks built around it to create relative political stability became increasingly unsustainable. As the economic crisis worsened in various African countries, so too did the capacity of the state to provide welfare services to the populace and patronage to the political and economic elite diminish.

With the decline of popular democratic politics and the collapse of the economies, social policy became equally eroded and downplayed. Social services and social infrastructures either decayed from sheer neglect or, where they existed in rudimentary forms, were appropriated by local barons and misused for political patronage.

## The crisis phase

To date, the crisis phase in the postcolonial period has not produced signs of resolution or relief. It has become more complex with the so-called economic-reform programs, which produced some changes in political and economic regimes in the region and redefined patterns of social relations between economic and social groups and ethnic and gender relations. Changes during this period have reorganized the colonial and early postcolonial social and class structures, creating new sets of winners and losers and leaving the vast majority of the population in the latter. In the political sphere, this phase opened up opportunities for political liberalization and for democratization in some countries, such as Benin and Mali, but it has not relieved the crisis in other chronically war-torn countries, such as Burundi, Rwanda, and Zaire.

As the accumulation and the legitimation models of many African political economies ran into trouble, several of these nations entered, in the 1970s, a phase of long drawn out economic decline. In some countries of West and Central Africa — such as Chad, Mali, and Niger — this was accompanied by drought, famine, and other severe ecological crises. In others, the crisis was compounded by political repression and monolithism, instability, wars, and conflicts. However, the debt crisis and the economic-recovery programs became a predominant feature of countries across the region. In a short period, economic decline and the debt crisis became the most critical problems. They were the outcomes of the combined effects of the initial colonial structure of African economies, the failure of the postcolonial regimes to correct these effects, and the pressures of economic globalization.

The collapse of commodity-export prices, which occurred in short cycles between 1960 and 1980, became more persistent, prolonged, and critical, leading to an export collapse in the 1980s (Culpeper 1987). Without going into detail, it suffices to say that this collapse was accompanied by declining agricultural productivity, increasing imports of food and other products, increasing debts, and a growing balance of payments deficit. Investments, particularly foreign investments, declined; unemployment began to rise; and poverty increased. Thus, whereas projections for the percentages of people living under the poverty line for the rest of the world show a decrease between 1985 and 2000, those for Africa show a consistent, if slight increase, from 47.6% in 1985 and 47.8% in 1990 to 49.7% in 2000 (Oxfam 1993).

The major IFIs, namely, the International Monetary Fund and the World Bank, designed a set of policies and strategies to respond to this crisis. These policies, if not directly designed by them, were implemented with their assistance and oriented by their philosophy and perception of correct economic strategy. These transnational responses to national problems, often aimed at "stabilizing" or "adjusting" economies, were formulated in market-reformist terms and conceived as palliatives for economies strangled or distorted by excessive state intervention and regulation, price distortions, oversubsidization of urban sectors, and heavy tendencies to state control and state monopolies.

The reforms, known as economic-stabilization programs, economic-adjustment policies or packages, economic-reform programs, or structural-adjustment programs (SAPs), involved a number of key features:

- Withdrawal of subsidies on essential products, such as foodstuffs, energy sources such as petroleum, and other productive inputs, such as fertilizers;

- Deregulation of agricultural prices and the elimination of marketing boards and other such intermediaries;

- Devaluation of the local currency;

- Reduction of public-sector employment and elimination or removal of subsidies for public-sector employees;

- Privatization or commercialization of parastatal and public enterprises;

- Commercialization of social services and infrastructures — such as education, health, water supply, and housing — by introducing higher user prices and cost-recovery measures;

- Increase in the use of indirect-taxation mechanisms and austerity packages, such as wage freezes, to augment public revenue; and

- Liberalization of labour laws to ensure a more market-driven economy.

That countries implement all or significant aspects of these measures was often a condition laid down by the IFIs for these countries' continuing to receive financial assistance. Between 1980 and 1989, 36 sub-Saharan African countries initiated 241 SAPs, many with multiple components (Oxfam 1993). This approach involves deregulation, withdrawal of subsidies, retrenchment of public-service employees, and commercialization of social services, which have all had profound impacts on employment and social provisioning. The economic crisis and the adjustment policies had far-reaching impacts on all aspects of life in most parts of Africa. Economic and social structures were transformed; polities and administrative systems, restructured; and individual and collective status, lifestyles, and psychology, affected in many ways, including a prolonged state of shock and multiadaptive compensatory behaviour (Aina 1989).

Structural-adjustment policies greatly affected social policies, the provision of social services, and the overall well-being of the population. Given the main elements of the reform package, social policy and social services were directly affected through either privatization, commercialization, or complete government withdrawal and neglect. It has been well documented that the impact of structural adjustment on social services severely affected health, education, water supply, and environmental sanitation. Most findings show that these either deteriorated out of neglect or became inaccessible to the majority of the people who used them during the early postcolonial period (Adepoju 1993; Bakker 1994; Gibbon 1995; Mkandawire and Olukoshi 1995).

Under these circumstances and with the extensive problems faced by ordinary people and communities in most West and Central African countries, they had little option but to resort to autonomous and creative means to satisfy their basic needs. Although they continued to suffer intense deprivations, they took steps to provide for themselves those services the state neglected or had no capacity to provide. In some ways, for these sectors of the population, the SAPs created new avenues for the delivery of social services, although at standards lower than those governments can provide; nevertheless, they have fulfilled real needs. Describing this experience mainly for the urban areas in Africa, Aina (1997b, p. 425) pointed out many facets of the impacts of SAPs and of popular responses to them in African urban centres:

> These ... include traffic congestion, floods, bad roads, blocked drains, overflowing and open sewers, erratic electricity and water supply, failing telephone systems, and mounting vermin-infested rubbish heaps. While the health and environmental hazards multiplied, health facilities, starved of essential resources and supplies and/or suffering from prolonged industrial action by dissatisfied personnel, failed to cope .... The basis of law and order was also increasingly eroded as economic pressures mounted while ill-motivated and underpaid security agents either could not cope or were too vulnerable in terms of their material needs .... To offer themselves some protection in their homes and settlements, communities organized vigilante groups and community watches .... These often administered instant justice by lynching suspected criminals. Although undesirable, this represents an expression of "self-help" organizing in response to difficult conditions.

This self-help element became an important aspect of social-service delivery and social policy in the "SAP era." It contained diverse features, including not only those of collective-community services but also those of commercialization and private initiatives. On the basis of the latter, the proponents of liberalization and privatization argued that this was only part of an ongoing trend. As Aina (1997b, p. 425) further noted,

> "self-help" in urban areas moved gradually from the "community development" efforts of the colonial and early post-colonial periods, which were often externally stimulated and directed by bureaucrats, to self-help (more as an autonomous, self-protective response based on real needs and pressures) in the provision of services such as waste disposal, drain-clearing and crime fighting. Where self-help (i.e. service provision not geared towards profit) was not well-developed, or could not take off, small commercial enterprises emerged in waste disposal, education, dispensing medicine, etc. These included efforts such as petty waste disposal units with wheel barrows and baskets, water-vending from buckets carried on heads and shoulders, and

"lessons" teachers instructing groups of children in backyards or front sheds. Wherever the state failed or was absent and the formal private sector would not go or imposed user charges that were too high, the urban poor organized to fill the gap either through collective non-profit responses or through small enterprises that charged affordable fees.

It is important to stress, however, that although the SAPs have promoted some forms of self-reliance and autonomous action, they have eroded many of the social-policy and human-development gains of the 1960s and 1970s in areas such as primary education, adult literacy, infant and maternal mortality, child nutrition, and the eradication of communicable diseases. With the deterioration and the lack of maintenance and renewal of the social infrastructures first established in the 1960s and 1970s, SAP public-spending cuts and a combination of bad management and neglect have reversed the gains of those decades. Agencies and groups concerned with the social outcomes of SAPs have forcefully highlighted this reality (Gibbon and Olukoski 1996). Effective momentum for this was created by the Adjustment with a Human Face books of the United Nations Children's Emergency Fund (Cornia et al. 1987). These brought the social-policy dimension back to the discussion of the design and implementation of the SAPs and created the basis for an adjustment era of social-policy efforts.

## Adjustment era in social policy

The transnational character of social policies requires looking at both their pervasiveness across the region and the new social-policy agenda that reflects such a phenomena. Social policies in the adjustment era have three major features in terms of both their agents and their implementation.

First, there is a new type of local, small-scale provider of social services. These differ from the conventional indigenous sources of social provisioning based on the social-solidarity systems of families, lineages, and kinship (Aina 1997a). These providers are often private initiatives operating along the lines of the informal sector, mainly for a fee. They involve a wide range of service provision, such as waste-disposal, selling water, education, and road-building, among others. What is interesting is that they are rudimentary, locally based products of individual initiatives and efforts.

A second feature of adjustment-era social policies is the expansion of the role of the community and volunteer actors in service provision, covering a wide range of institutional forms and social services. Their role includes provision of both voluntary and compulsory services, such as road-building, drainage clearing, environmental sanitation, social-defence neighbourhood watches, and vigilante groups. The institutionalization of these services takes different forms. In some cases, they are temporary arrangements set up in response to immediate community needs or threats, such as an increase in theft, and are dissolved after these needs are fulfilled. In other cases, such as in metropolitan Lagos, Nigeria, they have been transformed into more durable structures, such as neighbourhood associations or even cooperatives formed to make bulk purchases of commodities, such as building materials to upgrade homes, scarce foodstuffs, and other such items.

The volunteer sector has also witnessed the growth of both local and international nongovernmental organizations (NGOs), often initiated, encouraged, and funded by both private foundations and other multilateral and bilateral donors (Aina 1993). These new agents have come to play a major role not only in redefining social-policy priorities and concerns but also in formalizing the more universal application of institutional and management approaches in their implementation, including accounting systems and modes of financial reporting, management, governance structures, and even ideological and value systems for "NGO service culture, lifestyle and language" (Aina 1993, p. 140). In other words, in addition to carrying out what Fowler (Fowler 1992, 1995) described as the internationalization of welfare, NGOs are also internationalizing institutional structures, approaches, and ideologies.

A third feature — perhaps the most significant, because it has implied an extensive investment in resources and has in some cases involved formidable carriers and agents — is the emergence of social policies with an approach known as "social dimensions of adjustment" (SDA). This is a very important characteristic of current social policy and its transnational dimension, not only because the main agents are often IFIs, such as the World Bank, and the governments of countries in the region, but also because they are beginning to lay the basis for a postcrisis social-policy agenda in Africa.

This is particularly important because efforts to design and implement new neoliberal social policies are being harmonized and replicated across countries, affecting the lives of millions of people. These new social policies are designed and implemented not only with little or no debate in the countries affected but also with little or no real participation of the recipients in the identification of their needs. Despite this lack of regard for basic democratic and participatory principles, some of these projects are presented at the microlevel as participatory interventions. In practice, however, they are often designed by foreign specialists and usually managed and evaluated using indicators and benchmarks the participants have never been consulted about. They are usually therefore alienating, top-down interventions.

Two of the main elements of SDA policies and interventions are the social-action programs (SACPs) and the social funds (SFs). The SACPs operate with limited poverty-alleviation strategies and are often quite narrow in terms of their conception, implementation, and cost-effective attainment of their objectives (Hutchful 1994; Gayi 1995; Mhone 1995; Vivian 1995). In a World Bank document, Marc et al. (1995, p. 1) argued that

> in Africa, social action programs and social funds have taken different forms than in other regions. Social action programs and social funds are both considered social safety nets but in fact often have a broader mandate.

These medium-term, multisector projects are designed to intervene mainly to create employment and deliver basic social services. These interventions often involve multicountry projects, in some cases with programs applied in at least 14 countries in West and Central Africa and the initiative of the World Bank (Marc et al. 1995). In terms of objectives, according to Marc et al. 1995, p. 2), these SDA interventions

> are designed to achieve a variety of socio-economic, institutional and political objectives, including alleviating the effects of prolonged economic dysfunction, protecting those hurt by adjustment, providing support so that the poor may benefit in the longer term, setting up institutional mechanisms to reach the needy, and increasing political support for the adjustment program.

As lofty as these objectives are, some analysts of these efforts remain less than impressed by their impact or effectiveness on any of these counts (Hutchful 1994; Vivian 1995).

Comparative examinations of the projects stress the following points. They tend to be short to medium term; they focus mainly on public works and infrastructure-rehabilitation and employment-generation programs; they concentrate on building specific skills, particularly those at inferior, artisanal levels; they tend to rely on private-sector inputs, namely, through small-scale contractors and entrepreneurs, microenterprises, and the informal sector; and they favour the creation of alternative structures for social-service provision, either through the recruitment of personnel, boards, or other similar arrangements. Also, the projects are often demand driven, whereas clients are often self-selecting; the projects attempt to promote specific institutional, management, and operational approaches based on a belief in efficiency and the superiority of private enterprise; and these projects are often donor funded and funded from external sources.

These are the most salient characteristics of the SDA service-provision, public-works, and employment-generating efforts under way. In addition, these policies and programs have also been shown to be inherently limited in aspects such as male bias, long-term sustainability, scope (as they have difficulties reaching the poorest of the poor), and impact (as they tend to affect only a small proportion of the population). Their emphasis on political visibility has also been said to distort their conception and implementation, as well as hindering any serious effort to evaluate their impacts (Vivian 1995).

Based on experience in the past years, it is obvious that SDA efforts constitute a significant and important strategy for social provisioning in Africa. In many ways, SDA policies and programs represent a growing process of transnationalization of social policy; in the region, they are similar only to the policy-harmonization efforts of the colonial powers. However, these policies have greater range and reach than the colonial efforts. With the involvement of national governments, SDA social-policy efforts embody attempts to impose long-term social-provisioning strategies on their countries, in terms of not only the specific features of the social projects and programs but also the radical social-sector restructuring they impose. This in itself is a complex and often contradictory endeavour. As Vivian (1995, p. 19) argued,

> This type of social sector reform proposal constitutes an attempt to link the neo-liberal, market-based model of social provisioning to "alternative" approaches of participation and empowerment in a kind of "neo-liberal populism." This is an interesting concept. It implies that safety nets are not merely short-term palliatives ... but should rather be seen as part, of a process of long-term social restructuring.

These policies are then promoted using smoke screens (Mhone 1995) or "smoke and mirrors" (Hutchful 1994) and conceptual manipulations that hijack and appropriate popular and progressive notions — such as participation, empowerment, community, and equity — and then repackage them as central to the transformation of societies and economies. By adopting popular and progressive notions, these initiatives are made more acceptable, and questions related to how the new policies contribute to the reconstruction of West and Central African economies and societies and to authentic human development are never directly addressed. This is why Vivian's (1995, p. 23) call becomes imperative:

> Social sector reform models must be assessed in terms of their overall social efficiency and effectiveness as well as their impact on social development. Social policies have long-term effects on social divisions and social structures, and if safety nets become institutionalized as an alternative model of social service provisioning, a long-term question is raised. What will be the legacy of the neo-liberal approach to social service provisioning? Will it promote or retard progress toward social development and positive forms of social integration?

These are the type of questions that must be addressed to link transnational or even national social policies to the development process. Only by doing so can social policy for the countries of West and Central Africa become a means to support not only development but also the reconstruction needed to recover from the recent social, political, and economic crises and, of course, the SAPs.

# Conclusions: postcrisis social policy in West and Central Africa

As West and Central African societies struggle to emerge from the crises of the last two and a half decades, they face certain important issues. The very first is the challenge of social reconstruction. This must come from a clear and deliberate recognition of the disruptions and destruction of recent times. Virtually all sectors of social and economic life need programs or processes of reconstruction, including the economies, the social and political structures, and even cultural life. The past era of crisis and disruption has evidently not been the most conducive to launching a process of reconstruction of social structures and systems or moving ahead their positive transformation. In fact, such an era has been more a period of destabilization and destruction, which now requires rehabilitation and transformation.

Clearly, today, we need to rethink and rebuild the economic models for governing the countries of the region and to do so independently of the dictates or tutelage of either colonial powers or the managers of IFIs. Perhaps the greatest lesson from the crisis era is the recognition of the need to reconstruct and to learn from the mistakes of three or four decades of postcolonial economic development, which both Africans and foreigners have recognized to be a failure.

Another major demand for reconstruction is with respect to the political structures of African states. This is closely tied to the required changes in economic structure. The current wave of pluralism, multiparty democratization, and the struggle for a wide range of human and social rights provides a window of opportunity. But the debate about the meaning of democracy, participation, communities, representation, and decentralization needs to be revisited. There is a need to open up meaningful discussion on what these mean to different groups and how these might be integrated into new frameworks built to promote social justice and collective and individual well-being.

An important step in this process will be to rethink the nature and role of the state in Africa. This may imply moving away from the false state–market dichotomy so pervasive in the current development discourse. Another necessary step will be to identify the prospects in Africa for the emergence of "developmental democratic" states that simultaneously overcome the twin problems of economic development and democratic legitimation. States that are built on development and democracy and that build development and democracy.

With the construction of such a state must come a new and more constructive role for social policy. The eras of using social policies as instruments for exclusion or merely as means to political legitimacy are gone. We need to rethink and to integrate human development-oriented social-policy provisions with the totality of both nation-building and economic development. With development constructed as a more authentic human-centred undertaking in which various sectors and social groups participate and play an important role, the need for political legitimation will be reduced. So will be the need for policies as a means to sheer domination. In this way, the role and function of social policy in the development process is transformed from one that is instrumentalist to one embedded in the very process of creating a better society, constantly minimizing social and economic alienation, injustice, and inequity.

A transnational social-policy agenda can be both a positive and a negative force for human development and for collective well-being, depending on the contents and objectives of transnational social policies. If the objectives of transnational social policies do not have the well-being of people as their main concern, then they can become caught up in technocratic managerial systems aimed to increase the rationalization of distributional processes, rather than serious attempts to improve the human condition.

Transnational social policies can have positive outcomes, if they are designed and implemented in a framework of global concern to resolve the negative aspects of the contemporary human condition. This can be achieved through concerted efforts to address issues such as poverty and the lack of access for large numbers of people to opportunities and services needed to enable them to better their social and economic condition. This is the real challenge for any new social-policy regime and orientation in the context of current managerial, technocratic thinking and practice in addressing basic needs. By meeting this challenge, transnational social policies can contribute to a genuine process of social reconstruction and human development in West and Central Africa.

# CHAPTER 4

# SUB-SAHARAN AFRICA

## COMMUNITY-DRIVEN SOCIAL POLICIES

*Kwaku Osei-Hwedie and Arnon Bar-on*

In most African countries south of the Sahara, successive governments have, under diverse political-economic frameworks, set their development objectives based on ideological definitions of their national problems. In this context, the definition and the process of change of social policy in Africa have been dominated, led, and at times held to ransom by ideology.

Social policies are the collective efforts of a nation's people to address their basic welfare needs, related to health, education, employment, occupational training, housing, income security, and personal social services at the local or national levels. For the analysis of social policies in Africa, three distinctive periods may be identified. These are the colonial period, the first decades of independence, and the more recent era of macroeconomic structural adjustment. In the colonial period, the European powers took advantage of the military and technological weaknesses of Africa to exploit the mineral and agricultural wealth of the continent. In the process, they subjected all economic, social, and political activities to their interests. Thus, as a result of the lack of political control by Africans and the systematic expatriation of wealth, countries in the region became producers of an economic value that was lost to their people. As a result, countries in Africa became structurally dependent and so underdeveloped.

Underlying these changes in Africa's economy was the assumption that Africans were in a most elementary state of civilization, far below that of Europeans in the evolutionary ladder. This assumption led to two seemingly contradictory conclusions, formalized in the infamous ideology of apartheid. The first and dominant conclusion, was that only a certain level of African development was required to benefit the supposedly more advanced European capitalist system. Accordingly, the colonial regimes devoted only the resources needed to provide the minimum infrastructure and social services to accomplish this end. Thus, formal education, for example, was only introduced to make Africans efficient, reliable, and dedicated workers. Schooling, health, and related social services were restricted, therefore, to those segments of the population deemed potentially beneficial to the European capitalists. The second conclusion, opposed to the first, is that colonialism came about because of the Africans' need to advance beyond their state of development at that time and become "civilized." Thus, for example, religious education was established to improve the moral and social character of Africans. As the human-development objective was by far secondary to the other, capitalist objective, it was not included in any form of social policy but left entirely to the voluntary efforts of religious organizations, and the lack of an indigenous base made their services extremely rudimentary and ad hoc. The consequence was that African nations inherited from their colonial masters a social-service infrastructure that was close to nil and inherently residual.

At independence, nationalist governments sought to change both the conditions created under colonialism and the thinking behind them. This was a period of rising expectations that, coupled with nationalist sentiments, called for a parting with the past and a search for a new development ideology. Socialism — or more specifically, African socialism — thus became a vehicle to completely eradicate the colonial economy and its related structures.

African socialism emphasized the equality of all people and advocated equality of access to resources, services, and opportunities. Development efforts were thus geared toward structural transformation. Backed by rapid economic growth and the nationalization of a foreign-dominated private sector that provided buoyant government revenues, massive investments were made in infrastructure, from road construction to the new import-substitution enterprises given over to the parastatal sector.

The nationalization of private and foreign enterprises was wide in scope and included a proactive approach to social welfare within the socialist outlook on social development. Governments embarked on a manic spree of building schools, clinics, and other social and physical amenities, all under stringent state control. In keeping with the past, however, personal social services and social security remained underdeveloped. This was in part a legacy of a tradition that still regarded the family as the primary vehicle for personal security and in part due to the belief that under a socialist system, personal needs would be a reflection of individualism and a thing of the past.

In the mid-1970s, however, all these development efforts came to a stop. Across the continent, African economies started to experience deep, pervasive, and continuing economic crises, with zero or insignificant growth and high inflation. This led to rising foreign and domestic debts, increased unemployment, shortages of consumer goods, and deteriorating social infrastructures. Most governments' first response to these developments was to introduce price controls and subsidies for many popular consumer items and inputs for production, including fertilizers and seeds. However, these measures proved ineffective. As the situation deteriorated even further, the International Monetary Fund (IMF) intervened, introducing a new period in the history of African social policy: the era of structural adjustment.

The essence of the IMF's approach to structural adjustment is the neoliberal notion that the state must divest itself of direct participation in the economy and the provision of social services to make way for free-market exchange. Unfortunately however, the mechanisms introduced to reach this end, such as tightening the money supply and reducing public expenditure, compounded the already precarious economic status of most consumers. In a short period of time, it became increasingly clear that alternatives were needed to fill the gap left by the state. In the case of the satisfaction of basic needs, other bodies would have to step in, thus paving the road again for the volunteer sector to become the major provider of social services.

This chapter reviews the development path followed in social policies in Africa and its effects on social welfare. Three distinctive historical–ideological periods and their associated political-economic orientations are discussed as factors shaping the nature and scope of social provision. The analysis underlines how community-based social provision in the precolonial era gave way to voluntary and nongovernmental activities; how nationalist governments subsequently supplanted these modes of provision; and how in the wake of the structural-adjustment programs (SAPs), the trend has shifted again to community provision of social services. The chapter argues that such community-driven social policies are at best rudimentary, as the power of communities to exercise self-determination is largely constricted by the state and the organizations it has sanctioned to promote self-determination.

It should be pointed out that underlying many of these transformations have been substantial interregional, transnational influences stemming, in part, from a shared colonial experience under British rule, which brought most East and Southern African countries into close association with the Commonwealth of Nations. More recently, such ties have been further strengthened by the expansion of the Southern African Development Community, whose activities (much more like those of the European Economic Community) are increasingly influencing developments in its member countries' economies.

# The colonial legacy

Before the advent of colonialism, most sub-Saharan African societies were ethnic nationalities, organized around kith and kin, with authority exercised through a system of chieftaincy, clan elders, and heads of households. Given the mainly autarchic way of life of most people, this was generally adequate to meet most welfare requirements — from housing and the storage of food to personal support in times of bereavement — based on accepted reciprocity and equitable personal intimacies (Brooks and Nyireade 1987).

Colonialism changed the African landscape and permanently dented this social-support mechanism. A variety of reasons can be given to explain this phenomenon, not least of which are the promotion of money as the primary medium for exchange of goods and services and the introduction of a clear distinction between the homestead and the place of work. These developments lessened the need for reciprocity in attaining personal and family welfare (Ouma 1995). For example, when governments were trying to ensure an adequate supply of labour for European enterprises, they introduced taxation schemes. This made it necessary for Africans to seek employment to earn the cash they needed to pay taxes. Additionally, the removal of the hub of political power from the local population undermined the authority of the kinship system, which, in turn, reduced its ability to protect its socially vulnerable members.

Perhaps most importantly, the colonialists devalued the Africans, their organization, and their skills. This was the outcome of an ideology that promoted the colonial powers' own social, cultural, and economic supremacy. One of the most critical consequences of colonialism, crucial to explaining current social-policy patterns in Africa, was that all welfare activities were directed to meeting the interests of the nonindigenous population and these alone (MacPherson 1982). This approach was vigorously promoted and protected. It was also clearly articulated, for example, by Sir Godfrey Huggines, the Prime Minister of Southern Rhodesia: "I shall do all I can to develop the native if I am allowed to protect my own race in our own areas and, if I am not, I will not do anything" (SSW 1996, p. 20).

One of the practical implications of this ideology was that the welfare of Africans became subordinate to that of the colonialists and interpreted strictly in utilitarian terms. In health, for example, governments established hospitals and clinics for the general population primarily because the European enterprises needed healthy workers and the owners of these enterprises feared the spread of communicable diseases. Consequently, these services were rudimentary and inferior to those available to white people. The availability of services largely followed the pattern of European settlements, which meant that they were mainly urban based, despite the fact that most of the population was rural. In Zambia, for example, most health services were concentrated in the copper-mining belt and along the railroad line from where most African labour was recruited and worked.

This policy applied equally to education, as aptly demonstrated by events in Zimbabwe (then Southern Rhodesia). Between 1972 and 1976, only 4 years before independence, the ratio of government expenditure on education for black children and for white children was 1 : 12, or 40 Zimbabwe dollars (ZWD) per black child in comparison with 475 ZWD per white child (in 1998, 25.85 ZWD = 1 United States dollar [USD]). In contrast to black children, all white children were guaranteed full primary and secondary schooling. Also, black families were required to pay for their children's education, whereas their white counterparts were not. Consequently, of the 5 471 white children who started school in 1968, a total of 5 181 completed form IV, with a 5 % dropout rate, attributed mainly to migration. In contrast, out of every 1 000 black children in the same year, 250 never went to school, 340 had only incomplete primary education, and only 78 got to secondary school, of whom 45 reached form IV (SSW 1996).

Another example of this type of double standard is found in personal social services in Zimbabwe in the 1930s. The authorities were faced with growing rates of juvenile delinquency, prostitution, drunkenness, and the break up of families. However, the government restricted its concern over these phenomena only to their occurrence among the white settlers. When similar problems arose in the indigenous population, they were left to the police. When the newly established welfare departments did take an interest in the problems of black people, they attempted to solve these problems by moving the elderly and destitute from the towns and cities to the rural areas. Apart from the desire to keep the urban areas "clean," the reason for this policy was the assumption that black people's needs were "simple" and could be easily met by extended families and other mechanisms of the peasant economy. For this reason, too, old-age allowances were granted to whites only.

In sum, under colonial rule, Europeans received the highest priority, followed by those Africans immediately linked with the European economy. The problems of the rest of the African population were considered only if resources allowed or if they could be left to the humanitarian and missionary work of volunteers. Thus, in 1970, the church ran more than 60% of all rural health services in Zimbabwe; on the eve of independence, in 1980, non-governmental organizations (NGOs) owned 107 of the country's 177 secondary schools (SSW 1996). This, in turn, gave governments justification to remain aloof from such social services. However, the church and other volunteer organizations, relying mostly on charitable funding, were usually only able to offer the most basic of services, which were thus also of low quality. In health, for example, most Africans continued to rely on traditional medicine for a substantive part of their health care. However, the contribution of traditional medicine was unacknowledged and neglected, keeping it underdeveloped by contemporary standards of medicine.

## Gaining independence

Sub-Saharan Africa's independence and the ascension to power of nationalist governments raised a variety of expectations of socioeconomic change to foster greater equality and ultimately development. The newly formed political parties were instrumental in accelerating such changes as they tried to amass support to their cause. First among their promises was the guarantee of free education and health services for all, the improvement of housing, and the provision of other services, such as electricity, running water, and roads. Also important was the promise of popular participation in identifying needs and developing programs to address them. This was meant to allow people to taste political and economic powers that colonialism had denied them.

The prospects for satisfying such yearnings were also optimistic. Although it was recognized that all African countries suffered considerable economic backwardness, it was assumed that this was caused by decades of foreign rule resulting in insufficient investment, dependence on single metropolitan markets, and lack of education. When Africans gained control of their own destinies, the expectation was that they could build industries, develop cities and infrastructures, attract foreign investment and aid, and prove their development potential. The boom in world trade during the 1960s, with the growing demand for primary commodities, which were Africa's main line of exports, contributed to strengthening this optimism. Additionally, at that time, the continent was self-sufficient in food. In fact, it was a net food exporter.

At independence, as during the colonial period, ideology was again one of the major factors in the evolution of events. Partly as a reaction to previous forms of government but also because it was widely regarded at the time as an effective means to enhance the welfare of people *en masse*, socialism was adopted by most African governments. Socialist philosophies dominated the region from the end of the 1960s to the early 1990s. This was understood at that time to mean that government control of all natural resources and the major means of production and their use would be for the benefit of the nation as a whole. This led, first, to the adoption of social-sector policies as the primary instruments to create the new social order. Second, it led to the assumption that this would ensure that the necessary state resources were available to execute its policies and that the state would have sufficient control to manage society for its benefit. In the words of President Nkrumah (1967, pp. 52–53), socialism would allow governments to establish

> a society in which men and women will have no anxiety about work, food and shelter, where poverty and illiteracy no longer exist, and where diseases is brought under control; where our education facilities provide our children with the best possible opportunities for learning.

In hindsight, this may sound naive. However, to understand the postcolonial legacy that has shaped African social policy to date, one needs to appreciate the ambience of the time, the political atmosphere, and the euphoria of having independence after years of repression.

Socialist African governments took a structural view of social problems and took a proactive, rather than a reactive, approach to social-sector policies. In most cases, social-welfare programs differed from those in the West, which were characterized by a central policy concern with income transfers. In Africa, where most economies are dominated by subsistence-level agriculture, a very small sector of the population had income to be transferred to others, and even fewer could contribute to building national social-insurance systems. Consequently, what social-security system existed was restricted mainly to the civil service and a few other employment-based sectors of the economy, such as manual labour. Instead, the three most important areas of investment were education, health (including water supply), and price subsidies and controls. The importance of the latter is clear, given the proportion of income spent by the poor on basic commodities (Muzaale 1988). Put in another way, the emphasis was on social development, rather than on residualism, and consequently social assistance and other personal-welfare services remained largely underdeveloped.

With these principles and the necessary resources from the products of nationalization, governments went into a frenzy of compensating for past policies. This is illustrated by changes in the education sector. In Zambia, 880 000 new school places were created between 1964 and 1984 (Tembo 1995). In Zimbabwe, where free education was introduced overnight, the government established 5 500 primary and secondary schools in 6 years, a 220% increase over the preindependence era. Halfway through this period, school enrolment increased to 2.5 million, of which 420 000 were in secondary school; by contrast, the total enrolment was 800 000 in 1980, of which only 72 300 were in secondary school (SSW 1996). In the health sector, governments embarked on massive infrastructure building, with the aim (as in Zimbabwe) of ensuring that no one need travel more than 10 km to the nearest clinic. In Zambia, the total number of hospitals and health centres grew from 354 in 1964 to 1 006 in 1988, an increase of more than 160% (Tembo 1995). All health-care services were offered free of charge, at least to the poor, or at a standard, nominal price.

With these and other investments, especially in industry and water supply, Africa's first decade of political independence showed marked improvements in the situation of most of the population. In Zambia, for example, total public expenditures grew at an average annual rate of 19.3% between 1964 and 1970 and contributed to a more than 50% rise in new waged employment by 1973, doubling real earnings (Daniel 1985). This, plus a growth in social services, culminated in an overall enhancement of the welfare of the population. So well did most countries do on all universal social and economic performance indicators that it appeared unnecessary at the time to question the source of this progress or the prospects of its sustainability.

## A crises in the making

Looking back from the perspective of the 1990s, one sees these developments as almost unbelievable. Compare what is taking place in Africa today with parallel developments elsewhere, such as in the former Soviet Union, and with the economic recovery of some South American countries, and "it is difficult to believe," as the former President of Nigeria, General Olusegun Obasanjo, remarked "that we inhabit the same historical time" (Marcum 1988/89, p. 177). Recent reports on the state of the African continent are extraordinarily gloomy. They describe Africa as "moribund," "peripheral to the rest of the world," and "a human and environmental disaster area." In the view of the World Bank, whereas virtually every other region in the world is likely to experience an uplift in the quality of life by 2000, the situation in Africa will only get worse (Farnsworth 1990).

The obvious question is, what went wrong? Several factors may explain what happened. Financing the rapid expansion of the social infrastructure was facilitated by growth in the economy, often aided by continuing assistance from former colonial powers. This was invaluable to the success of governments in reviving the collective spirit of Africans, especially in rural areas, for it translated into the popularity of volunteering to help build clinics, schools, toilets, and wells. In Botswana, for example, albeit at that time one of the poorest countries in the world, colonial aid paid for the payroll of the entire civil service for 11 years after independence. Together with grants from the United Kingdom, this made up almost half of all government revenues (Morton and Ramsay 1987). However, this proved to be only a short-term measure.

Even as late as the early 1970s, when the global economy began to show signs of recession, Africa's social-development efforts continued to be strong. This was partly due to the introduction of international financial-compensatory measures that helped to weaken the impact of the first oil crisis in 1973. Another factor was the ability of many countries to attract bilateral assistance as their human-centred development models fitted well the basic-needs interest of donor agencies. In Tanzania, for example, the amount of foreign aid rose from 1% of gross domestic product (GDP) in 1961 to 16% of GDP in 1986.

Between 1973 and 1982, foreign aid from Scandinavian sources alone funded the construction of 400 dispensaries, rural health centres, and health-education and nutrition projects (Tungaraza 1990). As a result, expenditure on health rose by close to 200% in the 1970s; and in education, by 180%. This trend was also apparent in social security, which rose by 120% (Tungaraza 1990). Although total investments exceeded governments' own resources in most countries, the flow of foreign aid was a determinant factor in financing their expanding social infrastructure. All this, however, was still insufficient.

In general developmental terms, it could be argued that following independence most African countries made significant strides in uplifting the well-being of their populations. However, the situation of many people remained extremely harsh. In part, this was because in most African countries human-development indicators were very low to begin with. For example, in 1960, life expectancy at birth was 40 years, whereas it was 69 years in the industrial countries; the mortality rate for children under 5 years old was seven times as high; and adult literacy reached only 17% of that in the North, with university training almost nonexistent (UNDP 1992). In part, it was also because progress occurred over a relatively short period; as the situation improved, people's expectations rose proportionally.

However, overshadowing all other considerations that fueled the need for accelerated overall development was the mushrooming of the population. Improved medical care and the partial containment of diseases such as polio and malaria drastically cut infant mortality, thus contributing to rapid population growth. Africa's population was already increasing at an average annual rate of 2.6% in the 1960s. In the next decade, this increased to 2.9%, and by the late 1980s, it had risen to more than 3%. This implies a doubling in population every 22 years (Goliber 1989).

In theory, this growing population could have met its basic needs with an equal or a larger increase in productivity. This happened only to an extent during the 1960s. Farm output rose by around 3% a year, keeping pace with the rate of population growth. Since 1970, however, agricultural production grew at only half this rate. Part of this decline was and continues to be largely beyond the control of African countries — droughts, often made worse by overgrazing and by the rapid deforestation needed to provide fuel and shelter for a growing population, have been a factor. In part, however, the agricultural decline resulted directly from specific government policies. Governments seeking to transform their countries from primary-commodity producers into industrial manufacturers pursued import-substitution policies that led to the development of their own steel, cement, and paper industries. In this context, considerable efforts were directed to protecting these industries through heavy tariffs and subsidies, rather than targeting foreign markets and stimulating the economy by export growth. As a result, in a short time, these export products became less attractive abroad. Although establishing the heavy industries was relatively easy, African countries lacked the capacity to establish a high-tech sector. The result of this was a continuing heavy dependence on imports. To cover the resulting trade deficits, farmers were encouraged to grow tea, coffee, and cocoa for export, rather than food for domestic consumption. Ultimately, most countries ended up not only with a neglected agricultural base as a result of high investment in industrialization but also with an agricultural sector further curtailed by price controls that repressed the income received by farmers for the items they did grow.

Many other factors also made governments adopt strategies of internal-deficit financing, which ultimately affected the capacity of governments to respond to demands in the social sectors. In Uganda, for example, a drive to localize the economy led to massive capital flight abroad and a drain in the trained labour force with the expulsion of Asian entrepreneurs. Simultaneously, the country was engulfed in a web of political instability and in wars with neighbouring countries. At this time, African governments poured money not only into basic industrial infrastructure but also into large bureaucracies, oversized armies, and prestige enterprises, such as fancy parliament buildings and national airlines, paying for them by printing money and raising loans from abroad. In Zambia, for example, it was estimated that by 1980, total public expenditure had outstripped the gross national product by more than 50%, and government and other parastatal enterprises accounted for close to 80% of the country's total formal employment. But only a quarter of the income was collected through taxes.

These and other difficulties, both national (such as escalating civil wars) and international (such as the dramatic drop in the price of primary commodities), increased Africa's indebtedness in new ways. Earlier postcolonial borrowing had been driven primarily by the desire for rapid development: money was poured into industry, health, education, airports, roads, and water and electrification schemes. But the new borrowing was to pay for imported food, armaments, and a soaring civil service (often inept, because of a legacy of insufficient training, and more often than not chronically corrupt). Indebtedness grew at an accelerated pace. Defaults on loans rapidly produced a drying-up of capital from Western banks, which were never keen to invest in Africa in the first place; national economies came almost to a halt.

The social and human costs of this were devastating. The newly constructed schools, clinics, and hospitals could no longer be maintained. For the same reason, transportation, water delivery, and electricity supplies also staggered or, more often, degenerated. Concurrently — and, in the long-term perspective, more importantly — large numbers of trained personnel left for greener pastures, undermining the delivery of existing services and the development of new initiatives.

# Adjustment and change

Without an alternative framework for economic reform, the governments of African countries were under increased pressure to undertake sweeping reforms. On the one hand, chronic negative balance of payments triggered a shift in emphasis from industrial substitution to export-led industrialization. Because the state had until then played the major role in the economy, it became obvious that its functions would have to drastically change. On the other hand, it became evident that because large internal deficits and strong inflationary pressures accompanied the external deficits, reforms would have to include drastic reductions in the public sector and its expenditures.

This diagnosis was widely accepted. It might have led to the implementation of a range of corrective measures (Mkandawire 1989); however, in practice a neoliberal view of economic and social development became dominant, enabling international financial institutions (IFIs) to take control of the reforms, particularly the IMF and the World Bank. Thus, under the label of "structural adjustment," IFIs imposed the condition on their support that governments implement harsh austerity policies, first to reorient production toward exports and, second, to implement a general program of state withdrawal from active involvement in the social and economic sectors. By the late 1980s and early 1990s, SAPs were in place in more than 30 countries in sub-Saharan Africa.

Structural adjustment in Africa rested on two economic objectives: changes in the foundations of the economy and the achievement of an equilibrium in external and internal monetary balances. Therefore, as stated by Reinikka-Soininen (1990, p. 11), the SAPs involved

> a comprehensive set of economic measures designed to achieve macro-economic goals, such as improvement in the balance of payments, a more efficient use of the productive potential, an increase in the long-term rate of economic growth, and low inflation.

One of the strongly held assumptions underlying SAPs was that only efficiency in resource allocation and economic equilibrium can cause long-term growth. This meant that SAP measures were usually geared toward price mechanisms designed to induce substitutions in consumption and production. Thus, SAP recommendations were aimed at

- Removing or reducing price distortions and subsidies;

- Increasing depressed producer prices;

- Increasing domestic interest rates to promote saving and the efficiency of financial institutions;

- Promoting quick-yielding productive sectors;

- Restraining wages;

- Opening trade and capital markets to competition; and

- Managing external debts (Commonwealth Secretariat 1989).

In short, the primary aim of structural adjustment was to allow increased intervention of market forces in the control of the economy, thus reversing the ideological basis of government for most African countries before the SAPs.

The role and processes of SAPs as a means to reviving African economies have attracted considerable attention (Sahn 1994; World Bank 1994). In practice, however, several problems are associated with assessing the social impact of SAPs, especially when it comes to the weaker sectors in society. In part, this is due to undisaggregated statistics and a lack of substantive, reliable information and comprehensive household surveys (Demery and Squire 1996). In part, it is also due to problems related to the interpretation of available data. It has been difficult, for example, to clearly separate the effects of SAPs from the those of concurrent events (Commonwealth Secretariat 1989). This has become a problem particularly since the early 1990s, when many SAPs began to move beyond the strict realm of economic reform and tried to reorganize other aspects of society, including even gender relations and the democratization of political processes by facilitating multiparty elections and increased freedom of the press. One of the implications of the overall lack of social data is that most discussions of SAPs in Africa have had to rely on theory or the indirect evidence of modeling exercises (Bourguignon et al. 1991), on pan-African generalizations that incorrectly treat the continent as a homogeneous whole, or more commonly on largely anecdotal evidence (Watkins 1995). The following section discusses some of the social impacts of the SAPs.

## The social impacts

Because one of the primary aims of structural adjustment has been to liberate the economy from social and political influences, a major emphasis of SAPs to date has been on privatization. To this end, governments have implemented several interrelated measures. First, governments devalued exchange rates artificially overvalued to boost exports. Second, governments removed most price controls on basic commodities like the staple maize meal. In addition to reducing public deficits, this was also meant to stimulate the agricultural sector by increasing the price farmers receive for their products and thereby putting a halt to a serious social side effect: the rural–urban migration that was reaching untenable proportions. In Zambia, for example, in the first 16 years of independence, close to half the population migrated to urban areas. By 1980, the "rail provinces" — the Lusaka, Central, Copperbelt, and Southern provinces —

alone already contained more than 55% of the nation's population, up from 20% in 1964 (Burdette 1988). Third, governments divested themselves of the business enterprises under their control, reduced the size of their civil services, and diverted substantial funds from social services, generally regarded by the new neoliberal-thinking economists as unproductive.

Although the effectiveness of these measures over time remains subject to debate (Demery and Squire 1996; Hope 1997), it is generally acknowledged that over the short term they have brought a traumatic experience to much of the population. At the macroeconomic level, GDP per capita in sub-Saharan Africa as a whole declined in real terms between 1988 and 1992 by 1.0% a year, whereas per capita consumption, already at a minimum, fell in 23 out of 41 countries. It is, however, at the micro, that is to say more personal, level that SAPs have had their most direct social impact. In Zambia, for example, the divestiture by the government of its publicly owned businesses, ranging from mines and dairies to dry cleaners, left 85% of the population unemployed. By the end of 1996, out of a total of 9 million people, only 400 000 had formal employment. Further, although many workers were willing to take retrench-ment packages, their employers' cash flows were too meagre to pay them (Lamont 1996). Finally, even the mean years of schooling, in which govern-ments invested the most, had fallen (UNDP 1992).

Another strategy of the SAP for cost-recovery was to introduce user fees in key social-sector services, such as education, health, and water supply; in areas in which such measures were already in place, the approach was to dramatically increase user fees and to collect them more stringently. In the education sector, for example, many students have been forced to drop out of school because of their inability to pay higher schools fees. Owing to cultural factors, the most direct effects of these measures have been felt by girls. Users fees in education also contribute to increased urban–rural disparities, as the urban schools' con-stituencies are better placed to pay higher fees and more able to pay higher teachers' salaries, thus depleting rural schools of qualified teachers. Adeybayo Adedeji, former Executive Secretary of the Economic Commission for Africa, noted that "if things continue like this, Africa will have more illiterate people as a proportion of the population than at independence" (Commonwealth Secretariat 1989, pp. 27–28). The health sector has been equally affected. User fees in health were already a common practice, except for the poorest sector of the population. However, devaluation and budget cuts led to increases in the cost of drugs, which in turn led to a drastic reduction in the availability of drugs at clinics and hospitals. In Zambia, the real value of the drug budget in 1986 was a quarter of what it was in 1983 (Commonwealth Secretariat 1989). As in educa-tion, cutbacks in health have also had a greater impact on women, as they are the custodians of family health, especially of children.

Although most of these measures and their aftermath have been com-mon to many other developing countries, they caught African governments unprepared. Their civil societies had virtually no social safety nets to contain their adverse effects. In part, this was due to the governments' belief that the negative effects of these reforms would be short lived and so could be weathered if not by all, then by most of the population. Moreover, compared with other regions where neoliberal economic policies have been introduced, the African region had traditionally had institutionally underdeveloped personal and residual social services. This was due to a combination of factors. These included the colonial legacy that downplayed individuals' needs beyond the most basic — historically it had been assumed these could be met by the peasant economy; the legacy of a socialist outlook that places collective before individual needs; and the African kinship system that places responsibility for personal welfare on the extended family. In this regard, the profile of social policies in Africa under SAPs takes on a different dimension from those in other regions.

In addition, because the primary concern of some governments was social and not personal development, they even dismantled some of the few personal safeguards that were already in place or severely curtailed them as their economies deteriorated and resources became more limited. In Zimbabwe, the government decided as early as in 1980 to repeal its *Old Age Pension Act* (which at the time catered to whites only), instead of extending its coverage to the entire population. Although its importance was clearly recognized, this Act was deemed unfundable. Another cost-saving strategy was to keep the level of nominal income below which medical care was provided free of charge unchanged for 10 years, despite the country's roaring inflation.

Consequently, the measures in place in most countries to cushion the social impact of SAPs were very meagre. In some cases, the only safety net was food rations for the destitute and minimal cash-for-work or food-for-work programs intended to provide their recipients with just enough to sustain their physical health. In Botswana, the food package originally meant for a single person was provided to feed the entire family. The same applies to the cash-for-work program ("drought relief"), in which participation was also restricted. In Swaziland, public assistance was so small that recipients were paid only once every 3 months because the amounts on their social-assistance cheques would be otherwise less than their transportation costs for collecting them (Khumalo 1992).

Under these conditions, most governments have been forced to revise their entire set of social policies. From using their limited resources to promote social welfare across society, they have had to begin using them residually as a corrective tool to manage the social malfunctioning of the market economy — to compensate for or, more precisely, to cope with "economic diswelfare." Moreover, governments have had to do this literally overnight and in the light of the dictates of the SAPs, which demanded as little public investment as possible. All this took place at a time when the sick in hospitals already had to rely on relatives for a change of bedding; schools were operating without books or desks; and people were going back to using unsafe water sources as taps ran dry (Mabote 1996). In Zimbabwe, less than 5% of those employed in the formal sector qualified for free health care, compared with 46% in 1982 (Sanders 1992).

The "new" ideology of residualism — in effect, a return to colonialism — translated into three key phenomena in terms of social development: the active retargeting of the neediest among the needy, more by default than intent; the restressing or reemergence of self-help or local autonomy under the disguise of decentralization, local participation, and partnership; and the reintroduction of private welfare, undertaken mainly by NGOs.

## Targeting the neediest of the needy

Many African governments, cognizant that some of the direct social-reform measures and the trigger-off impacts of SAPs would aggravate an already difficult situation and aware of the probable political effects, introduced some cushioning mechanisms aimed to help the most vulnerable groups: the Programme of Action to Mitigate the Social Costs of Adjustment in Ghana; the Programme for Alleviation of Poverty and Social Cost of Adjustment in Uganda; the Social Action Programme in Zambia; and the Social Dimensions Fund in Zimbabwe. All these programs were drawn up alongside the SAP economic measures, but more often than not they were introduced belatedly.

Very early in the process, some of these programs began to encounter serious obstacles. Arriving at a definition of *vulnerable groups*, for example, was not an easy task. Different programs adopted different, often conflicting, strategies. Thus, in Zimbabwe, which had one of the broadest public-assistance programs in Africa, one approach was to tighten the eligibility criteria so that help would be available only to the most needy. This led to the enactment of the *Social Welfare Assistance Act* of 1988, which restricted public assistance to the elderly, the chronically ill, the disabled, and the dependants of indigent people. Before the implementation of this Act, all persons had been able to receive assistance provided they proved that they were destitute and had no other significant source of assistance. At the same time it promulgated this Act, the government extended the provision of health care free of charge across the board by significantly raising the income threshold for fees to be paid, from 150 ZWD to 400 ZWD, although this sum took no account of family size (SSW 1996). In recognition of rural–urban disparities, the government exempted all families in rural areas, whatever their income, from the newly introduced schools fees, and in the urban centres poor families were expected to apply to the Social Dimensions Fund for help. In contrast, in Zambia, which used a system of food subsidies, only urban-based heads of households earning less than a specified amount per year were eligible for coupons they could exchange for heavily subsidized corn meal. The system did not apply to rural communities, except in provincial towns of predominantly urban provinces, as it was assumed that rural dwellers were self-sufficient in food production.

However, even when these measures were implemented, they often proved to be insufficient. Many people, especially workers on commercial farms, who were fairly isolated, remained unaware of the availability of these services. In most cases, even if they were informed, they could do little to use the services because the program offices were located in major cities, out of reach of much of the population. Also, assistance programs usually dealt with only newly added service costs, not with those already in place. Thus, for example, in all African countries, families contended not only with school fees but also with other associated expenditures, such as a school-building levy and the costs of children's school uniforms, which many families could ill-afford and which the funds failed to cover.

Even more detrimental, however, was the fact that governments allocated insufficient funds for these programs. As a result, the programs were often unable to cover even some basic contingencies for which people were eligible for assistance. As often occurred, governments found it easier to sustain some particular arrangements rather than others. In Ghana, for instance, most assistance funds were earmarked to enable retrenched workers to venture into new occupations. In Senegal, the funds were used to set up small businesses (UNDP 1991). In both cases, little was left for other groups.

The lengthy delay in processing benefits has become even worse because of underfunding. This problem has been further compounded by an increasingly frustrated staff unable to carry out its duties. To implement most of the new policies effectively, the officers responsible have had to investigate the claimants. However, one of the major difficulties is inadequate transportation. This is due in part to the small number of vehicles available, the low allocations to cover mileage costs, and the poor maintenance of vehicles, some of which were donated directly from abroad and are expensive to repair, as parts have to be imported. Consequently, officers often just wait for clients in their offices. For their part, clients are often unable to cover transportation costs to reach the offices, or when they are able to, they receive little attention because the officers, often not being much better off than their clients, are busy attending to their own affairs. As a health worker remarked, "before [the SAP], nurses discussed medicine, now all they talk about is how to 'deal'. Instead of giving health education to a patient, you find a nurse busy asking a patient where this or that can be procured" (SSW 1996, p. 62).

## Decentralization, participation, and partnership

To revitalize the economy and bridge financial gaps in the social sectors, central governments decentralized management and administration, including social services. Most governments embraced this measure with great enthusiasm. At independence, African countries inherited highly efficient administrative structures and forms of governance. For example, fewer than 100 officials ran all of Botswana, a country the size of France, albeit with a minuscule population (Morton and Ramsay 1987). Situations like this were possible, first, because of the limited aims of colonial regimes (that is, keeping law and order, facilitating economic exploitation, and, at times, introducing small-scale improvement projects, all of which required few supportive services) and, second, because of the civil services' fusion of political and administrative authority. This allowed local authorities to be personal representatives of the heads of governments in their respective places of operation, leading to extreme centralization down to the lowest levels.

Independence found much of this structure wanting. To establish development policies, new governments needed, first, to build the institutional capacity to provide services requiring, among other things, a much larger civil service. Second, because the members of this service had to be dissociated from the previous administration, governments wanted to localize public servants and divest them of their all-embracing powers. Third, they wished to give the people an effective voice in running their affairs.

The most common mechanisms introduced in several countries to address these three issues, almost immediately after independence, set out to revive the village as the basic unit of administration in the rural areas and to establish town councils in the urban areas. Villages and town councils were made, at least on paper, the effective development units, linked to the main urban centres by a string of similar development institutions at district and provincial levels. One of the most sophisticated of these models was introduced in Tanzania. After 1972, elected village councils were given the authority to make bylaws, raise revenues to finance local development, and carry out activities that they had previously had little involvement in, such as road works and water-supply projects (Mutahaba 1989). More often, however, as in Botswana, Zambia, and Zimbabwe, the lower levels of the structure had less effective authority.

With only slight variations, under this model, the first stage in policy formulation was to bring problems to the attention of one of the village-level committees, popularly elected at the *Kgotla* or its equivalent village-based mechanism.[1] Issues would then be taken up by the Village Development Committee (VDC). The VDC was also elected at the *Kgotla* and divided into committees dealing with substantive areas, such as education, health, and agriculture, that were expected to formulate proposals for village-wide development. The VDC was also expected to provide the link between the village and

---

[1] In Botswana, for example, the *Kgotla* is the central decision-making agency of a village and serves as the village's administrative and judicial centre. It is presided over by the local chief, and all adult community members are expected to attend to discuss public affairs.

central and local government structures (Silitshena 1989). For example, the VDC identified the needy in the village, brought them to the attention of social workers, and arranged for them to receive public assistance.

Following this village-based approach to policy formulation, the VDCs' recommendations would move up through the administrative structure to district and, ultimately, national levels. From the Ward Development Committees, composed of the VDC chairpersons, suggestions were to be forwarded to the District Development Committee to be subjected to technical analysis. Depending on the outcome of these deliberations, the recommendations were to be sent to the Provincial Development Committee for further technical and budgetary analysis, and if approved, they were then to be recommended to Cabinet and to Parliament for adoption. This last step was usually to be taken by the relevant ministry charged with ranking the policy proposals from all the country's districts and provinces. When a community's plans were to be carried out, or the government wanted to consult its constituency, the same path was to be followed but in reverse.

In theory, this process of policy formulation was neat and clear, but in reality it remained a statement of intent, not a program of action (Chikulo 1985). This was due to a combination of both local- and central-government constraints. Local governments were weak, first, because of an absence of any tradition of local government beyond traditional forms of governance that had been undermined by colonial rule and, second, because of a lack in all but a few localities of an economic base to support local governments. With many new responsibilities, local governments ran into functional overload.

Other factors added to the complexity of the situation. One set of factors was related to the drive to localize personnel. These were associated with a decline, first, in performance, as a result of the induction of a large number of functionaries ill-prepared to take up their new positions and, second, in supervision, which was entrusted to newly elected councillors, who had none of the experience and competence needed to exercise this type of responsibility. Consequently, to get things moving in the new, decentralized environment, many functions formally devolved to the village and district levels reverted over the short-term to "proper" officials, who were found mainly in the central government. The situation was further aggravated by the fact that development projects and budgets formulated at the village level were often very unrealistic, much akin to a child's Christmas shopping list. For example, a small settlement of 500 residents might decide that it must establish a secondary school. In the middle of a dryland, already suffering from lack of water, a community wanted to begin a vegetable-growing project. The estimated costs of such projects were often severely trimmed as they moved up the ladder. By the time they reached the final decision-making level, they bore little resemblance to the original proposals (Hyden 1980). Even when projects were approved, it often took so long to discuss them that by the time they were adopted they were already outdated and ripe for review or their "good implementation" had attracted the centre's displeasure, as it was not prepared to see alternative power structures emerge. With time, the lower-level organizations, especially the villages, became demoralized and stopped taking their role seriously. This disaffection was compounded by the practice of using the villages, under the guise of their participating in self-help projects, more as instruments for the extraction of labour than as organs to influence decisions — a practice that Salole (1991) aptly called "the taxation of the beneficiaries."

Overall, the centralization process itself proved resilient to change. Three reasons can be given to explain this. First, centralization was originally seen as a key means to consolidate the process of nation building. This was to respond, in part, to the legacy left by the European carving up of Africa. When boundaries were drawn without regard to differing ethnic groups or even to earlier conquests of neighbouring lands by successful tribes, few governments attracted the loyalty of their citizens, except perhaps for kin of the group in power (Kennedy 1993). Second, centralization was a means to make the public service accountable to the dominant, often sole, political party, described in typical doublespeak by former President of Zambia, His Excellency K. Kaunda, as a policy of "decentralization in centralism": "a measure whereby through the Party and Government machinery, we will decentralize most of our Party and Government activities while retaining effective control of the Party and Government machinery at the center in the interest of unity" (Mutahaba 1989, p. 98). Third, the centralized form of governance largely fit the determined role and paternalistic nature of political leadership in African societies, in which people regard their leaders as the guardians of their personal and social well-being and regard their public servants as the extension workers of those leaders. This explains, for example, the frequent reference to African presidents as the "father of the nation." When taken literally, this notion often leads to a system of central patronage in which, at least theoretically, all civil servants are appointed personally by the president and accountable to this person alone (Mutahaba 1989). Thus, as the years passed, Africa saw the progressive diluting of the autonomy enjoyed by local governments. Its replacement by a hierarchy "allowed only as much discretionary power as was necessary to implement central policy directive[s]" (Chikulo 1985, p. 351), which, in effect, made much of government and service administration revert to the prefectural system of the past.

Today, SAP reforms are once again turning this situation around. Neoliberal policies assume that, by analogy with the free-market dynamic, effective public decision-making can only be made either directly by people's individual preferences or by individuals through the preferences of their communities. When these assumptions are reinforced by pressure from Western donors to make African governments more democratic, the outcome is the lessening, if not the ending, of central-government planning and control. However, the governments themselves have become concerned because, despite the progressive coverage of essential social services and many development programs, the trickle-down effect of economic activities, especially to rural areas, has been disappointing, and most of the rural population still lives in poverty. This can be partly attributed to difficulties in expanding and diversifying rural economies; however, increasingly, in line with some of the underlying assumptions of structural adjustment, the fault is found to lie with the technocrats who conceive and implement development programs. Technocrats are thought to find it easier to disperse money than to build institutional capacity at grassroots levels; thus, they not only contribute to, but also encourage, dependence. In Botswana, for example, under one of many programs to stimulate agricultural production among smallholders, farmers were paid to plow, destump, and plant their land in rows, which is to say, they were paid to do the work they would have done normally. Agricultural demonstrators, consequently, were turned into administrators, measuring the land plowed each season, and farmer committees became gatherings to receive handouts (Morna 1989). Likewise, the National Policy on Destitution in 1980 stipulated that eligible destitute persons receive monthly rations but made no provision for their rehabilitation or return to productive life. To change this situation, found throughout much of the rural economy, the new approach has been to encourage communities to take greater responsibility for their own development and to allow governments to concentrate on their overall strategic and facilitating roles.

This renewed focus on the community as a development base poses several major challenges. First, for this strategy to be a significant departure from the past, development responsibility and control have to shift substantially from central and provincial to district and community levels. This would also require a significant change in development activities. Both types of changes would require the substantial reorientation of the civil service, which, in practice, is used to administering, rather than facilitating, development operations. With such a reorientation, there is also the risk that governments will again invest mainly in capacity-building for their own personnel through new in-house retraining. An associated factor mitigating against decentralization is the importance attributed to social networks in Africa. This often leads people in positions of lesser authority to expect "leadership," in the sense that it is often considered politically prudent for the government, not the community, to solve local problems and to be seen to be doing so.

Second, to achieve any degree of success, community-based programs inevitably require significant financial inputs. In this respect, however, the room to manoeuvre has become severely curtailed. The poverty of their constituencies limits independent sources of income for local councils, especially in the rural areas. Also, as one aim of the entire exercise is to balance the public budget, the spending of central governments, too, is very restricted. Thus, as a recent document on the topic states, "it is expected that the budget line [for community-based programs] could be set at a level that would provide community members with sufficient motivation to participate, while remaining relatively modest in terms of national budgets" (GOB 1995, p. 3). In practice, this is tantamount to saying that no further funds for these programs are available.

Finally, hurdles have to be overcome at the local level. Two decades after grassroots participation in policy formulation was largely abandoned, village organizations, like their bureaucratic counterparts, have come to perceive development mainly in terms of service-infrastructure provision and less in terms of improved livelihoods. For example, in a recent village-planning exercise in four villages in Botswana, almost all the plans developed by the village organizations referred to government-provided services. Only on a few occasions, and even then, only after considerable prompting from development workers, did local organizations come up with anything that they could do for themselves (Prinsen et al. 1996) Also, village-level organizations are often not truly participatory and are therefore inadequate for consultation. Attendance at village meetings, for example, has declined considerably, as has people's willingness to participate in voluntary activities. Not uncommonly, the elderly, usually men, dominate most village affairs, despite their lack of proficiency in government procedures. This situation raises serious concerns about any move toward community-development strategies, particularly in the area of basic needs, without first focusing on substantial capacity-building to equip villages with the participatory and management skills required to formulate, run, and monitor their development programs.

## The reintroduction of private welfare: development, capacity-building, and partnership

Economic and social vacuums seldom stay as such. In Africa, declining employment led rapidly to the growth of the informal sector, already widespread because of wages being literally at starvation levels. In the social sphere, the virtual collapse of the welfare state stimulated the role of private enterprises in providing key social services and encouraged the reintroduction of the volunteer sector, now under the banner of NGOs. Thus, a third outcome of the reforms affecting social policy has been the involvement of NGOs.

In the years immediately following independence, most African governments tried to face the demands for social-policy development alone. The volunteer sector, mainly church-led organizations that dominated the provision of social services, were either banned or marginalized, being upstaged many times over by the public sector. In other cases, the volunteer sector's mode of operation, working directly at the grassroots level, was deemed subversive in the socialist outlook of the times, with the result that some of these volunteer organizations were closed (Mwansa 1995).

With their treasuries depleted and participation, self-help, and partnership given priority, governments allowed the reemergence of NGOs. Priority was given to those NGOs dealing strictly with humanitarian (residual) assistance and those that might contribute to community development, for example, through capacity-building. Often, however, the operations of these organizations remained under suspicion. In Uganda, for example, the government vets all NGOs. Indigenous organizations are subjected to additional rules to ensure a tighter control than is the case with nonindigenous NGOs. Some of the major attractions of NGOs for African governments are that most of their funding comes from nongovernmental sources and that among their professed aims is the promotion of local ownership and popular participation through development programs. Although there is undoubtedly evidence of local ownership and popular participation, to many these characteristics of NGOs are a double-edged sword.

Recent experiences of the role of NGOs in social policy point to various areas of concern. In theory, NGOs and the multilateral and bilateral organizations that fund and advise them help governments formulate social policies, contribute resources toward transforming these policies into action, and operate, during their implementation, within the parameters set by governments. But, it is not uncommon for NGOs to come with their own preconceived definitions of problems, in many cases dictated by their own interests. One result of this is that although local decision-makers are usually involved in the policy process, their participation is often reduced to identifying problems in accordance with the NGO's or the funder's priorities. Mwansa (1995, pp. 72–73) noted that "the state then merely acts as a passive recipient ... . Driven by poverty and want, ... [it] cannot afford to challenge the NGO lest the assistance is taken to another country."

A typical example of this dilemma occurred recently in Zambia. Following lengthy consultations, a local authority compiled a list of the residents' most urgent needs. Unable to meet these needs, it hoped that an NGO participating in preparing the list would help. However, the NGO had its own agenda, which did not include addressing any of the most pressing needs identified by the community (Mwansa 1995). Although this in itself posed little problem, given that the magnitude of the community's needs made any help welcome, it shows how the NGO's response aimed at needs that were low in the residents' priorities. This example also shows that even under a different approach, there is an entrenchment of old practices that bypass local ownership in planning and implementing community actions and ignore the importance of local capacity-building.

A second concern, closely connected to the first, is that many of the NGOs' agendas are under foreign domination, thus undermining their effectiveness in social policy and program implementation. In many cases, the agendas of NGOs, as well intentioned as they may be, are not locally grounded: they inadequately reflect the outlook, attitudes, and cultures of their intended beneficiaries. A current example is the Women in Development approach. The focus of this approach is to increase women's productive efficiency with the hope that this will have multiplier effects in other spheres, such as their ability to take care of their children. Although few critical studies have been done in this area, preliminary evidence suggests that instead of improving women's quality of life, programs conceived within this framework end up increasing women's already heavy workload. As a result, these programs become unsustainable because many of their recipients abandon them early in their implementation (Manyire and Asingwiire 1996).

A third concern is that much of the work of the NGO movement is undermined by its own structure, in particular its financing, labour, and mode of accountability. Financially, almost all NGOs, including the indigenous organizations, rely heavily on external funding. Although the argument can be made that such help may be unavoidable during a program's infancy, it seriously challenges the sustainability of the NGO's efforts once this external support ends or is withdrawn. In 1993, for example, four NGOs were established in Botswana to address the problem of the increasing number of street children. Within 3 years, with their seed money exhausted, all but one folded; the remaining one cut its operations to the bone. Another example occurred in South Africa: after apartheid ended, many international organizations and donors funding social programs began to channel their assistance to this country, severely curtailing their operations or even ending them elsewhere.

In terms of their labour structure, NGOs often lack sufficient local labour to run their programs. In many cases this is compensated for by donors bringing in their own experts. However, the lack of local expertise poses particular problems. Many of the foreign experts are not only unfamiliar with local customs but also unaware of the problems this creates. Thus, for example, if using foreign experts proves to be sustainable, it provides even less incentive to train local workers. Even when local expertise is available, the numbers are usually so small that NGOs tend to simply redeploy it, rather than contributing to its expansion. NGOs are often able to pay better wages, so many draw experienced workers away from the public service, leaving it depleted. Thus, in effect, the NGO is substituting for, rather than complementing, services already provided.

In terms of accountability, NGOs, in a large part because of their structure, are more accountable to donors than to the communities they are meant to serve and to support. This often means that they are expected to demonstrate effectiveness in concrete, measurable outcomes. One of the consequences of this expectation is that NGOs are often driven to adopt practices that essentially contradict their very mission. An example is found among large multinational NGOs engaged in housing. True to the mandate of working with beneficiaries, families receiving assistance must contribute in kind to their future dwelling. However, as building a house takes a certain amount of skill, family participation is limited to moulding bricks. In the interest of efficiency, the construction is left to professionals. The final result is that the NGOs end up doing the work for people, rather than building their capacity to do it themselves or teaching them the skills to enable them to be self-sufficient.

Some of the constraints facing NGOs might simply be a result of NGOs' being in their early stages of development. There are indications, for example, that funding agencies are attempting to improve the social-policy performance of NGOs. The World Bank, recognizing the magnitude of the negative effects of structural adjustment in the social sectors and the much slower-than-expected pace at which economic recovery is occurring, is putting a premium on grass-roots participation, insisting that all its projects incorporate participatory techniques. What is more important to recognize, however, is that no matter what their weaknesses have been, NGOs provide essential basic-needs services that in their absence would be unavailable, especially for the most vulnerable members of society.

## Conclusions

The changes taking place in social policy in Africa show not only the complexity of the field but also the magnitude of the work still to be done. A multitude of problems besets social policy in Africa. Basic social services remain fragmented and at times confused in their objectives. Many primary needs in health care, education, social security, housing, employment, and water and sanitation continue to go unmet. What services are provided have neither the scope nor the depth to cover the array of demands of most of the population. Yet, despite these weaknesses and the fact that governments continue to shift responsibilities to individuals, families, and communities, most people still look to the state to meet their welfare needs.

The internal capacity of governments to meet social-welfare expectations can be disputed, if only because of the size and depth of the needs. But the methods governments have used to accomplish this task have always been informed by ideology, as underlined by the current political-economic framework and by transnational development agendas. Social provision in Africa from the colonial period to the present has been predicated on, and dictated by, the predominant ideology, which has also determined the role of the major actors in the process.

Generally, the core institution in social provision in Africa has been and continues to be the family, through its informal systems and networks. But changes in the social systems, the demands of modernization, and rising social expectations call for an increasing role for a formal system of social provision to supplement the contribution of individuals and families. This has been the case since the 1960s, when most African states achieved independence.

Within a decade or two of independence, efforts to compensate for past neglect catapulted upward most people's standards of living in all spheres of life. However, the socialist ideology accompanying this process failed to establish an efficient and productive economy able to deliver consumer goods and social services at a higher level of economic development. This, in turn, led to the failure of early development efforts. Attempts at reforming the economy were unsuccessful. The former socialist regimes are now trying to make the transition to the market economy, hoping that this change will serve their people better. In this respect, the wheel has come full circle. As the economy becomes an autonomous sector, so social policies emerge as a distinct sphere of action for correcting the negative effects of the market economy. Like the economy, social policies are entering the purview of a distinct set of institutions, with their own principles and practices (Mishra 1995).

When neoliberal economic strategies were introduced in the West, unlike in Africa, there were well-established social infrastructures in place to cushion the effects of the new economic practices on the poor. Severe as the expenditure cuts and cost-recovery measures are, children still go to school and few, if any, die of hunger. As big as the numbers of those affected, for example, the numbers of the homeless, they are still manageable, both in absolute and in political terms. This is not the case in Africa. Even worse, every social indicator shows that the situation is bound to deteriorate further.

But this is not the only unique feature of African social policy. Traditionally, social policy has been a concern strictly of the state or a matter for the nongovernmental activities that a country's citizens design for their individual and collective protection. Today, however, in most African countries, IFIs, multinational agencies such as the various organs of the United Nations, and donors and foreign-aid NGOs are as influential in determining social policy as local politicians and communities. In fact, they are demanding, and more often than not they are receiving, desks in the ministries responsible for their areas of operation; representatives of these organizations have, in effect, taken over social-policy formulation, in many cases reducing local politicians' participation to that of attending parliamentary debates.

One of the major problems with this situation is that all these organizations are pulling in different directions, as dictated by their respective ideologies (Deacon 1995). The IMF, for example, with its strong emphasis on private welfare, is promoting the targeting of the neediest. If one abided by conspiracy theories or attributed to the IMF more cunning than it deserves, one could argue that the IMF's policies are actually meant to change African society from its foundations. Most of its policies seem geared to replacing cooperation of the kinship system with competitive individualism and encouraging large differences in social status, as a reflection of the fact that dominating behaviour increases with the competition for resources.

Other organizations, like the International Labour Organization (ILO) and many NGOs, promulgate more democratic social policies. The ILO, for instance, is increasingly instrumental in introducing Africa to social-insurance schemes that emphasize a considerable degree of vertical distribution delivered through a tax-benefit system. However, as these schemes are based on the ability to make financial contributions, and thus on employment, it is doubtful that those who need their protection the most, the poor, will ultimately benefit. Zimbabwe, for example, introduced a pension plan in 1994 that is to be implemented in three stages. It is a contributory program to which employees pay 3% of their salaries up to a ceiling that their employers match. Phase 1 covers all private-sector employees. However, this is a minuscule part of the labour force. Although extending coverage to civil servants in phase 2 will be easy, this will not be so for phase 3, planned to cover communal farmers and informal-sector workers, as their incomes are low and irregular.

Ironically, the common thread in all these efforts is the call for families and communities to be more extensively involved in meeting their own social and economic needs, both in symbolic and in practical terms. This also coincides with political reforms resulting from structural adjustments that demand more efforts at democratization and its associated stress on empowerment and decentralization. However, unless communities are given practical skills and greater discretion and control over resources, it is difficult to imagine how, or indeed why, they should increase their participation and take on the difficult task of establishing structures and mechanisms to carry out grassroots social-policy projects.

With sufficient efforts from outsiders, assembling groups of people and working with them to formulate ideas for community development activities is often possible. But to date, experience has shown that this process fails on at least two counts. First, and most often, the majority of the ideas generated at the grassroots level relate to extension of the provision of outside services, such as education, health, and government-sponsored employment-substitution programs. Far rarer are realistic income-generating schemes with outputs that go beyond ensuring mere physical survival for participants. Second, all these initiatives lapse quickly unless community members have a strong incentive to continue their participation when the outsiders are gone. In principle, it can be argued that this incentive could be enhanced if communities are given effective authority to carry out their ideas, such as by decentralizing budget allocations. Yet, this approach is treated with caution, as it is argued that (1) it will still take time to strengthen the administrative capacity and accountability of community organizations; and (2) most of the noncommunity inputs required for development can be obtained more easily and at a lower cost through government-procurement channels (Schemetzer et al. 1992). Consequently, as providing for people is easier and politically more effective than developing their capacities, development remains the domain of technocrats, be they in government or in NGOs.

If African experience with reforming social policies shows one thing, it is that although policy matters, in practice it is not the only thing that matters. Poverty cannot be eradicated by policies merely with that intention. Policy options are constrained by the economic conditions and social and cultural structures that shape development opportunities. When an economy collapses (which weakens government), the vacuum is immediately filled — in this case, mainly with foreign organizations that, though their intentions are good, bear the risk of recolonizing Africa.

# CHAPTER 5

# SOUTHEAST ASIA

## THE DECENTRALIZATION OF SOCIAL POLICY

*Trinidad S. Osteria*

At the end of World War II, Southeast Asia was a region with pressing development problems as a result, in part, of high levels of poverty and rapid population growth. However, half a century later, the economy has grown at an unexpected and unprecedented rate. Rapid economic growth has paved the way to improved standards of living and reduced poverty.

Although history, geography, population, natural resources, and global economic, political, and social agendas for reform have influenced the growth of most countries in the region, a determining factor has been the shift in national economic policies. Increased industrialization has become the foundation of development in the last two decades of the 20th century.

The countries of Southeast Asia (Brunei, Cambodia, Indonesia, Laos, Malaysia, Myanmar, Philippines, Singapore, Thailand, and Viet Nam) are all at various stages in the transition from agriculture and labour-intensive manufacturing to higher technology and skill-intensive production in conjunction, with further development of the service sector. They have generally adopted open trading systems, maintained low rates of inflation, and followed prudent fiscal and monetary policies. Large inflows of foreign direct investment helped these countries to increase industrial capacity and adopt new technologies (Dowling and Castillo 1996). The critical economic policies that led to the formulation of poverty-alleviation and social-development measures were fiscal and monetary probity, open trade, human-resource development, and infrastructure investments that reflected economic and social priorities (Hughes 1994).

This chapter examines the most recent economic developments in Southeast Asia, the effectiveness of macroeconomic management, and the current social-policy response to the globalization and regionalization of the economy, with particular emphasis on decentralization policies. Against a background of continued strong growth in regional trade, the key role of social policy is assessed in recognition of the critical social problems associated with economic growth. The constituent countries' experience of economic growth is analyzed in terms of social impacts and current policy-reform initiatives. Finally, by looking at the lessons learned, this chapter reviews decentralization as a modality for social development.

## Economic growth, social policies, and transnational influences

In many countries in Southeast Asia, standards of living doubled between the 1960s and the 1990s. Population growth was significantly curtailed. However, continued economic growth placed pressure on labour markets, extended productive capacity, and threatened the conditions needed for price stability. Hence, controlling inflation without slowing down growth has been among the prime concerns of public policy in many of these economies. With a rapidly globalizing international environment, Southeast Asia has faced intense competition in external markets, underscoring the need for skills and technology to support continued industrialization. The transitional economies of Cambodia, Laos, and Myanmar and, to a lesser extent, Viet Nam, faced the challenge of continuous structural adjustment from a centrally planned to a market-driven economy, requiring the capacity to implement foreign-assisted projects and new production and distribution systems (Dowling and Castillo 1996). Both local industry and multinational enterprises were crucial to promoting the growth of new industries. Multinational enterprises have been particularly important in sectors such as electronics and chemicals from which new products and technologies have emerged. The rapid growth of both foreign and domestic investment in export-oriented, labour-intensive manufacturing has been a major feature of growth in Southeast Asia (Booth 1995). Multinational corporations (MNCs) relocate production to developing countries to take advantage of the rapidly growing domestic markets and cheaper labour there, to cut production costs, and to expand market shares worldwide.

As in other regions, governments in Southeast Asia have been key actors in growth and development. Empirical evidence shows that the poorest countries within the region are those that have suffered from internal strife. Democratization of governance has progressively claimed more support, and possibilities for growth have been widely acknowledged. The principal policies used to ensure equitable outcomes for growth and its sustainability have been aimed to create employment and education.

However, many imperfections evolve with this type of economic growth, for policies required for rapid growth are generally resisted by privileged groups in society. High-income earners, for example, may successfully avoid taxation, throwing the burden of development on the poor and reducing the amount of public saving available to invest in infrastructure (Hughes 1994). Taxation has been viewed as a means to fund the operation of political-, economic-, and social-sector services. Countries in the region increasingly use indirect value-added taxes that impact on consumption rather than savings. The growth of employment was marked by the creation of opportunities for female workers in both the formal and the informal sectors of the economy. They played an important role in labour-intensive industries that are mainly export oriented. Together with access to education, employment opportunities transformed the role of women in the family and society in the region (Hughes 1994).

Expansion and improvement of educational coverage, quality, and access are among the main social challenges for the region. As the economy grows and financial resources become more readily available, the demand for education and training increases. Health is promoted by economic growth as a means to improve the well-being and productivity of the population, and social welfare provides a safety net for the disadvantaged, marginal, and disabled. However, the *Human Development Report 1996* (UNDP 1996) indicated that reinforcing the relationship between equity and growth has more far-reaching policy implications than simply changing sectoral policies. It affects policy-making through, for example, job opportunities; access to land, physical infra-structure, and credit; social expenditure; gender equality; good governance; and the creation of an active civil society to play a vital advocacy role, mobilize public opinion, and shape human-development priorities. In 1995, the region adopted the threefold goals of poverty alleviation, employment expansion, and social integration as its social-development theme. Where a standard of growth has been achieved, the further task is to ensure equitable distribution of these gains and to strengthen social cohesion. To this end, the region's governments were encouraged to decentralize and devolve authority in the delivery of social services. These governments continue to pursue cooperation with nongovern-mental organizations (NGOs), the private sector, and the people. Structural-adjustment programs will have to be designed in a realistic manner to reflect the inevitable lag in the effectiveness of supply-side responses (UNESCAP 1995).

## The social-development landscape

In 1997, the total population of Southeast Asia reached about 497.3 million. The population and development indicators in Table 1 show a region where fertility trends declined and the annual rate of population growth averaged 1.6% (UNESCAP 1991a). This profile reflects a number of factors. Over a short

**Table 1.** Population and development indicators, Southeast Asia, 1997.

| | Population | | Crude birth rate (per 1 000) | Crude death rate (per 1 000) | Fertility rate | | Contraceptive prevalence rate[b] (%) | Source |
|---|---|---|---|---|---|---|---|---|
| | Mid-1997 (thousands) | Annual growth rate[a] (%) | | | Total (per woman) | Ages 15–19 (per 1 000) | | |
| Southeast Asia | 497 261 | 1.6 | 24.2 | 7.5 | 2.9 | — | 43 | |
| Brunei | 309 | 2.7 | 23.3 | 3.0 | 2.9 | 21 | — | Brunei Darussalam (n.d.); UNDESIPA (1996) |
| Cambodia | 10 481 | 2.0[c] | 31.8[c] | 11.6[c] | 5.2[c] | 23[c] | 13[c] | Long et al. (1995); NIS (1996); UNDESIPA (1996) |
| Indonesia | 201 435 | 1.4 | 22.4 | 7.9 | 2.6 | 45 | 47 | Ananta and Nurvidya Arifin (1991) |
| Laos | 5 192 | 3.1 | 44.3 | 13.7 | 6.7 | 51 | — | UNDESIPA (1996) |
| Malaysia | 20 977 | 2.1 | 25.6 | 4.8 | 3.3 | 29 | 31 | UNDESIPA (1996) |
| Myanmar | 46 755 | 1.8 | 27.4 | 9.9 | 3.3 | 36 | — | UNDESIPA (1996) |
| Philippines | 70 631 | 2.0 | 28.7 | 5.8 | 3.7 | 41 | 25 | UNDESIPA (1996) |
| Singapore | 3 429 | 1.5 | 16.0 | 5.0 | 1.8 | 8 | — | SDS (1996); UNDESIPA (1996) |
| Thailand | 60 602 | 1.0 | 17.8 | 7.4 | 2.0 | 60 | 64 | NESDB (1995) |
| Viet Nam | 77 450 | 1.9 | 25.6 | 7.0 | 3.2 | 35 | 35 | Duy (1994) |

(continues)

Table 1 (continued)

| | Life expectancy at birth (years) | | Mortality (per 1 000 live births) | | Sex ratio (males per 100 females) | Age class (%) | | | Source |
|---|---|---|---|---|---|---|---|---|---|
| | Male | Female | Infant | Maternal[d] | | 0–14 | 60+ | 65+ | |
| Southeast Asia | 64 | 67 | 44 | 423 | 99 | 33 | 7 | 5 | |
| Brunei | 73 | 78 | 9 | 60 | 113 | 33 | 5 | 3 | UNDESIPA (1996); United Nations (1996b) |
| Cambodia | 52 | 55 | 103 | 900 | 94 | 42 | 5 | 3 | Ananta and Nurvidya Arifin (1991); SDS (1996); UNDESIPA (1996) |
| Indonesia | 63 | 66 | 51 | 650 | 100 | 32 | 7 | 5 | United Nations (1996b) |
| Laos | 52 | 55 | 87 | 650 | 98 | 45 | 5 | 3 | UNDESIPA (1996) |
| Malaysia | 70 | 74 | 11 | 80 | 102 | 37 | 6 | 4 | UNDESIPA (1996) |
| Myanmar | 58 | 62 | 79 | 580 | 99 | 35 | 7 | 4 | UNDESIPA (1996) |
| Philippines | 66 | 70 | 36 | 280 | 101 | 38 | 5 | 3 | UNDESIPA (1996) |
| Singapore | 75 | 79 | 5 | 10 | 102 | 22 | 10 | 7 | IPSR (1996); UNDESIPA (1996) |
| Thailand | 67 | 72 | 31 | 200 | 100 | 27 | 8 | 5 | Duy (1994); United Nations (1996b) |
| Viet Nam | 66 | 69 | 38 | 160 | 97 | 36 | 7 | 5 | Duy (1994) |

(continues)

Table 1 (concluded)

| | Gross enrolment ratio[e] | | | | 1997 (%) | Urban population | | Population projected to 2020 (millions) | Source |
|---|---|---|---|---|---|---|---|---|---|
| | Primary school | | Secondary school | | | Annual growth rate (%) | Human Development Index[f] | | |
| | Male | Female | Male | Female | | | | | |
| Southeast Asia | — | — | — | — | 37 | 3.7 | — | 652.2 | |
| Brunei | 111 | 104 | 67 | 74 | 58 | 2.2 | 0.872 | 0.4 | UNDESIPA (1996); United Nations (1996b) |
| Cambodia | — | — | — | — | 22 | 5.7 | 0.325 | 15.9 | Ananta and Nurvidya Arifin (1991); SDS (1996); UNDESIPA (1996) |
| Indonesia | 116 | 112 | 48 | 39 | 37 | 4.1 | 0.641 | 253.7 | United Nations (1996b) |
| Laos | 123 | 92 | 31 | 19 | 23 | 5.7 | 0.400 | 9.3 | UNDESIPA (1996) |
| Malaysia | 93 | 93 | 56 | 61 | 55 | 3.4 | 0.826 | 29.8 | UNDESIPA (1996) |
| Myanmar | 107 | 104 | 23 | 23 | 27 | 3.6 | 0.451 | 64.3 | UNDESIPA (1996) |
| Philippines | 111 | — | 81 | — | 56 | 3.7 | 0.665 | 99.9 | UNDESIPA (1996) |
| Singapore | — | — | 85 | — | 100 | 1.5 | 0.881 | 4.1 | IPSR (1996); UNDESIPA (1996) |
| Thailand | 98 | 97 | 38 | 37 | 32[g] | 2.8 | 0.832 | 70.5 | Duy (1994); United Nations (1996b) |
| Viet Nam | 111 | — | 35 | — | 21 | 3.4 | 0.523 | 104.2 | Duy (1994) |

Source: UNESCAP (1997, chart). Contraceptive prevalence rate: United Nations (1996a, table A.6); gross enrolment ratio: UNESCO (1995, table 3.2); Human Development Index: UNDP (1996); infant mortality: WHO and UNICEF (1996); urban population (except recent data): United Nations (1994).

[a] Exponential growth rate. The rate takes into account international migration and thus may not equal the rate of natural increase.
[b] Prevalence rate for modern methods among married women of reproductive age; most recent data available.
[c] 1995.
[d] 1990.
[e] 1993. Gross enrolment ratio = number of students enrolled at specified level per 100 persons in applicable age group (e.g., ages 6–12 for primary school).
[f] A higher value indicates a higher level of human development.
[g] 1996.

period, steady advances were made in public health, including increased access to health care for pregnant women, improved nutrition levels, reduced infant mortality, and increased child survival. Progress in infrastructure and social services in most countries led to the large-scale provision of potable water and basic education (improving literacy rates) and the dissemination of reliable and affordable methods of contraception (WHO 1989). At present, the region's urban residents account for some 37% of the total population. However, it is projected that by 2000, almost half of the population in the region will be living in urban areas. This process of development represents a historic transformation from the traditional economic base, which was predominantly rural and agricultural.

The implications of these demographic changes for fundamental social-policy issues are wide and far reaching. The urbanization process, for example, has proceeded at a particularly rapid pace, adding a number of new cities with populations of 1 million or more by 1995. Large agglomerations face the broad range of new social problems that often accompany urban sprawl. The close association between urban centres and industry, as well as the spread of industrial-support services, has resulted in a steady inflow of workers into metropolitan areas, primarily at the low end of the wage scale (UNESCAP 1992a). In fact, most rural-to-urban migrants become part of the informal sector of the economy, resulting in the transfer of rural poverty to urban settings. The poverty of migrants in the midst of urban affluence, the loosening of family ties, the promotion of materialist values by the media, the alienation that comes with increasing urbanization, and the inability of industry to meet the job expectations of a growing population lead to a sense of anomie, futility, and dissatisfaction, often manifested in crime (UNESCAP 1991b).

## The social implications of economic growth

The first half of the 1990s witnessed a surge in economic growth per annum in many countries of Southeast Asia, ranging from 1.7% in the Philippines to 10% in Singapore in 1990. Economic growth in the region was spearheaded by Malaysia, Singapore, Thailand, and Viet Nam. Inflation decelerated slightly, as most countries were able to contain the upward pressure on prices in the face of tight labour markets and capacity constraints. Laos, Myanmar, and Viet Nam, however, remained burdened with double-digit inflation. Exports grew rapidly but the current account deficit of the region increased to 20.5 billion United States dollars (USD) in 1995 — an increase from 8.1 billion USD in 1994. On the strength of their economic performance, some countries in the region have made optimistic growth projections for the 21st century. The Malaysian government's Vision 2020, for example, envisages its economy catching up with Western levels by the first quarter of the 21st century. The targets set by the Indonesian government for economic and social development from 1994 to 2019 forecast that economic growth per annum will accelerate from 6.2% in the Sixth Five-Year Development Plan period (1994–99) to 8.7% in 2014–19 (Booth 1995).

This economic surge is reflected in the remarkable pace of growth of the gross domestic product (GDP) of most of these countries. Malaysia, Singapore, Thailand, and Viet Nam, for example, recorded economic growth rates of more than 9% between 1994 and 1995, and in 1995, Indonesia registered an annual growth rate of GDP of more than 7%. The economic recovery in the Philippines, which started in 1993, was sustained in the subsequent 2 years at 5% (see Table 2). This progress was also accompanied by improved saving and investment rates but also by increased infrastructure requirements and shortages in skilled human resources, all of which translated into higher costs driven by income growth (UNESCAP 1996).

In Cambodia, the reform process broadened and accelerated in 1989 with the restoration of private-property ownership and liberalization of foreign trade. After 20 years of war and dislocation, the country's human resources were depleted, requiring substantive improvements in education and health services. The country had major macroeconomic imbalances, including high fiscal deficits and inflation. The privatization of state enterprises has been undertaken, and foreign and local private investment has been encouraged. The transition has progressed quite rapidly, although the country still suffers from the legacy of war and internal strife. Table 3 presents a comparative overview of the region.

Indonesia has shown strong overall growth as a result of rapid growth in both the industrial and the service sectors. Agricultural output improved, and rice production benefited from changes in the price-incentive structure. Performance in the industrial sector also improved. Strong private investment — 36% of GDP in 1995 — supported by substantial inflows of foreign direct capital accounted for the increase in gross domestic investment. Development expenditures increased slightly in real terms, with the major part of outlays directed to roads, education, and subsidies for regional development (Dowling and Castillo 1996).

In Thailand, rapid growth has brought about large changes in the structure and dynamics of the economy. The World Bank has argued that Thailand has grown by following structural-adjustment policies, by attracting direct foreign investment, and by creating a favourable environment for exports without intervening directly in the capital market (Phongpaichit 1996). Throughout the 1980s, the urban population grew by about 4 million people, with the pool of rural labour acting as a source of urban labour supply. However, two problems were encountered: growing upward pressure on wage rates and the mismatch of skills and education to market requirements.

**Table 2.** Economic indicators, Southeast Asia, 1994 and 1995.

| | Growth rate, real GDP (% per annum) | | Changes in consumer prices (% per annum) | | Balance of payments on current account (millions USD) | |
|---|---|---|---|---|---|---|
| | 1994 | 1995 | 1994 | 1995 | 1994 | 1995 |
| Southeast Asia | 8.0 | 8.1 | 6.8 | 6.7 | −8 132 | −20 492 |
| Cambodia | 4.0 | 7.0 | 26.1 | 9.8 | −107 | −164 |
| Indonesia | 7.5 | 7.6 | 9.6 | 9.0 | −2 800 | −8 000 |
| Laos | 8.0 | 7.1 | 6.7 | 18.4 | −202 | −247 |
| Malaysia | 9.2 | 9.5 | 3.7 | 3.5 | −4 147 | −7 600 |
| Myanmar | 6.8 | 7.7 | 24.1 | 22.7 | −275 | −294 |
| Philippines | 4.3 | 5.2 | 9.0 | 8.1 | −2 800 | −3 000 |
| Singapore | 10.2 | 9.1 | 3.8 | 3.2 | 11 951 | 13 000 |
| Thailand | 8.7 | 8.6 | 4.6 | 5.8 | −8 419 | −12 458 |
| Viet Nam | 8.8 | 9.5 | 14.4 | 12.7 | −966 | −1 729 |

Source: ADB (1996, pp. 23–24).
Note: GDP, gross domestic product; USD, United States dollars.

**Table 3.** Selected socioeconomic indicators, Southeast Asia, 1994.

| | GNP | | Growth rate, real GDP (%) | Growth rate (%) | | |
|---|---|---|---|---|---|---|
| | Total (millions USD) | Per capita (USD) | | Agriculture | Industry | Service |
| Cambodia | 2 360 | 240 | 4.0 | 0.0 | 7.5 | 7.5 |
| Indonesia | 167 630 | 880 | 7.5 | 0.5 | 11.2 | 6.9 |
| Laos | 1 500 | 320 | 8.0 | 8.3 | 10.7 | 5.6 |
| Malaysia | 68 670 | 3 520 | 9.2 | −1.0 | 12.4 | 9.9 |
| Myanmar | — | — | 6.8 | 6.1 | 8.9 | 6.8 |
| Philippines | 63 310 | 960 | 4.3 | 2.6 | 5.8 | 4.3 |
| Singapore | 65 840 | 23 360 | 10.2 | 5.6 | 13.4 | 8.4 |
| Thailand | 129 860 | 2 210 | 8.7 | 5.5 | 9.9 | 8.5 |
| Viet Nam | 13 780 | 190 | 8.8 | 3.9 | 14.0 | 10.0 |

Source: ADB (1996, pp. 18–19).
Note: GDP. gross domestic product; GNP, gross national product; USD, United States dollars.

Under these circumstances, the Thai government's response was twofold. First, it imposed a minimum wage adjusted upward annually on the basis of inflation and passed a new *Social Security Act* in 1989, creating a basic system of labour welfare by increasing the minimum wage. These initiatives generated an increase in informal employment. Recruitment on a subcontract basis meant paying less than the minimum wage; children and illegal-migrant labourers were drawn from neighbouring countries, China, Laos, and Myanmar. Second, the Thai government undertook a number of measures to combat shortfalls in skills and education. It increased the number of extension courses for skills training, implemented a crash program to extend secondary schooling, put in place a cheap-loan scheme to encourage private investors to build more schools, and provided student loans. To improve higher education, the government channeled more money into the education budget. The privatization of university education led to the establishment in 1994 of 26 private universities and technical colleges with more than 125 000 students (Dowling and Castillo 1996). In addition, in the late 1980s, the Thai government privatized road construction, land transportation, and communications, with mixed results.

Viet Nam's economic reform and performance have received high commendations from the major multilateral lending institutions. Viet Nam's GDP growth rate in 1995 was 9.5%, with industry and construction constituting 30.3% of the total. Trade flows also increased markedly in 1995, with exports rising by about 30%. As more export-oriented and import-substituting foreign-investment projects enter production, this will have a positive impact on Vietnamese trade (Freeman 1996).

The recovery of the Philippine economy, which started in 1993, was further strengthened in 1995. Political stability, macroeconomic management, and structural reforms encouraged private-sector confidence and eased infrastructure constraints. The main source of growth was the industrial sector, which expanded by more than 8% (Dowling and Castillo 1996). However, the more quickly expanding sectors — real estate, transport, and communications — have limited potential to create massive and sustained employment. In this context, an important challenge has been to ensure that subsequent growth generates enough employment to alleviate poverty on a broader scale. At present, the only governmental redistributive program is agrarian reform, and this program also has adverse effects on agricultural investments and productivity (De Dios 1995).

The economic pattern of the region (see Table 4) has high associated social costs. The increasing pressure of population and industrialization led to extensive deterioration of the environment. The lack of effective industrial-regulatory measures contributed to occupational risks, disabilities, and deaths among workers and residents in the vicinity of the industrial estates most affected by industrialization.

Other associated costs have included the effects on the traditional family. Although the traditional family remains the norm in Southeast Asia, it has come under increasing pressure from changing social and economic realities. As a result, policymakers face the new and difficult challenges of maintaining social stability and enhancing social programs in the context of economic expansion. Among the important concerns policymakers face are the erosion of family ties resulting from geographic mobility, a growing preference for having a smaller family, more individualistic tendencies among youth, the growing needs of an aging population, and new roles for female caregivers as they enter

**Table 4.** Gross domestic saving, capital formation, and resource gap, Southeast Asia, 1995.

| | % of GDP | | |
| --- | --- | --- | --- |
| | Gross domestic saving | Capital formation | Resource gap |
| Cambodia | 8.3 | 21.5 | 13.2 |
| Indonesia | 35.8 | 37.8 | 2.0 |
| Malaysia | 37.2 | 40.6 | 3.4 |
| Myanmar | 12.2 | 13.0 | 0.8 |
| Philippines | 14.7 | 22.3 | 7.7 |
| Singapore | 52.0 | 33.2 | −18.8 |
| Thailand | 36.5 | 43.1 | 6.6 |
| Viet Nam | 19.0 | 27.1 | 8.2 |

Source: ADB (1996, pp. 18–19).
Note: GDP, gross domestic product.

**Table 5.** Selected trade and assistance indicators, Southeast Asia, 1994 and 1995.

| | Official development assistance, 1994 (Millions USD) | Merchandise exports, 1994 (Millions USD) | Total trade, 1995 (% of GNP) | Foreign direct nvestment, 1995 (Millions USD) |
| --- | --- | --- | --- | --- |
| Cambodia | 336.8 | 490 | −5.4 | 69.0 |
| Indonesia | 1 642.1 | 40 054 | −1.7 | 2 109.0 |
| Laos | 217.7 | 300 | −5.8 | 60.1 |
| Malaysia | 68.2 | 58 756 | −8.8 | 4 348.0 |
| Myanmar | 161.6 | 771 | −0.9 | — |
| Philippines | 1 057.5 | 13 304 | −2.5 | 1 861.0 |
| Singapore | 16.9 | 96 826 | 13.3 | 3 411.0 |
| Thailand | 578.2 | 45 261 | −8.0 | 147.0 |
| Viet Nam | 897.1 | 3 600 | — | 1 048 |

Source: ADB (1996, p. 47).
Note: GNP, gross national product; USD, United States dollars.

the labour force. At the same time, Southeast Asia has made impressive advances in life expectancy and other health indicators, owing to governments' emphasis on primary health care and to international development assistance (see Table 5).

For example, most countries in the region have considered universal primary education and literacy important social-development goals. Many governments are also increasing their commitments to secondary, vocational, and nonformal education to achieve the goals of Education for All. By 2000 the Education for All approach aims to reduce levels of illiteracy in the region to 50% of those prevailing in 1990, with emphasis on female literacy. The target is to ensure that at least 80% of primary-school-age children complete primary education. To respond to economic restructuring and technological changes, governments in the region are also significantly expanding education that targets youth and adults. Such prioritization reflects these governments' recognition that a diversified and trained labour force is required to operate in a competitive, technologically sophisticated, and global economic environment (UNESCAP 1992a).

The Southeast Asian experience of rapid economic development raises important questions relevant to understanding social policy from a transnational perspective: Has there been congruence between economic-resource allocation and social expenditure? How can the social and economic sectors be effectively integrated into the overall development planning of these countries? Could a new development paradigm be formulated that more directly identifies the socioeconomic transformation processes, issues, problems, and concerns of the region?

## Trends and patterns of social expenditure

Until the late 1990s, Southeast Asia could be described as the most successful developing region in terms of growth and employment. However, the economic scenario points to a wide spectrum of development situations. At one end, the chief Asian "tiger", Singapore, is transforming itself with remarkable growth into an industrial economy. At the other end, the transitional economies, Cambodia, Laos, and Myanmar, still face acute problems of poverty, despite recent GDP increases. Indonesia, Malaysia, and Thailand form a second tier of newly industrialized economies. These governments recognize that economic growth is by itself insufficient to realize the required qualitative social changes. Deliberate policy interventions are required to ensure that economic development proceeds fairly and equitably and helps to raise people's quality of life. Sectoral economic policies enable countries to derive the maximum gains from trade, adopt new technologies, alleviate poverty, and promote social integration. However, as shown in Table 6, the burden of external debt and debt servicing is severe on these countries, making them draw resources from much needed social programs.

The Asian Pacific Ministerial Conference in 1995 enunciated that (UNESCAP 1995, pp. 31–32)

> Macro economic stability should not be pursued at the cost of the needs and interests of the poor and vulnerable sections of the population as this may well compromise social stability. Structural adjustment programs must correspond to the economic and social conditions of individual countries and should be designed realistically to reflect the inevitable time lags in the effectiveness of supply side responses. Decisions concerning adjustment should include a full examination of alternative ways of securing macroeconomic stability, structural change and improved efficiency from the perspective of social equity.

**Table 6.** Debt indicators, Southeast Asia, 1994.

| | Total external debt–GNP ratio (%) | Total external debt–exports ratio (%) | Total debt service–exports ratio (%) | Concessional long-term debts (%) | Total external debt (millions USD) | Debt service payment (millions USD) |
|---|---|---|---|---|---|---|
| Cambodia | 83.5 | 375.9 | 0.4 | 100.0 | 1 943.4 | 2.0 |
| Indonesia | 57.4 | 195.8 | 30.0 | 36.4 | 96 499.6 | 14 791.9 |
| Laos | 135.6 | 803.1 | 7.7 | 99.8 | 2 080.1 | 20.0 |
| Malaysia | 36.9 | 37.7 | 7.7 | 92.8 | 24 766.6 | 5 042.3 |
| Myanmar | — | 578.0 | 15.4 | 92.8 | 6 502.0 | 173.0 |
| Philippines | 59.3 | 160.6 | 18.5 | 34.6 | 39 301.6 | 4 534.1 |
| Singapore | 11.9 | 6.0 | — | — | 7 688.0 | — |
| Thailand | 43.1 | 103.1 | 15.6 | 21.6 | 60 990.4 | 9 237.2 |
| Viet Nam | 161.3 | 510.7 | 6.1 | 92.3 | 25 115.4 | 300.1 |

Source: ADB (1996, p. 47).
Note: GNP, gross national product; USD, United States dollars.

**Table 7.** Key social indicators, Southeast Asia, 1994 and 1995.

| | Adult literacy rate, 1995 (%)[a] | | Gross enrolment ratio, 1994 (%)[b] | | | |
|---|---|---|---|---|---|---|
| | | | Primary school | | Secondary school | |
| | Female | Male | Female | Male | Female | Male |
| Cambodia | 22 | 48 | 46 | 48 | — | — |
| Indonesia | 78 | 90 | 112 | 116 | 39 | 48 |
| Laos | 44 | 69 | 92 | 123 | 19 | 31 |
| Malaysia | 78 | 89 | 93 | 93 | 61 | 56 |
| Myanmar | 78 | 89 | 104 | 107 | 23 | 23 |
| Philippines | 94 | 95 | 111 | 113 | 75 | 71 |
| Singapore | 86 | 96 | 107 | 109 | 71 | 69 |
| Thailand | 92 | 96 | 97 | 98 | 37 | 38 |
| Viet Nam | 91 | 97 | 99 | 105 | 40 | 43 |

Source: ADB (1996, pp. 43–44).
[a] Refers to population aged 15+.
[b] Gross enrolment ratio = number of students enrolled at specified level per 100 persons in applicable age group (e.g., ages 6–12 for primary school).

In the broad context, however, social indicators reveal that although literacy rates have remained high in the region, they have not done so in Cambodia or Laos, where gender disparities also still exist, as females lag behind in literacy and educational attainment (Table 7). In the health sector, the physician-population ratios remain basically low across the board, and variations in childhood malnutrition and in access to sanitation facilities can be also observed (Table 8).

Given this general profile, adequate social-policy formulation will require considerable investment in education and health. Current ratios of government

**Table 8.** Health indicators, Southeast Asia, 1985–93.

| | Persons per physician | Daily per capita protein supply, 1992 (grams) | Daily per capita calorie supply, 1992 | Child malnutrition, 1994 (% under age 5) | Population with access to safe water, 1988–93 (%) | | Population with access to sanitation, 1988–93 (%) | |
|---|---|---|---|---|---|---|---|---|
| | | | | | Urban | Rural | Urban | Rural |
| Cambodia | 9 727[a] | 50 | 2 021 | 20.0[b] | 65 | 33 | 81 | 8 |
| Indonesia | 7 028[a] | 61 | 2 752 | 38.7 | 68 | 43 | 64 | 36 |
| Laos | 4 446[a] | 63 | 2 259 | 40.0 | 54 | 33 | 97 | 8 |
| Malaysia | 2 302[a] | 60 | 2 888 | 23.3 | 96 | 66 | ND | ND |
| Myanmar | 3 565[c] | 64 | 2 598 | 31.2 | 37 | ND | 39 | 35 |
| Philippines | 9 689[d] | 52 | 2 257 | 29.6 | 85 | 79 | 79 | 62 |
| Singapore | 722[d] | 82 | 3 000 | 14.4 | 100 | — | 99 | — |
| Thailand | 4 425[e] | 54 | 2 432 | 13.0 | 87 | 72 | 80 | 72 |
| Viet Nam | 2 491[d] | 52 | 2 250 | 44.9 | 39 | 21 | 34 | 14 |

Source: ADB (1996, pp. 45–46).
Note: ND, not determined.
[a] 1994.
[b] 1985.
[c] 1992.
[d] 1993.
[e] 1991.

expenditure in the *Human Development Report 1996* (UNDP 1996) included two elements. First, it included the public-expenditure ratio defined as the percentage of national income that goes into public expenditure. In 1994, this ranged from 9.3% in Myanmar to 26.2% in Viet Nam (Table 9). This ratio is contingent on the ability of the governments to collect taxes and other revenues. As a proportion of GDP, taxes ranged from 3.8% in Myanmar to 20.2% in Malaysia. Second, the report included the social-allocation ratio, which is the percentage of public expenditure earmarked for the social sectors. In the case of education, for example, this ranged from 9.4% in Indonesia to 19.6% in Thailand (in the countries of the region, people basically pay for their own tertiary education).

Across the region, governments realize that sustained and successful efforts in resource mobilization rely on the participation of civil society, such as private business, philanthropic people and institutions, and NGOs. Effective intervention for equity and poverty reduction requires some exclusively allocated funds, meaning that the nonpoor should benefit little from these funds. In most countries in the region, a higher premium is placed on price stability. Governments curb widening deficits through spending cuts in social services. Large debt-service bills for domestic borrowing may themselves preempt social services and fuel inflationary expectations. Poor tax administration, the small formal sector, and tax evasion weaken resource mobilization. Trade liberalization in the region will imply a reduction in taxes collected from import tariffs. At the World Summit for Social Development, a concrete new proposal for the mobilization of financial resources was the 20 : 20 compact, by which both the recipient and donor governments would commit at least 20% of their total respective national aid budgets to basic social services (UNESCAP 1996).

## Globalization and social-policy reform

The 1990s marked an accelerating trend toward closer integration of the world economy. Major advances in microelectronics, information exchange, communication technologies, and trade liberalization have been conducive to this integration process. In addition, international conventions, such as the General Agreement on Tariffs and Trade, served to strengthen these influences.

The countries of the Southeast Asia region have been markedly affected by the globalization process. Intraregional trade has been growing rapidly, and MNCs operate in most of these countries. Japanese firms, for example, have relocated their production in Southeast Asia, assisted by the appreciation of the yen and by rising wages at home. These trends have serious impacts on the region's employment and labour situation. At one level, competition is increased for exports and foreign investment. At another level, the emphasis is growing on investments in human resources as a means of maintaining

**Table 9.** Government finance indicators, Southeast Asia, 1994.

| | Taxes (% of GDP) | Total expenditures (% of GDP) | Fiscal deficit (% of GDP) | Health (% of GDP) | Education (% of GDP) | Education (% of total expenditures) | Housing and community amenities (% of GDP) |
|---|---|---|---|---|---|---|---|
| Cambodia | 6.0 | 16.5 | 6.7 | 0.4 | 1.0 | — | — |
| Indonesia | 14.6 | 16.0 | -0.2 | 0.7 | 0.8 | 9.4 | 1.6 |
| Laos | 9.4 | 24.4 | — | 1.3 | 10.3 | — | 0.3 |
| Malaysia | 20.2 | 25.0 | 0.3 | — | 5.2 | 16.9 | 0.2 |
| Myanmar | 3.8 | 9.3 | 2.9 | — | — | — | — |
| Philippines | 16.0 | 13.7 | -0.9 | 0.5 | 3.1 | 10.5 | 0.3 |
| Singapore | — | — | — | — | — | — | 1.3 |
| Thailand | 17.2 | 16.1 | -2.7 | 1.1 | 4.4 | 19.6 | — |
| Viet Nam | 19.7 | 26.2 | 1.5 | — | — | — | — |

Source: ADB (1996, pp. 33–34).
Note: GDP, gross domestic product.

**Table 10.** Southeast Asian countries
to which Japan is top donor, 1993.

| | Amount (Millions USD) |
|---|---|
| Singapore | 18.16 |
| Indonesia | 1 148.89 |
| Philippines | 758.39 |
| Thailand | 350.15 |
| Laos | 40.43 |
| Cambodia | 61.34 |
| Brunei | 4.52 |

Source; JMF (1994).
Note: On a net-disbursement basis. USD, United States dollars.

competitiveness in the global market. The underlying fear is that globalization will lead to job losses in some areas as capital moves freely between countries (UNESCAP 1995). As the leading exporter of capital and merchandise and the principal donor of overseas development assistance (ODA; Table 10), Japan, through trade, investment, and technology transfer, has played a crucial role in promoting international economic interdependence in the Association of Southeast Asian Nations (ASEAN), founded by Indonesia, Malaysia, the Philippines, Singapore, and Thailand and later joined by Brunei and Viet Nam. Japanese ODA provided to ASEAN amounted to 35% of the bilateral ODA to developing countries in 1992. In the Japan–ASEAN Tripartite Cooperation Project, for example, Japanese and ASEAN technical personnel work together

**Table 11.** Trend of Japan's direct investment in ASEAN, 1987–94.

|  | 1987 | 1988 | 1989 | 1990 | 1991 | 1992 | 1993 | 1994 |
|---|---|---|---|---|---|---|---|---|
| **ASEAN** | | | | | | | | |
| Projects (*n*) | 523 | 825 | 970 | 898 | 687 | 508 | 487 | 437 |
| Value (millions USD) | 1 524 | 2 713 | 4 684 | 4 082 | 3 696 | 3 867 | 3 042 | 4 957 |
| **Brunei** | | | | | | | | |
| Projects (*n*) | — | — | — | — | — | — | — | — |
| Value (millions USD) | — | — | — | — | — | — | — | 15 |
| **Indonesia** | | | | | | | | |
| Projects (*n*) | 67 | 84 | 140 | 155 | 148 | 122 | 115 | 116 |
| Value (millions USD) | 545 | 586 | 631 | 1 105 | 1 193 | 1 676 | 813 | 1 759 |
| **Malaysia** | | | | | | | | |
| Projects (*n*) | 64 | 108 | 159 | 169 | 136 | 111 | 92 | 51 |
| Value (millions USD) | 163 | 387 | 673 | 725 | 880 | 704 | 800 | 742 |
| **Philippines** | | | | | | | | |
| Projects (*n*) | 18 | 54 | 87 | 58 | 42 | 45 | 56 | 75 |
| Value (millions USD) | 72 | 134 | 202 | 258 | 203 | 160 | 207 | 668 |
| **Singapore** | | | | | | | | |
| Projects (*n*) | 182 | 197 | 181 | 139 | 103 | 100 | 97 | 69 |
| Value (millions USD) | 494 | 747 | 1 902 | 840 | 613 | 670 | 644 | 1 054 |
| **Thailand** | | | | | | | | |
| Projects (*n*) | 192 | 382 | 403 | 377 | 258 | 130 | 127 | 126 |
| Value (millions USD) | 250 | 859 | 1 276 | 1 154 | 807 | 657 | 578 | 719 |
| **World** | | | | | | | | |
| Projects (*n*) | 4 584 | 6 076 | 6 589 | 5 863 | 4 564 | 3 741 | 3 488 | 2 478 |
| Value (millions USD) | 33 364 | 47 022 | 67 540 | 56 911 | 41 584 | 34 138 | 36 025 | 41 051 |

Source: JMF (1994).
Note: ASEAN, Association of Southeast Asian Nations. USD, United States dollars.

to assist in the resettlement of Cambodian expatriates. Japan also gives priority to helping ASEAN countries deal with environmental degradation and related problems (Tan 1994). Indonesia remains a major recipient of Japanese development assistance. The total volume of Japanese trade almost tripled in the region between 1987 and 1994 (Table 11).

Southeast Asian countries have instituted numerous measures at the subregional level to address economic issues. In 1967, for example, ASEAN was established to promote regional economic cooperation and security (Baker 1995). The Asian Free Trade Area identifies products scheduled for tariff reductions — such as oils, chemicals, fertilizer, rubber products, and electronics — with side effects on the trade capabilities of various partner nations, Overall, however, the trade potential of these countries, despite geographic proximity, has remained relatively untapped because of political sensitivities calling for a reorientation of trade and investments in a more unified and larger regional market. Thus, the establishment of Asia–Pacific Economic Cooperation was part of the response to the expressed need for region-wide economic structures in the Asia–Pacific region. Building a sense of regional community was deemed to be highly relevant to coping with the realities of interdependence and to bringing collective leadership to these new global economies.

The trend toward nondiscriminating multilateral economic systems is catalyzed by two factors. First, governments are increasingly willing to accept massive structural changes to maintain the efficiency of their economies, as demonstrated by sweeping, unilateral reforms to open their markets to international investment and competition. Second, these economies tend to achieve integration across political boundaries, creating larger zones of integrated production for global markets (Drysdale and Elek 1995). Globalization brings a complex set of external influences that affect the whole range of public policy-making. However, the vastness and heterogeneity of the region have raised fears that the economically weaker nations would be dominated by more economically competitive ones (UNESCAP 1995).

## The social impact of globalization

The pattern of macroeconomic adjustment in the region raises a number of concerns. First, structural-adjustment measures, even when they are successful in increasing exports, saving, investment, and economic efficiency, risk neglecting the human factor and sidetracking the social goals that countries expect to achieve. Second, macroeconomic policies may deepen the disadvantage of the most vulnerable groups, which often suffer a disproportionate share of the negative effects of economic restructuring, including unemployment, wage losses, higher taxes, and reduced social spending (Table 9). Third, if social-development strategies are not integrated within the overall development framework, they undermine rather than stimulate the desired levels of progress (UNESCAP 1991b).

Within this context, the impact of the mass media on the popular culture has been instrumental in changing values in the societies of the region. The new values promoted by globalization involve consumerism, individualism, and materialism, especially among a growing middle class alienated from the poorer groups. The process of cultural globalization draws from the influence of factors as diverse as television, movies, newspapers, magazines, and music; capital products, technology, and information crossing national boundaries; mass international tourism; and the advertising industry.

## Regional social policy and planning

Despite the generally progressive economic climate in Southeast Asia, the assessment of the regional social-development situation indicates that social development has not kept pace with economic growth, as shown in Tables 2 and 7. This lack of congruence has been attributed primarily to the absence of a clear and common vision among national policymakers about the specific social-development objectives they should pursue and also to a lack of appreciation of the specific policy measures (UNESCAP 1991b). Some policymakers, for example, have conveniently assumed that the benefits of economic progress, though emanating from the top of the economic hierarchy, will automatically diffuse to the lower levels, eventually benefiting all members of society. Income inequalities are thought to be subsequently narrowed because all social groups ultimately benefit from economic development through employment opportunities and higher wages. However, empirical analysis has failed to validate these theories in Southeast Asian.

In fact, the pressures on the state to take prime responsibility for the provision of social services have increased. The traditional social-welfare safety nets provided by the family and the community have deteriorated as a result of increasing urbanization, industrialization, and corresponding migration patterns. At the same time, other social institutions, particularly nongovernmental organizations (NGOs) and the private-business sector, are increasingly co-opted to supplement the role of the state. Until recently, government interventions consisted primarily of formal programs in education, health, social welfare, and income security. Meanwhile, NGOs emphasized the delivery of "hands-on" social services at the grassroots level. However, past responses to social issues in the area of basic needs have often been piecemeal, providing, at best, partial or temporary remedies. In recent years, more proactive approaches have been taken. Also, social-development goals and targets in national development plans are being considered in local planning, and statistical facilities are being strengthened to permit the collection, analysis, and dissemination of data for social-policy formulation and monitoring. This is reflected, for example, in the Medium-Term Philippine Development Plan, in Thailand's National Economic and Social Development Five-Year Plan, in Indonesia's Repelita VI, and in the indicative plans of other countries, such as Viet Nam (UNESCAP 1992b).

National action programs encompass several functions. These include the intragovernmental and intersectoral coordination of social-development policy, planning, and programing; targeting of specific social groups, such as the disadvantaged and other vulnerable sectors; training of personnel to deliver social services; monitoring and evaluation of programs; and allocation of resources. Where substantial social-development impact has been achieved, further tasks include universalization of social gains and strengthening of social cohesion. Eradicating poverty, for example, requires focusing attention on the needs of social groups whose specific disadvantages or vulnerabilities impede their participation in the development process. Concerns about creating employment are not only about improving working conditions and redistributing the benefits equitably but also about raising labour productivity in the presence of rapid technological change and international competitiveness of industry. Across the board, however, the broader social-development objective is the quest for social integration as an equating factor, with poverty eradication and employment generation serving as the necessary preconditions (UNESCAP 1994).

Governments vary in their approach to poverty alleviation. Indonesia's Presidential Instruction Program on Poverty Alleviation galvanizes the efforts of all government agencies, communities, and enterprises for socioeconomic development in less-developed villages through integration, mutual cooperation, self-reliance, and decentralization. The ultimate goal is to create and enhance productive employment, financial assistance to poor families, and community solidarity. Under the Social Protection umbrella, the goals of Indonesia's Sixth Five-Year Development Plan (1994–99) include social development of isolated communities; assistance to the poor and the elderly; rehabilitation of the disabled, juvenile delinquents, and victims of drug abuse; and enhancement of community participation in development activities.

In the Philippines, the Social Reform Agenda focuses and synchronizes programs for targeted families and communities. The aim is to meet the people's basic needs through agrarian reform, institution-building, and effective participation in governance. Under the project for the Comprehensive Integrated Delivery of Social Services, communities are encouraged to identify their "minimum" basic needs and to formulate their own community-development plans. The Government Service Insurance System and the Social Security System have increased the benefits of state employees and have broadened the definition of the private-sector employee to include the self-employed. To counteract the adverse effects of structural adjustment, some of the welfare measures include food assistance, housing, financial support, training, and employment.

In Viet Nam, the national program on poverty alleviation focuses on economic development through self-reliance, primarily in rural mountainous areas and among minority groups. In Thailand, programs to create rural employment aim to assist farmers during the lean (nonharvest) seasons through the implementation of water-supply projects, infrastructure development, and a comprehensive social-insurance scheme initiated in 1990. The first stage in the implementation of this scheme (1991–96) provided financial support in cases of sickness, maternity, work-related disability, and death. The second stage, from 1998 on, will introduce old-age pension and family benefits. Unemployment-insurance benefits are also envisaged for the future (UNESCAP 1996).

Most governments formulate long- and short-term social-development strategies, and the various government ministries implement specific sectoral programs. But the most recent development is to decentralize initiatives, transferring the planning and implementation of social programs to local governments. Various approaches to institution-building in areas of social development have been initiated. In such efforts, the significance of people's participation and the involvement of local-government units (LGUs) in social-development planning and implementation has been increasingly recognized. Greater attention has been paid to enhancing the role of NGOs, the private sector, and civil society in the planning and delivery of social services.

## Decentralization: an approach to social-policy reform

Experience with social-policy development in the region shows that in terms of feasibility and, in most cases, impact, the state has been at the centre of the policy and planning process. State planning bodies have traditionally taken responsibility for translating policy goals into implementable programs, with resources largely supplied by government and directives issued by relevant government agencies. At the same time, ideals often identified with social progress have been considered attainable only if objectives of national unity, political feasibility, security, economic growth, self-reliance, and human-resource development are achieved. In this context, the social-development activities of governments have ranged from planning at the macrolevel to providing basic services — such as health, education, and welfare — through designated ministries. Social policies have thus been traditionally determined at the highest administrative levels of government because of the perceived political sensitivity of many of their social goals, including empowerment of the poor and popular participation.

In addition to financial constraints and the need for cost-reduction measures in the provision of social services, one of the key issues raised by critics of these national social-development efforts is whether centralized and uniform social programs are adequate to deal with problems often rooted in local realities, lack of participation by stakeholders, and political manipulation of traditional social relationships. Policies formulated at the central-government level tend to result in uniform programs for very diverse settings. They thus often fail to consider local participation in the implementation process, tend to express elitist and hierarchical values, and are unsuited to address existing social problems at the local level. Thus, social-development plans are often designed after specific targets, to be achieved using provincial and local governments resources, have been identified. The implementation of social-development programs in health, education, and welfare is becoming the responsibility of local governments and local structures that deliver services to each sector.

However, this approach raises a new set of issues. The differing socioeconomic contexts of geographic regions within a country, for example, require area-specific policy instruments and institutional arrangements. The devolution of responsibilities in social policy-making, planning, and administration to lower government units is pertinent only if the mechanisms to attain the established social goals are appropriate and relevant to the local circumstances (UNESCAP 1992b). Because local governance in social-sector policies is viewed as a political and social process emanating from the citizenry, the challenge is to build pluralistic civil-society institutions capable of fostering active and responsible citizen participation in policy formulation and implementation.

Presently, enough evidence indicates that the objectives of social development in the region can only be achieved within a policy context that promotes local governance and the maximum involvement of the constituencies and beneficiaries. This implies that political and social conditions need to support the development of self-governing mechanisms with sufficient latitude for local initiatives. In practice, although many governments have espoused decentralization as a national policy, central governments still have a lot more control over policy formulation and program implementation than nongovernmental partners and people's organizations do. Recognizing this, the *Manila Declaration on the Agenda for Action on Social Development in the ESCAP Region* (UNESCAP 1995, pp. 13–14) recommended that

> the governments encourage and implement decentralization and devolution of responsibility and authority, including fiscal authority, in the planning and delivery of social services. Relevant institutions will be empowered to assume increasing responsibility and authority for social development. The governments will pursue constructive cooperation with non-governmental organizations ... private enterprise, and the people to ensure that social development policies and programs are directed to meet the aims and aspirations of all social groups. Through such cooperation and strengthening the means of effective popular participation, governments can be brought closer to the people, improving performance and ensuring that people's concerns are taken into full consideration in policy-making, planning, programming, implementation, and evaluation.

The decentralization of social policies thus responds to a number of concerns. First, it recognizes the importance of local initiatives in promoting social development within the overall development framework of a country. Second, it acknowledges the inadequacy of centralized approaches to social development. Third, it results in a proliferation of approaches to the development of social policies and programs that take into account a wider range of local-level considerations. Fourth, it reflects a growing recognition of the importance of local initiatives, self-reliance, and participation. Fifth, it recognizes the need to ensure that social-policy reforms are planned and implemented in the local context so as to respond more directly to real needs (MacPherson 1989). The decentralization of social policies ultimately responds to the view that local governance increases political leaders' critical awareness of their responsibilities, fosters community initiative and commitment, and reduces dependence on central government. In practice, however, despite the frequent claims about "development from below" and "bottom-up" planning and decision-making, experiences indicate a definite need for a substantive theory of local governance. Until now, studies and programs have focused on the legal-institutional aspects of decentralized organizations, with little analysis of the power structures and little understanding of the dynamics within and among institutions (Ruland 1990). What was conceived as decentralization in the Southeast Asian region in the 1980s was in reality deconcentration. As such, it involved the distribution of administrative responsibilities within the central government and the transfer of responsibilities from central ministries to the field staff. This, however, failed to include the responsibility to formulate policies or make policy decisions.

The literature on local government in Southeast Asia has focused on five major models of governance: legal and institutional, normative, circular causative, penetrative, and comparative (Ruland 1990). The legal-institutional model basically views a local government's performance in terms of the powers and functions of local authorities, including local autonomy, financing, personnel management, and procedures. Drawing from Western experience of political development, local governance within this perspective was deemed a precondition of economic development. However, adherence to a purely legalistic view of self-government has a convenient way of sidestepping the political pitfalls arising from increasing discrepancies between the neatly designed legal provisions to decentralize, on the one hand, and encroachment on civic rights, on the other (Ruland 1990). In practice, relatively little consideration is given to local decision-making processes and procedures, associated leadership support, central–local interactions, or resource allocation mechanisms, although this approach was taken in the late 1970s In the Philippines, for example, the Marcos' regime showcased the creation of neighbourhood communities (*barangays*) as a form of grassroots democracy. In Malaysia, the restructuring of local government and the enactment of the *Local Government Act* were moves to rationalize the lowest tier of government and improve its efficiency. In Thailand, the Bangkok Metropolitan Administration strongly depended on national authorities in program implementation, despite its being a decentralized geographic structure (Patom 1978).

The normative model of local governance focuses on the promotion of democracy, popular participation, local autonomy, and transparency in decision-making. An example of this approach has been the creation of autonomous social movements, such as those for the empowerment of landless peasants, the urban poor, and labourers. The circular-causative model explains the lack of local autonomy and the existence of weak local institutions as consequences of underdevelopment. In this regard, Riggs (1995) proposed the concept of institutional and growth poles. In his view, a strong development-oriented central government can stimulate local administrative structures and promote economic development by concentrating resources in strategic-growth regions. This concept has been adopted in more industrialized countries in the region, such as Japan, Korea, and Singapore.

The penetrative model emphasizes the influences of supralocal forces and vertical political interactions on local governance. The community is seen as the focal point of political and bureaucratic influences from national and local authorities that translate into decisions according to the relative influence of each group. Community-power analysis focuses on the role of the elites in local politics and the importance of attitudes, values, and resources for local decision-making.

Using the comparative model to understanding local governance, Osteria has attempted to examine the variety of decentralization approaches adopted by four countries: Indonesia, Philippines, Thailand, and Viet Nam (Osteria 1996). This study noted that social policies in these countries have initiated people-centred approaches to social development to achieve the goals of the alleviation of poverty, employment expansion, and social integration. The fact that the social-policy strategies developed in these countries were closely linked to those targets reflects the recognition that these objectives could not be achieved through central-government initiatives alone. Osteria's study showed that basic reforms are required in both the political and the administrative structures to shift the locus of decision-making in social-policy reforms from the central ministries to the local governments. It also showed that decentralization has been implemented in different ways by different governments in the region.

Social-policy decentralization has been broadly defined as the transfer of planning, decision-making, and administrative authority from the central government to LGUs or NGOs. In Thailand, for example, after the Fourth National Development Plan (1977–81), the Thai government put in place policies to decentralize basic economic services, to increase rural production; and social-development planning to extend these services to most people. Linkages were also developed between national and provincial plans. Urban-development strategies decentralized the growth from the Bangkok Metropolitan Area to other urban centres. The system of education was modified to move more autonomy in education policy-making from the central to the regional and local levels. Public-health management in planning, implementation, budget allocation, decision-making, and personnel decisions devolved to provincial administrations. The Thai government further stipulated that operational plans at the provincial and community levels take into account local conditions and policies for national development (Leoprapai 1996). Subsequent national plans reiterated this focus in the social-development field. In practice, however, the policy pronouncements still need to be transformed into local initiatives.

The 1986 Philippine Constitution stated that decentralization policy is a substantiation of a democratization philosophy. The Constitution mandated Congress to enact a local-government code to institute a system of decentralization affecting the powers, responsibilities, and duties of LGUs in the allocation of resources. Powers of taxation were also granted to address the financial concerns created by decentralization of the social sector at all levels (Osteria 1996).

Indonesia's First National Five-Year Plan (Repelita I, 1969–73) stated that regional planning was the sole responsibility of sectoral ministries. The central-government ministries were expected to plan, implement, and monitor their projects through their representative officers at the provincial and municipal levels. Based on the recognition that such an approach leads to unequal development, subsequent five-year plans shifted the development objectives to equity and welfare distribution through increased participation of the regions (Van den Ham 1989). Although an administrative framework for decentralization was in place, much debate arose about the extent to which responsibilities and decision-making were to be devolved to the regencies. A two-tier system has complicated the structure because alongside the autonomous local-government structures are the local branches of the central government that carry out various functions and activities in the field (Malo 1996).

Viet Nam demonstrated its adherence to decentralization tenets in its 7th Party Congress pronouncements and in general provisions of the People's Councils and People's Committees, which underscored the need for "broadening the scope of responsibility and power at the local levels" (Bui 1996, pp. 152–153). As the state's local organ of power, the People's Councils are responsible for implementing the terms of the Constitution. As such, they issue resolutions related to educational development, culture and cultural preservation, children's welfare, and maternal and child health. They formulate policies and guidelines to create employment, improve working conditions, and raise living standards. The decentralization mandate (Viet Nam 1992) is explicitly stated as follows:

> to continue to reform the state through a clear structure where power is distributed to the local levels and to redefine the functions and tasks of the provincial, district, and commune levels to specify the organization at each level.

Decentralization has been effectively implemented, as reflected in activities to alleviate poverty and the activities of local health units. However, with the introduction of further economic reforms, concern is raised about the system's ability to respond adequately to emerging social needs (Bui 1996).

## NGOs and decentralization schemes

Under decentralized social-sector schemes, NGOs have become partners of local administrators in forging administrative, policy, and institutional reforms, such as policies and programs dealing with poverty alleviation and social integration. In this role, NGOs often build on the participation of traditional safety nets, such as kinship ties, the family, and the community.

The people-centred development thrust in social-policy reform underscores the active participation of all citizens, in concert with the government, in attaining social-development goals and targets. Traditionally, the NGOs have had functions in local social development: implementation of self-help initiatives, delivery of basic social services, funding, and technical and other support services. Many NGOs in the Asian region started primarily as welfare and charitable agencies that provided relief services to alleviate the conditions of disadvantaged and marginalized populations. However, over the years, they have taken on more diversified and expanded roles, empowering people's organizations and serving as agents of development for the poor and underdeveloped communities (UNESCAP 1995). More recently, NGOs have become involved in policy advocacy, paying more attention to the systemic and structural elements perpetuating social inequities. In this regard, NGOs complement the tasks of local governments by building people's capacities to participate meaningfully in community development, by providing basic services, by increasing employment opportunities, and by assisting grassroots organizations.

However, underlying tensions between local leaders and NGOs have resulted from differences in perceptions, strategies, and motivations related to the provision of specific services, which in some cases leads NGOs to refuse to cooperate with local governments (UNESCAP 1995). Local-government leaders, in turn, often view NGOs with caution, seeing them as having the potential to threaten their power and authority and expose them to public accountability. Despite the proliferation of NGOs over the past decades, their long-term and large-scale impacts have generally been questioned. The reasons for this are complex and evolve from a host of factors, including weak organizational structure; strategies that are perceived as being inappropriate; and the restriction of their activities by existing government attitudes and policies. In some countries such as Viet Nam, though, the state creates or assists NGOs, and they are virtually indistinguishable from the state apparatus. Thus, for example, the government helps trade unions, women's unions, and youth unions by providing funds and logistical support, and these organizations work in coordination with the People's Committees in social programs (Bui 1996).

In other countries, licencing and accreditation of NGOs by government have been viewed with concern. The fear is that the licencing standards "could turn into another mechanism of state control on behalf of entrenched attitudes and vested interests opposed to social reform and change" (UNESCAP 1995,

p. 47). For example, the Philippines has developed no clear policy guidelines on NGOs or their relationship with local governments. They are, thus, highly unstructured, and their relationship with local governments is often based on personal contacts (UNESCAP 1990). As a result of frequent turnover of local officials, NGO workers not uncommonly have to deal with new officials who are unaware of existing linkages or the tasks expected from them. In addition, many NGOs continue to be based in the capital or in cities and have been unable to expand their resources to rural areas and the populations most in need of their services. In Indonesia, some government agencies are reluctant to get involved with certain NGOs because the agencies lack information about their operations. In fact, some provincial officials have a controlling attitude toward NGOs and still regard them with suspicion. The Malaysian government has a dual attitude: it collaborates with the NGOs, particularly in implementing formal-education policies and youth and women's development programs, but confronts the NGOs when they seek to make the social and political systems accountable to the public (UNESCAP 1990).

The approach to social-policy decentralization in the Southeast Asian region has not been uniform. In Malaysia, for example, the federal government administers decentralization at various levels. Central-government policy- and decision-making machinery is extended to the local grassroots level or to the village communities. The District Action Committee coordinates and integrates information and communications regarding economic and social development. Through this committee, federal- and state-level policy decisions and directions are conveyed to the various departments and villages. However, one of the problems encountered with this approach is the lack of integration and coordination in policy formation among the multitude of agencies involved in program planning at the local levels, with a resultant overlap in functions. Likewise, most of the social-development programs at the district level tend to be planned and implemented on a sectoral basis, resulting in inefficient allocation and distribution of resources. This is compounded by a related problem: the lack of grassroots participation and self-determination in the decision-making process (Choo 1989).

In the Philippines, the 1991 *Local Government Code* specified the health, education, and welfare functions to be devolved to the local level. However, the effective implementation of this Code was constrained by insufficient financial resources, uneven administrative capacity of local-government leaders, lack of workable mechanisms to harness or tap the support of NGOs and the private sector, and lack of monitoring and evaluation standards (Osteria 1996). The Thai government considered decentralization of administrative authority to local governments as one of eight key policy measures established to pursue the following goals:

- Decentralizing more public functions to LGUs;

- Distributing more revenue to LGUs;

- Holding elections of local administrators at all levels;

- Creating an enabling environment in the formulation of local policies; and

- Supporting LGUs in their administration of social-sector functions (Leoprapai 1996).

In Indonesia, the implementation of decentralization took various forms, ranging from actual decentralization to "deconcentration" (Malo 1996), with local branches of sectoral ministries holding the responsibility for carrying out social-sector functions.

However, for most government officials in Southeast Asia, decentralization implies a radical transformation in the direction and implementation of policies. It reflects a paradigm shift that alters the major front lines of attitudes and behaviour in local governance and the exercise of power. In practice, this means that local officials, beyond being political leaders, must also become area managers. As such, they must be able to set the direction of their localities' development plans while implementing various social-sector initiatives in partnership with NGOs and their constituencies. The new structure implies that local officials shift from being mere beneficiaries of government's largesse to being partners and critical collaborators in local governance.

Among the major constraints on local officials implementing decentralization schemes are the following:

- Inadequate resource support;

- Basic reluctance of central governments to transfer responsibilities, personnel, and equipment to local governments, as central governments perceive local governments as being incapable of undertaking the specified tasks;

- Fear that devolution leads to local power abuse, warlordism, and elitism, which are basic cultural features in parts of the region;

- LGUs' inability to carry out the prescribed activities;

- Nebulous roles and responsibilities of local leaders and sectoral field agents;

- Absence of monitoring and evaluation standards;

- Unclear power-sharing mechanism between LGUs and NGOs;

- NGOs' and government agencies' opposing perceptions of the implementation of decentralization programs;

- Differential viewpoints regarding the decentralization modalities for the social sector at the local level; and

- Low levels of public accountability.

Four factors affect the success or failure of decentralized programs in most countries in the region:

- The degree to which central-government political leaders and bureaucracies support decentralization and local governments in cases in which responsibilities are transferred;

- The degree to which the dominant behaviour, attitudes, and culture of local leaders are conducive to decentralized decision-making;

- The degree to which policies and programs are appropriately designed to promote decentralized decision-making and management; and

- The degree to which adequate financial, human, and physical resources are made available to the local governments in cases in which responsibilities are transferred.

## Conclusions

Economic interdependence in Southeast Asia has increased at a phenomenal pace with increasing international trade and investment flows. This interdependence has been propelled by market forces that surmount official and private barriers to trade and investment. Four factors account for this:

- Substantial income expansion as a result of sustained economic growth and increased trade;

- Unilateral trade liberalization with the reduction of official trade and investment barriers;

- Complementary formation of economic structures through direct foreign investment; and

- Emergence and elaboration of cooperation schemes (Tan 1994).

These countries have also been successful in raising saving and investment rates while attracting essential capital from abroad. However, policymakers are facing the challenge of maintaining social stability and enhancing social programs in the face of economic expansion. Industrialization and urbanization result in large-scale rural-to-urban migration and the proliferation of slums and squatter settlements. Although social indicators have recorded improvements in standards of living, large disparities still exist between rural and urban areas in standards of living and in access to, and use of, educational and health services. Despite noted increases in government expenditures on social services, their percentages in GDP and total government expenditures remain low (≤10% of GDP and 20% of total expenditures). Financial allocations to social services are vulnerable to overall macroeconomic difficulties, such as debt servicing. Higher taxation, increased prices, and reduced social spending may further disadvantage vulnerable groups. Reductions in subsidies and devaluation of local currency can increase food prices and result in malnutrition of low-income groups.

The Southeast Asian governments have underscored the role of good governance in social development through decentralization and devolution of responsibility and authority in the planning and delivery of social services. Institutions within the purview of local government have to be empowered to assume increasing responsibility and authority for social development. Equally important for good governance are efforts to get relevant groups to actively participate in policy-making, planning, and programing so as to improve the effectiveness of social-development interventions and ensure the equitable distribution of development benefits. Regional experience has revealed that dynamic involvement of the total network of social institutions, including NGOs and popular organizations, is required for effective and sustained development. Cooperation in research of critical concern also has an important role to play in strengthening future policy and program development.

## Lessons from social-sector decentralization

The governments in Southeast Asia, irrespective of ideology, have had a common preoccupation with sustained social development to ensure progressively higher levels of well-being of their populations. However, decentralization to achieve this end has varied between and within countries, both in how it has been implemented and in the type of responses it has evoked.

After several years of experimenting with decentralization as a way to reform social policies, countries in the region are now in a position to observe each other's social-policy performance and learn from each other's experiences. This review of these experiences yields a number of lessons.

First, if the implementation of decentralized policies and programs requires local leaders to assume the tasks of social-sector planning and implementation, then the leaders need to have an ideological commitment and the implementers need to have the necessary technical skills. Experience shows that the skills required for policy formulation, program implementation, and resource mobilization can be acquired through training with the assistance of locally appropriate modules and programs.

Second, beginning early in the process of policy change, those designing policy reforms and policy-decentralization strategies need to identify and mediate the inherent conflicts between sectoral ministries and LGUs to achieve the smooth implementation of programs. Although it is not unusual for many central sectoral ministries and LGUs to claim commitment to the tenets of decentralization, little progress is sometimes made in translating policies into effective action. One of the impediments to decentralized programs is the prevailing top-down approach to policy implementation. To overcome this, implementers need a meaningful, flexible, and participatory strategy; stakeholders must be involved, beginning at the initial stage of policy formulation.

Third, it is important to have the active joint participation of government agencies and NGOs in planning and implementing social programs at the local level. Effective community-based social organizations are, for this reason, another important element in implementing decentralization strategies if local leaders' actions are to realistically reflect local needs, mobilize community resources, and enforce the decentralization mandate. Village leaders, for example, can find the balance between community social needs and program inputs. The key factors, however, are local organizations that substantively involve the people and provide skills and institutional management capacity through participatory actions.

Fourth, local governments must systematically address the issues of resource identification and mobilization to adequately finance social services. Overall, however, the effective implementation of decentralized social-sector programs depends on predetermined requirements, such as organizational structure, a functional bureaucracy, and mutually supportive horizontal and vertical relations in the management of policies and programs.

Fifth, organizations at the lowest level of the hierarchy are often in a better position to address local problems. This depends on the capacity and creativity of local leaders and their constituencies. However, effective leadership at the local level is the critical factor in implementing and sustaining decentralization initiatives. Local leaders can draw from their strong family, community, and political linkages to mobilize resources for social-sector programs. It is not unusual for their lack of skills for carrying out organizational activities to be offset by their ability to provide traditional legitimacy, apply informal procedures, and mobilize community support. In many cases, given the passivity of most beneficiaries, a major way to enhance prospects for local social action is for leaders to co-opt the beneficiaries as major stakeholders in the programs.

Finally, the delegation of responsibilities to local governments often raises issues of public accountability of local-government officials. A way to help them internalize the notion of accountability is to involve NGOs and the communities in program implementation. In this way, accountability becomes broad based. Leaders are more likely to manage programs that support local needs if they are held accountable to their constituencies. Accountability can be built into the structure of local systems if decision-making is shared by the local governments, sectoral field agents, and NGOs.

When responsibilities are transferred from central to local governments, the latter often have to introduce measures with long-term impacts on the sustainability, efficiency, and effectiveness of decentralized social-sector programs. In such cases, the central agency is expected to contribute direction, technical support, databases, and resources to help local governments develop a structure and operational system. Quite often, this process presents a number of constraints. Implementers indicate that local governments often lack the ability to meet social-sector demands. They take over social programs and staff with existing arrangements based on a previous central structure designed to provide specific services. However, they are incapable of providing the same support that the central agency contributed to the program in terms of staff, equipment, and supplies. A second crucial concern of local governments is the identification of specific tasks and activities of the service-delivery units under decentralization. What social-sector programs, services, inputs, and supplies will be required by local governments? What specific program can they undertake, given their resources? These are some of the issues that local leaders and sectoral field agents have to address. Experiences show that it is essential that technical and monitoring standards be developed in cooperation with sectoral agencies and NGOs. A third concern has to do with vertical and horizontal linkages. Social-sector programs must establish linkages to ensure that the community is given the appropriate services. An important element in such contexts is networking among the various local-level units; among sectoral field units; among public, private, and NGO service providers; and between the service providers and the population.

Overall experience in the region shows that strengthening local governments supports the aim of linking social-development efforts to the population at large. This is for several reasons. For one thing, local governments have the ability to meaningfully address social-sector needs at local levels, given that social-development problems are locality and population specific. For another, the coordination and collaboration of entities at local levels can help to establish holistic and culturally acceptable local programs. However, for this approach to be operational, responsibilities must be relinquished to LGUs, leaving central authorities with the responsibility for macrolevel initiatives aimed at achieving the country's overall development goals. Under these conditions, decentralization creates an atmosphere of collective commitment and shared responsibility. And this atmosphere encourages initiatives at all levels to allow people to make decisions affecting their lives. A decentralization modality is promoted that is people oriented, sustainable, and relevant to people's needs and interests.

# CHAPTER 6

# THE AMERICAS

## EDUCATIONAL REFORM, EXTERNAL FORCES,
## AND INTERNAL CHALLENGES

*Jeffrey M. Puryear*

The most striking feature of educational systems in Latin America and the Caribbean today is change. The region's dramatic shift toward open economies, democratic governance, and state decentralization has made education crucial to continued economic success and social development. Global competition requires workers who understand science and technology and can adapt to rapidly changing conditions. Democratic rule requires citizens who are better informed and more responsible. The decentralization of public administration is placing a new emphasis on citizen participation, autonomy, and responsibility in provincial and municipal settings.

Schools are not responding to these new demands. More children go to school now than ever, but the education that most receive falls far short of the requirements for economic success and social advance.

The problems are striking. Latin America has the highest repetition rates in the world, with nearly a third of all primary students repeating a grade each year. The cost of teaching these repeaters has been estimated at several billion dollars annually. Only half the students who begin primary school will complete the cycle, leaving far too many children without a basic mastery of language and mathematics. In virtually every international test of reading, mathematics, and science, Latin American students perform poorly in comparison with students elsewhere. The region's involvement in the international scientific community is marginal. Despite having more than 8% of the world's population, Latin America and the Caribbean accounted for just 0.6% of the resources invested worldwide in research and development in 1990 and 1.5% of the scientific articles published worldwide in 1993.

Teachers tend to be poorly trained, to have a low status, and to have few incentives for professional excellence. Pedagogy is dominated by the "frontal" model that rewards the memorization of facts and fails to develop student capacities to question, explore, work in groups, and learn on their own.

Educational systems are also remarkably inequitable. Students from the poorest families score dramatically lower on achievement tests than do middle- and upper-class children. Most primary-school repeaters are poor and attend low-quality public schools. But public funds have been used disproportionately to expand secondary and higher education — levels of education most of the poor do not reach — rather than to improve public primary schools. For much of the region, good education is still a privilege of the wealthy and upper-middle classes, given at expensive private schools (IADB 1996; Puryear 1997).

Public- and private-sector leaders are deploring the inadequacies of existing schools and calling for reform. Governments everywhere are revising their education policies. Bilateral and multilateral assistance institutions are offering to help governments improve the quality and quantity of their investments in human resources. The long-standing problems of the region's school systems have become all too apparent. Reform has become the norm.

Almost as striking is the fact that much of the impetus for reform is coming from sources external to the educational systems, rather than from those internal to it. The challenges of global competition have forced governments to pay more attention to the quality of their work forces and to the schools that produce them. The information revolution has shortened the time it takes to communicate about policy innovation from one country to another and has made it easier for countries to compare their efforts with those of their neighbours. Foreign assistance institutions have become promoters of reform and the bearers of new approaches. The context for policy debate in education has increasingly become regional and global, rather than simply national. Education ministries are being pressed by heads of state and nongovernmental technocrats to produce better education more efficiently. Change is being imposed on education systems from without, rather than from within.

As a result, education has become one of the most dynamic sectors of national policy-making in Latin America and the Caribbean. Major reforms are being attempted, and even greater reforms are being discussed. Ministries of education are delegating significant responsibility to provincial and municipal bodies. The management of schools is being decentralized, and parents and employers are being asked to participate. National testing regimes are being established. Concepts that have traditionally been resisted by actors within the educational system, such as parental choice, competition among schools, community involvement in school management, and performance-based pay systems for teachers, are now on the policy agenda.

What are we to make of these challenges that globalization poses to the status quo within educational systems in this region? Do they signal a renaissance in the region's social-policy systems? Do they represent inappropriate meddling by outside forces? Can they promote economic growth and social equity? Can they make schools better? Will they persist?

This chapter argues that we are witnessing a fundamentally healthy process, with significant potential to improve education in many countries. The pressures for change coming from outside the educational systems constitute an important corrective to the deeply conservative forces that dominate most public-education systems in the region. Such outside pressures should be welcomed, rather than feared. This chapter also argues that these challenges do not guarantee better schools. The required innovations must be tested and adapted. Moreover, significant forces are opposed to reform. Real progress will depend on how public-education systems — and governments more broadly — respond to these new ideas. Those that develop clear goals for their schools, measure new ideas by their potential to help achieve those goals, and decide to address the formidable political obstacles to change will be able to take advantage of the rich mixture of policy suggestions emerging from experience around the world.

The next sections discuss the various factors affecting educational reform in the region, as well as some views on the positive and negative influence of these factors. This chapter concludes by outlining some of the key issues in need of further consideration in social-policy reform in general and in educational reform in particular.

## Factors in educational reform

Several factors that spur education reform derive from the region-wide shift to open economies and global competition. Two of these factors are especially important. The first is the growing centrality of knowledge as a production factor. The second is the increasing global character of information, communication, and economic activity. Both these factors are sharply increasing the demand for education. They are establishing a new and compelling economic argument for educational reform. They are also causing powerful actors outside educational systems — politicians, business leaders, development-assistance institutions (DAIs), and civil society more generally — to press for better schools and a better quality of education.

## The growing centrality of knowledge

Many analysts argue that knowledge is central to post-industrial society and that its importance will only grow in the future (Drucker 1989; Reich 1991). Production, which in its most primitive form requires little more than capital and labour, now depends more and more on technology (Dahlman 1989; Lall 1990). We are experiencing a scientific and technological revolution that is sharply increasing the value added by knowledge to production. As technology expands and as technological cycles become shorter, the key to remaining competitive is to be able to create, evaluate, adapt, and exploit technology.

Because technology depends ultimately on human resources, competitiveness is increasingly based on an educated work force, rather than on capital or natural resources. The spread of new technologies is creating a need for employees who know how to use them. Those who work directly with knowledge and information are becoming more central to production. For example, advances in microelectronic technology have led to the rapid spread of computerized machine tools, robotics, and computer-assisted design — all of which can be used to perform a variety of tasks and to produce a variety of products. They enable firms to change products rapidly in response to shifting demand but require a work force well versed in the fundamentals of technology and able to absorb and apply new knowledge on the job. Similarly, firms rely increasingly on sophisticated computerized databases and communications systems for their daily operations, requiring levels of knowledge and adaptability rarely needed by workers even a decade ago. Biotechnological advances have produced major gains in agricultural production but require workers who can interpret written instructions and properly combine complementary inputs, such as irrigation and fertilizers (Middleton et al. 1993). In more general terms, economic success now requires countries to develop a national technological capability, a key component of which is an adequate stock of high-quality scientific and technological human resources. Countries need graduates who understand modern technology and can adapt it to local conditions. They must be able to monitor emerging technologies, assimilate and adapt them, and devise appropriate strategies to exploit them (Lall 1990; Dahlman 1991).

This line of thinking has reinforced the idea that human resources play an increasingly important role in economic competitiveness and growth. An impressive body of theory and evidence now suggests that investments in human capital, particularly in education, enhance economic competitiveness (Schultz 1961; Becker 1964; Barro 1991).

We know, for example, that a strong relationship exists between school enrollments — particularly at the primary level — and subsequent economic growth. Countries that expanded enrollments sharply during the 1950s and 1960s experienced higher rates of economic growth during the 1970s and 1980s, even after other factors that contribute to growth are taken into account.

A recent World Bank study found that sustained investments in primary schooling several decades ago were critically important to the success of the eight rapidly growing economies of East Asia — the "tigers" (World Bank 1993a). The historical evidence on this issue is so strong that many economists argue that at a certain threshold in human-capital accumulation economic growth accelerates.

We also know that education makes farmers more productive. A study of 18 low-income countries recently concluded that 4 years of primary schooling made farmers, on average, nearly 9% more productive than those with no education. When complementary inputs are available — such as fertilizer, new seeds, and new machinery — the impact rises to 13%. A study in Peru showed that an additional 1 year of schooling for a farmer increased annual output by about 2%. Most economists argue that education not only makes farmers produce more with the same quantity of inputs but also enables them to absorb new information and makes them more willing to try new techniques (Lockheed et al. 1980).

Finally, we know that the rates of return to investments in education are high, particularly in low- and middle-income countries. Workers with more education earn more money. The social rates of return to primary and secondary education in Latin America and the Caribbean have recently been calculated at about 18 and 13%, respectively, even without including possible spillover benefits that may accrue to employers (and to society) from having more educated workers. Those rates are generally higher than the long-run opportunity costs of capital (that is, the rate of return to alternative, noneducational investments). They suggest that education — at least, at the primary and secondary levels — is an excellent investment.

On the basis of these findings, governments have shifted attention to education and health and have sought new policies and priorities in key areas of social and human development.

## Globalization

Most spheres of human activity are becoming progressively altered by globalization. Communication is increasingly global. Knowledge and the news of events in one country are readily available to people in another. Culture is rapidly transmitted from one country to another. Increasingly, our reference point is the world, rather than the nation-state (ECLAC and OREALC 1992; Marshall and Tucker 1992).

Globalization has had its most dramatic impact on economic competition. With open economies, trade becomes a global activity, and investment and technology become global commodities. Investment capital is actively sought, and flows of investment capital are global, rather than national. Competition becomes global, rather than national. As nations open up to the outside world, they identify promising new technologies, adapt them to local conditions, attract foreign investment, and monitor global markets for the best opportunities. The result is a global push for higher productivity, which causes employers to seek new technologies and workers who can apply them successfully. Remaining competitive under these conditions depends increasingly on the skills of a nation's work force.

Some economists even suggest that globalization is creating a new stage of capitalism. Earlier, the dominant principle was "scientific management" (known as Taylorism), in which skilled managers and engineers directed relatively unskilled line workers in carrying out specialized, repetitive tasks (Marshall and Tucker 1992). Capital and corporations were more national than international and relatively stable. But the emerging global economy is much more competitive and much more dynamic. Producers must be able to adapt rapidly to a constantly changing marketplace. They need managers who can quickly move from one technology to another and production workers who can think for themselves and act on their own accord. Producers must invest not only in plant and equipment but also in a productive work force. In a world of global capital flows and rootless corporations, a country's work force is one of its few dependable assets.

## The spread of new ideas

Globalization has spawned a third factor fueling change: the spread of new ideas about the ways education is provided. The debate about education has become global. New developments in economic theory, social policy, and public administration are transmitted rapidly around the world and discussed with great authority by local analysts and policymakers. Development banks, aid agencies, and international nongovernmental organizations (NGOs) transmit extensive information on the structure and performance of national educational systems. Schools are increasingly compared cross-nationally in terms of their costs, output, equity, and efficiency. Today, policymakers inside and outside the education sector have at their disposal a powerful store of ideas, data, and analyses they can apply to assessing national educational systems.

Examples abound. Detailed education statistics for most countries are widely available from the United Nations Educational, Scientific and Cultural Organization (UNESCO), the World Bank, and the Inter-American Development Bank (IADB). International educational comparisons, such as the Third International Math and Science Study (Schmidt et al. 1996), UNESCO's biannual *World Education Report* (UNESCO 1995), and the Organisation for Economic Co-operation and Development's Education at a Glance project (OECD 1995), have become important sources of global comparative analysis of the evolution of educational systems. Policy measures endorsed at the World Conference on Education For All in Jomtien, Thailand, in 1989, have significantly altered the terms of the debate about educational policy in Latin America (WCEFA 1990). World Bank publications on educational policies have often become important benchmarks for policymakers in Latin America (Lockheed and Verspoor 1991; World Bank 1991, 1995b). IADB is producing powerful comparative analyses of the ways education is provided (Behrman 1993; IADB 1996). Cross-national comparisons of national educational systems have become almost commonplace (Puryear and Brunner 1995; Álvarez and Ruiz-Casares 1997).

The abundance of information and analyses has led countries to pay far greater attention to foreign experiences and ideas when considering educational reform. Countries are comparing their performance in education with that of countries around the world. National policymakers are just as likely to suggest adopting an approach tried in Chile, Singapore, or the United Kingdom as to use approaches developed locally. Local practice is increasingly influenced by practice abroad, and policymakers are less likely to try to reinvent the wheel. An extraordinary cross-fertilization of ideas about the ways education is provided is under way.

## New actors in educational policy

Over the last few years, a host of new actors have come to play important roles in educational reform. Some of these actors, such as development banks and bilateral assistance agencies, are international. Many others are national but are external to national educational systems. All have become important factors pressing for change. Their efforts have often engendered significant resistance from those who have traditionally dominated educational systems, particularly teachers' unions and ministerial bureaucrats.

Among the strongest of the new actors have been heads of state. Whereas in the past educational policy was lower on the political agenda and more often left to ministers of education, today presidents — such as Fernando Henrique Cardoso in Brazil, Eduardo Frei in Chile, and Cesar Gaviria in Colombia — have increasingly taken up the banner of educational reform, making it a central feature of their political platforms. Convinced that poor-quality schools are a major bottleneck to economic growth and social advancement, they are charging ministers of education with reform agendas and providing them with political support. Often, they are aided by technocrats from sectors of government other than education, particularly ministries of finance and planning, or from nongovernmental think tanks, whose views of educational policy are based firmly on modern economic theory. Such think tanks have on occasion proposed radical changes, such as cutting subsidies to higher education (as in Nicaragua), sharply reducing the power of education ministries (as in Argentina), promoting competition among public schools (as in Chile), and breaking up the monopoly of teachers' unions (as in El Salvador).

Although their success has varied greatly, heads of state are becoming central players in the promotion of educational reform in Latin America and the Caribbean.

Sectors of civil society — the consumers of education — traditionally little involved in educational policy have also begun to play important roles in debating and promoting educational reform. In the Dominican Republic, for example, two NGOs with strong business connections — Educa and Plan Educativo — worked with the academic, business, and professional communities to develop educational-reform plans that eventually had a strong impact on government policy (Zaiter 1997). In Nicaragua, a radical decentralization program for education has as its centrepiece the systematic involvement of parents in local-school management.

Argentina, Brazil, Chile, Ecuador, and El Salvador have all established programs to bring diverse social sectors together to discuss educational policy. Nongovernmental groups in Brazil, Colombia, the Dominican Republic, Guatemala, Nicaragua, Peru, and Venezuela have worked since 1995 to generate a sustained process of national debate and discussion about educational reform among political, business, and professional organizations, under the Partnership for Educational Revitalization in the Americas (PREAL). PREAL is a hemispheric partnership of public- and private-sector organizations working for educational reform in Latin America and the Caribbean, jointly managed by the Inter-American Dialogue, in the United States, and the Corporation for Development Research, in Chile. The partnership promotes informed debate on policy alternatives, identifies and disseminates best education practices emerging in the region and elsewhere, and monitors progress toward improving educational policy. Participants include governments, nongovernmental actors, researchers, international organizations, universities, and the business community. Business leaders are showing increased interest in local and national educational policy (Puryear 1996). The emphasis in all these initiatives has been to develop consensus regarding educational problems and their possible solutions among actors outside the educational system. Although their impact is not easy to assess, in large part because the road to policy change is seldom short or direct, several accounts suggest that consumers of education are beginning to play more important roles than in the past (Hernández Mella 1997; Reimers and McGinn 1997).

A third group of actors playing increasingly important roles in the reform of education are the DAIs. These include organizations as diverse as development banks, international organizations, bilateral aid agencies, NGOs, and consulting firms. Some of them, particularly UNESCO and the United Nations Children's Fund, have long been active in education in Latin America. Others, such as the World Bank and IADB, have recently increased their work, becoming much more significant sources of information, analyses, and financing than in the past (McMeekin 1996).

Several characteristics make DAIs particularly powerful in educational reform. First, they are often significant sources of funding. Although public expenditures on education dwarf even the sums available from the development banks, most public funds are closely tied to ongoing operations (particularly salaries) and cannot be easily shifted to other uses. By contrast, funds from DAIs tend to be flexible. They can be used to select, adapt, and evaluate new programs, giving them a significance far in excess of their share in public spending on education. In Latin America, funding from DAIs often constitutes a major source of discretionary public spending on education. During the 1990s, funding for education from DAIs averaged more than 1.3 billion United States dollars annually. Loans constituted most of this support, and they came almost entirely from the development banks (McMeekin 1996).

Second, DAIs often produce some of the best information and analysis regarding education in the region. By virtue of their multinational character, human resources, and considerable funding, DAIs are extraordinarily well positioned to be key sources of information, analyzing national efforts, transferring policy innovations cross-nationally, and drawing policy conclusions. For example, the World Bank has become the single best source of data and analyses regarding education in Latin America and the Caribbean. Its technical reports, country analyses, and policy documents are required reading for both academics and policymakers, including those who disagree with the World Bank's conclusions. IADB recently stepped up its analytical work and is also becoming an important voice on educational policy. A comprehensive educational policy paper produced by the Economic Commission for Latin America and the Caribbean and UNESCO's regional office for Latin America a few years ago has had a major impact on policy debate (ECLAC and OREALC 1992).

This information is often of value to national governments. The development banks in particular have become a source of knowledge and experience not generally available locally and otherwise difficult to secure. Governments often seek to work with development banks as much for their technical expertise as for their money.

Third, DAIs also provide political resources, such as legitimacy, clout, and cover, that are very useful to policymakers. For example, the blessing of a development bank or an international organization often helps to convince otherwise sceptical or neutral national groups to accept reforms. Economists from development banks may have more success than ministry-of-education officials in convincing those at ministries of finance and planning that certain educational policies are advisable. Also, DAIs provide governments with a convenient scapegoat for politically unpopular policy decisions. In the face of complaints, the involvement of a DAI allows the government to suggest that there was no real alternative — "the Bank made us do it."

DAIs can perform these political functions precisely because they have the image of the impartial, authoritative expert whose word is based on science and reason, rather than on ideology or partisan politics. This expert status enables DAIs to depoliticize decisions — bestowing a nonpolitical stamp of approval on government decisions, which helps counteract allegations of political partisanship and patronage.

Often, DAIs use their expert status prescriptively, criticizing national systems and policies, taking clear stands for or against certain policies and tying their support to those stands. They have also taken a top-down approach, working almost exclusively with top governmental officials and only occasionally developing contacts with other stakeholders in educational policy.

Overall, then, the educational establishment in Latin America is being challenged to a degree not seen in the recent past, by forces that are largely external to its educational systems. Some of these forces are international; others, including heads of state, ministries of finance and planning, and technocrats based in local NGOs, are national but often work closely with international DAIs to develop reform policies. The demand for education is changing rapidly; the supply is under fire.

## Counterreform

Pressures for change in the Americas' educational systems have not surprisingly met with significant resistance. Much of that resistance has come from teachers' unions, universities, and ministerial officials. Some has come from politicians and from some in the academic community. Considerably less resistance has come from parents, students, and employers — with the exception of university students who defend tuition-free higher education.

Those resisting change have mounted a variety of arguments. One of the most common emerging recently is based on the notion that a neoliberal model is being forced on the country by foreign interests. The argument is that foreign actors, led by the International Monetary Fund and the World Bank, are forcibly imposing a cruel and inappropriate model on national educational systems. According to this argument, the motive for this model is to cut public spending, reduce teaching only to narrow, vocational topics that can be measured by tests, and shift education away from the public sector and into private hands. It is argued that the neoliberal model tends to be totally insensitive to national conditions and goals and to the needs of the poor. The discussion is often dominated by catch phrases — such as *privatization and competition* —

which are assumed to refer to things so objectionable as not to even merit serious consideration (CEA 1997).

This is of course a powerful argument. It arouses fears of foreign encroachment on national autonomy and fears of sacrificing education for financial gains. The issues are often presented in highly emotional terms that divide disputants into two sharply divided camps — one good and one bad — and that make reasonable discussion and consensus-building almost impossible. Too often, the result has been conflict and stalemate.

Even more striking is the extent to which the current debate about educational reform is dominated by the traditional suppliers of public education — heads of state, the ministries of finance, planning, and education, and the teachers' unions. As striking is how little the consumers of public education — parents, students, and employers — participate in the debate. This state of affairs is simple enough to explain. Traditional systems of public education have created strong vested interests. Ministries of education control power and jobs. Well-organized teachers' unions hold a national monopoly on teaching positions. Politicians often control patronage within the educational system. These groups constitute a powerful political force in education; they benefit directly from the existing system and have strong incentives to resist change (Hausman 1994; Montenegro 1996; IADB 1996). The teachers' unions also have a powerful mechanism — the strike — to influence educational policy.

Of course, the consumers of education also have interests at stake. But their interests are less direct and less visible, and they have fewer mechanisms to defend their interests. Most have little information about educational policy and no experience discussing it. The business community, traditionally unexposed to international competition, has paid little attention to public educational policy. Middle- and upper-class parents generally send their children to private schools and do not have to suffer the deficiencies of public education. Thus, these groups — which control decision-making in public educational policy in most countries — have no compelling incentive to improve the quality of public schools; their interests are not directly at stake. The poor have no choice but to send their children to local public schools, regardless of their quality, and possess few mechanisms to influence educational policy. As a result, most of the effective interest in public educational policy in Latin America is with the suppliers of education, rather than the consumers. The supply has to a significant extent become the demand.

Today, then, the growing forces seeking to reform schools in Latin America and the Caribbean have come face to face with powerful vested interests in traditional approaches to education. Despite considerable initiative, new thinking, and serious effort, fundamental changes have often been stymied. A major political battle is holding up reform. Genuine, pressing needs to improve education are going unmet.

# Conclusion: issues and possible solutions

Several issues have emerged in the debate about educational policy in the Americas that merit consideration by governments and others concerned with making schools better. First, it is important to realize that new ideas are not the problem. Schools are very conservative institutions. New approaches are crucial to making sure that they do not fall behind in their mission. The availability of information and experience, foreign or otherwise, provides an extraordinary opportunity to identify promising approaches and to speed up eventual improvements. The Luddite impulse, which is so common in the debate on reform, needs to be firmly resisted. Governments should make it clear that good ideas are welcome, whether they come from a local municipality, Thailand, or France.

That does not mean that all new ideas are good, however. Governments also need to take a critical approach to new ideas and an experimental approach to applying them. Governments need to have a strong technical capacity to evaluate experience elsewhere, determine which innovations hold the most promise, and adapt them to local needs and conditions. Governments also need to recognize that introducing even the most promising of new ideas can be extraordinarily difficult and requires great care. That means establishing — inside or outside government — a solid cadre of national technical advisors who can deal with foreign technocrats on even terms. These cadres should be charged with identifying promising new approaches, adapting them to local conditions, and devising strategies to introduce them, monitor their implementation, and adjust them as needed. New ideas may be good, but governments need to make them their own.

Second, the terms of the debate need to be changed. Too much time is spent debating policies in terms of their associated ideologies, models, and backers. Whether an innovation is leftist or neoliberal, market or nonmarket, or promoted by teachers' unions or by the World Bank is beside the point. None of these labels reflects the real priorities of schools. Most of these labels are distractions, designed to promote the agenda of one or another vested interest. Instead, governments should insist that learning be placed at the centre of the debate, followed closely by equity and efficiency. Policy innovations should be judged first in terms of their probable impact on learning. If they improve learning, they deserve consideration, regardless of their source or associated ideology. Similarly, policies should be assessed in terms of how they affect equity — a major problem for most Latin American societies — and whether they promote the more efficient use of scarce resources. Only by keeping an eye on the goals of learning, equity, and efficiency are governments likely to successfully negotiate the rising claims of diverse interest groups.

Third, governments need to add a political dimension to their efforts to reform education. The dominant approach to reform — in which technocrats come up with new policies and governments adopt them — is simply inadequate. Instead, there needs to be a process in which stakeholders from all parts of civil society — parents, business leaders, churches, the media, labour unions, and professional associations — participate in setting goals for the educational system and in discussing policy options. Emphasis should be on the kinds of schools needed to enable a country to achieve its social and economic objectives. The process should include agreement on how to measure progress toward the goals selected and participation by stakeholders in monitoring progress.

This applies particularly to teachers, who have always been excluded from reform planning and have responded with fierce resistance. But it also applies to the consumers of education, particularly parents and employers, who traditionally have little information about schools and have not played an important role in calling for better education. By building broad agreement on problems and ways to address them, governments can help create a crucial element in making reforms succeed: a more sophisticated demand for education (Reimers and McGinn 1997). Once policy decisions have been made, their character and merit should be explained to the country, including the use of the media to reach a broad audience. The public needs to understand why certain policies have been chosen, how they relate to national goals, and what these policies are supposed to accomplish. The public also needs to realize that progress will take time, that quick fixes are uncommon in education. Even the most compelling reforms need to be marketed.

Fourth, DAIs need to use less prescription and more discussion in working with countries. They need to pay more explicit attention to the political obstacles that governments face in promoting reform and help devise appropriate strategies to address them. DAIs should find ways to reach a broader range of education stakeholders — particularly those outside government. DAIs should also recognize the need in most cases to adapt and adjust new approaches. This does not mean that DAIs should sacrifice technical excellence for political expediency; rather, they should recognize that technical excellence often has important political prerequisites and that failing to address these prerequisites places technical excellence in jeopardy.

The unprecedented challenges to traditional school systems have made education a remarkably dynamic sector of national policy-making in Latin America and the Caribbean. But real improvement will depend not only on the quality of new ideas but also on the quality of the implementation strategies that governments devise. Only governments that work with broader sectors of civil society to develop a clear vision for their schools and address intelligently the serious political obstacles that stand in the way of change are likely to make real progress in making schools better.

# PART III

# CONCLUDING REMARKS

# CONCLUSION

## WHAT TYPE OF SOCIAL-POLICY REFORM

## FOR WHAT KIND OF SOCIETY? ·

*Daniel Morales-Gómez and Mario Torres A.*

Social policies are undergoing radical reform. The agendas leading these changes show similar characteristics across sectors, countries, and regions. At the same time, the experiences to date show considerable differences in the implementation and impacts of these changes. Reform efforts include the privatization of education, health, and social-security services; moves toward market-oriented provision of social services; decentralization and deconcentration of services, relying on local governments and communities for their delivery; establishment of fee-for-service schemes; targeting of social provision to specific populations; and increased bottom-up participation in policy design and implementation.

The inspiration for these changes no longer rests with the welfare-state model of the 1940s and 1950s (Taylor-Gooby 1991; Hunsley 1992; Moon and Dixon 1992). Quite the contrary, the drive to reform public policies in the social sectors has its source in a philosophy of economic liberalism (Saul 1995; Vilas 1996; Petras 1997). Today, the reform of public policies in general, and of social policies in particular, is only one expression of what some argue is the rise of a new development paradigm that is redefining the role of the nation-state. One of the main expressions of this neoliberalism is the implementation of programs for economic reform based on the liberalization of prices, deregulation of markets, elimination of subsidies, elimination of trade barriers, privatization of state operations, and opening up of competition at all levels. Other manifestations include new forms of economic integration and partnerships and free-trade agreements assisted by increasing economic globalization, freer capital-investment flows across countries, heavier dependence on the role of information and communication technologies, and greater movement of labour across borders (UNRISD 1997).

In this scenario, social-policy reform is one component of an international development-policy agenda attempting to address a wide range of issues, including employment, poverty, low standards of human and social development, the negative conditions affecting particular population sectors, and economic growth. Many countries are thus under increasing transnational pressure to respond to complex development demands, in addition to those affecting their national economies. In part, because of the recognition of social development as an integral dimension of economic growth and, in part, because of changes in the role of the nation-state, governments have to respond to demands for more and better human and social development — demands that originate not only from within their national borders but also from transnational sources. Public policies are thus less and less an exclusive domain of the nation-state as defined by territorial or cultural boundaries. Many questions are raised by this phenomenon. Three seem to be at the top of the list: What is the meaning of current policy-reform approaches in the context of globalization? What is known about the effects and impacts of ongoing experience in social-policy reform? What kind of society are these new policies likely to create?

## Globalization and transnational influences

Some of the lessons drawn from Africa, Latin America, and Southeast Asia show that addressing questions raised by globalization requires one to revisit the meaning of globalization in light of its impacts on human development. These lessons also show a need to acknowledge that most of the factors that shape globalization today are not new. In various forms and ideological expressions, the role of capital flows, trade, and geopolitical relations between countries at different development stages have been present since the emergence of imperialism in the past century (Magdoff 1969; Bukharin 1973; Petras 1978).

What today is labeled globalization is the expression of a complex net of power relations between nation-states, perhaps only with broader and deeper ramifications than in the past. Thus, for example, despite the importance attributed to structural adjustment as a set of measures driving policy reforms, in the broader picture they are no more than a set of conditional measures reflecting relations of power between rich and poor countries that are different from those imposed by economic, political, and cultural imperialism in the past. The perception that nation-states have less power than before because of globalization is also relative. The history of this century is full of examples documenting how vulnerable political and economic systems are when examined in light of power relations between developed and developing economies. The colonial history of countries in Africa and that of the dependence of Latin America on more developed economies reinforce this view.

What is new about globalization and its transnational dimension in the late 1990s is the rapidity with which globalization is taking place and the depth of its effects on the makeup of societies. This is due, in part, to the collapse of the East–West divide and, in part, to an unprecedented revolution in information and communication technologies, which is speeding up the effects of two fundamental features of globalization: the liberalization of trade and the rapidity of capital flows (Tanaguchi and West 1997). The depolarization of the world has resulted in the transformation of traditional centre–periphery relations, making them truly transnational. Yet, at another level, there is a new depth and scope to the impacts of these transnational forces. With primary emphasis on the economic, political, and military relations between more and less powerful countries, the forces of globalization reach areas that until recently were strictly national domains. In essence, transnational influences are directly affecting the capacity of societies to shape their basic social-provision systems, the mechanisms protecting their cultural identity, and the values underlying their national development plans and forms of governance.

To an extent, globalization is a label identifying yet another more subtle and complex but no less evident process of social transformation at the end of the 20th century. Ultimately, globalization represents a process of profound penetration of local ethical systems by a set of values brought about and sustained by economic imperatives, trade, and mass communication. In this context, the impacts of transnational influences on countries' vulnerability are more likely to be perceived as long term or irreversible than when the effects of globalization are reduced to a purely economic dimension. Nowhere is this more evident today than in the transformations of the public policies and systems on which social and human development depend.

Although this is not the first time in history that powerful ideas and values have been key ingredients in relations between countries and between cultures, today the recipient societies seem to offer more fertile ground for them to take root. The values, ideas, images, and goals underlying transnational influences portray an abstract, ideal society, where economic progress, technological development, social upward mobility, and individual success blend together as an appealing, short-term, achievable objective. The only requirement for this ideal society to become a reality is the desire and willingness of its citizens to change and to adjust their social structures, institutions, and political and economic practices to a predefined blue-print that belongs to no particular nation or culture. This penetration of local value systems is assisted by the wide spread signs of a successful capitalist system. For some, this is encapsulated in the notion of a "new world order," framed in a neoliberal ideology, which presents itself as sustained by and promoting value-neutral goals of efficiency, order, and democracy, equal opportunity for success, open access to knowledge, free flows of capital, and new forms of partnership based on more horizontal power relations.

These pressures on the large majority of the world's population in the South have an impact that can no longer be explained solely as an outcome of underdevelopment. Globalization is a two-way street. Explosive demographics in developing countries, for example, are forcing traditional local structures to change. Because of these numbers, the effects of poverty, alienation, and social exclusion in developing countries have spillover effects on wealthier countries. It is difficult to ignore, for example, that the rural–urban social and economic structures in the South are overflowing with millions looking for opportunities for a better social and political niche. This has dramatic impacts on political institutions, cultural practices, solidarity systems, forms of governance, and labour markets. Tade Aina (this volume) and Kwaku Osei-Hwedie and Arnon Bar-on (this volume) show that the combination of population growth and limited resources in Africa is one of the factors at the root of the development crisis in that continent. To a lesser extent, this is also true in countries the world over.

However, some transnational influences are positive. International pressure for minimum environmental standards, basic human rights, and minimum provision of essential services — such as those needed to provide immunization, nutrition, and literacy — are positive transnational influences. Nevertheless, the combined effects of globalization forces on developing countries are likely over the long term to weaken rather than strengthen the capacities of these countries to make independent policy decisions.

Although globalization brings about increased interdependence between countries at different stages of development, this process may make developing countries in the periphery more vulnerable. Andrés Pérez Baltodano (this volume) argues that globalization reduces the capacities of modern societies both to overcome contingencies and to provide citizens with a sense of "ontological security." This is particularly relevant to understanding the ways transnational influences are reshaping social policies in developing countries. In a globalized world, the state has less capacity to create social safety nets without either external assistance or drastic cost-saving measures. This is the case for many developing countries, where the welfare state has been traditionally weak or nonexistent and where there is no welfare-state institutional base to minimize the impacts of social-policy reforms induced from outside their borders.

The current drive to change the social-policy agenda is, in part, an effort to adapt policies on the assumption that economic growth would be staged and demographic growth would be slow and, in part, an effort to bring existing human and social capital up to the levels of economies and productive systems operating globally rather than locally. However, globalization is taking place in a world in which economic growth has been inequitable and demographic trends have been explosive. In this context, globalization has differential effects on the makeup of social policies, depending on the case and conditions of the affected countries and their status in the world economy. In this regard, Luis Ratinoff (this volume) argues that the vulnerability created by globalization is not the same for all societies. For developing countries, it is likely to be even harder, as they need to deal with previously existing conditions of dependence, scarcity of resources, and lack of control over policy decisions and instruments. However, even if globalization makes states more vulnerable and dependent on external factors, the state is institutionally in most cases still the only instrument for mediating the impacts of this process on societies.

One of the public-policy challenges emerging with globalization is thus to make the state more effective and efficient in its role as mediator of transnational forces and still effectively promote social and human development. Another no less critical challenge is to make private interest into a positive force in social change. Globalization may provide access to new resources of capital, technology, knowledge, and people, but even in such circumstances, transnational influences represent quite different opportunities, depending on the case, and may lead to very different social-policy systems.

## The meaning of social-policy reform

Some of the chapters in this book have shown that the notion of social-policy reform conveys different meanings in different settings to different actors. Although policies that address social development and basic needs have been in place in various forms in the modern state, the view that these policies are part of an interrelated public-policy system is relatively recent. The need to look at public policies from an integrated perspective is partly a need to minimize the predominance of economic policies in setting development goals. In part, it is also the result of predicating as a universal model the pattern of state–civil-society interactions born out in industrialized, developed countries.

In light of this, social-policy reform today has at least two predominant meanings. On the one hand, the notion of social-policy reform serves as a value framework and orientation regarding the governance of the systems responsible for equity and social justice. On the other hand, social-policy reform is seen as an ongoing process of change in a number of public policies and programs, with a view to readapting, changing, or eliminating them through efficient and effective technical solutions. According to the former view, social-policy reform is a value orientation guiding public-policy decisions concerning allocation of resources. According to the latter, it is a *de facto*

readaptation of selective public policies to a new pattern of sociopolitical organization no longer based on the welfare-state model; the concern is now with
the introduction of corrective measures in a governance system to change the
design, objectives, or forms of delivery of social-policy programs, seeking
greater efficiency and a closer and more effective response to the problems of
vulnerable groups. Often, these two meanings complement each other and set
the profile and the direction of various approaches to public-policy reform.

Common to most approaches to social-policy reform in the West in the
1980s and 1990s is the rejection of the welfare-state model. The classic port-
folio of social-support systems has changed, including the principle of univer-
sality, a central-government management system, free-access to basic services,
and state-driven provision of key services such as education, basic health care,
and social security. This is happening despite the differences in the modalities
and significance of the welfare-state model from country to country and
between developed and developing countries (Lynn 1992; Esping-Andersen
1994; Muller and Wright 1994). In most of the developing countries, the clas-
sical welfare-state model never materialized to the extent that it did in the
North. In other countries, as in postcolonial Africa, where it was more a
theoretical-political construct than a feasible policy option, the welfare state
was never fully present. In other regions, such as in Latin America, some countries enjoy advanced welfare-state models. Despite this diversity, policy reform
has acquired fundamental importance in the management of public-policy systems. The notion of social-policy reform thus provides a conceptual and analytical framework for examining the relationships between different
approaches to dealing with the management and redistribution of social and
economic capital.

At this point, it is useful to distinguish between the concepts of social-
policy reform and social reform. Social policies are instrumental to social
reform, which is a broader process. Social reform is defined by international
agencies, such as the Inter-American Development Bank (IADB) and the United
Nations Development Programme (UNDP), as the policies, specific instruments, and processes to incorporate all sectors of the society into the process
of growth in a context of better welfare (BID–PNUD 1993). In this regard, policies and policy instruments to achieve a more equitable distribution of the benefits of economic growth, the progressive incorporation into society of
excluded sectors, and the adequacy of the supply of and demand for goods and
services for the satisfaction of basic needs and for human development are key
components of social reform.

Social reform involves the promotion of equity through a broad system
of public policies, approaches, institutions, and services to provide opportunities for all. Social-policy reform is one means to doing this more efficiently and
effectively. In this sense, social reform and social-policy reform are more than

just actions taken for the sake of the poor or just the means to transfer resources to alleviate social problems (Iglesias 1993). Both are ways to reach a broader goal: to make society intrinsically more equitable and just. If this is accepted as a point of departure in conceptualizing social-policy reforms, it becomes of great importance to determine the type of society pursued by a reform process and the types of policy put in place to achieve it. What should the societal aim guiding the agenda of social reform be? This is the main question.

Social-reform processes with single-issue agendas — such as modernization, fiscal balance, improved quality of life in urban centres, the environment, creation of productive employment, or improved quality of labour — are often insufficient (Emmerij 1993a), and they are unlikely to lead to sustainable change. Some critics would even argue that single-issue policy reforms currently implemented, for example, in economics, the environment, education, and health are not conducive to social reform over the long term but respond to short-term political objectives. In this regard, the integration of social-policy reform plays a critical role.

## Framework and dimensions of social-policy reform

In light of the above, the current notion of social-policy reform must be understood broadly as the process of global trends changing the parameters of the welfare state in its various versions in both developed and developing societies through sectoral public-policy approaches and specific governance measures, such as targeting, decentralization, fees for service, and privatization. This view of social-policy reform, however, must be placed within the framework of the values it promotes and the various dimensions of its implementation.

### A value framework

The current approaches to social-policy reform are oriented to a large extent by the goals of neoliberalism. This, in turn, rests on a value system that emphasizes reliance on the market's capacity to stimulate higher levels of performance in public-investment decisions and in the provision of social services.

A central argument for this approach is that by relying on market mechanisms for the satisfaction of basic needs and for the allocation of resources governments can simultaneously achieve several desirable objectives. First, the market allows a government to attain intrinsic social benefits from the free competition between the supply of and demand for social services. The underlying assumption is that the market naturally selects the best, the cheapest, or the most convenient service. Second, the market is the easiest way to mobilize available resources from profit and nonprofit organizations. Implicit is the view that under other circumstances these resources would not be channeled to meet social goals or to the target groups. Third, the market leads to the development of independent citizens with a capacity to make choices based on individual preference. The assumption here is that the market promotes the free consumption of social-sector services and avoids clientelism, dependence on state provision, and, ultimately, waste.

The utopianism of globalization rests on the belief that open markets will eventually destabilize the oppressive conditions causing poverty and exclusion. In practice, however, this view of the role of the market is misleading. Although trade serves as an avenue for innovation, one needs to distinguish between the ideal of the free exchange of goods and services and the actual existence of markets open to all population sectors. Open markets in developing countries are more a project than a reality. The utopianism of globalization rests on the view that markets are open, at least in principle, to all members of society, with access limited only by taste, preference, or power to consume. In practice, in developing societies, one finds small, local, fragmented markets. It would be a mistake to consider the free flow of goods and services across borders as indicative of markets open to all social sectors for it may indicate only the circulation of merchandise among preexisting markets.

The overall rationale for this thinking is based on a complex set of ideas about what makes a modern society work effectively and efficiently. For example, it is assumed to be a society in which political concerns favour social justice, one in which the majority of the population, particularly the poor, do not suffer most of the impact of fiscal overexpenditure caused by poorly functioning systems of social-service provision (MacKintosh 1995). In this scenario, the answer is to reduce costs by reducing expensive state bureaucracies and by relying on a mechanism — the market — to secure an unbiased minimum balance. A related view is that, in an increasingly global environment, facilitating long-term economic and social recovery is not just an internal, national responsibility. Countries must honour their debt and show efficiency in public management to avoid alienating the international financial community and the private sector, both with resources that are indispensable. A complementary view is that if abuse and waste are to be avoided, access to services may no longer be an inherent personal right. Rather, the community and the individual must take responsibility for their own welfare. This can be achieved in different ways: through direct participation, fees for service, or taking actions to avoid poverty becoming a way of life and therefore a permanent state of welfare dependence. These carrot-and-stick arguments are believed to make public-system reforms a vehicle for the reduction in social spending and a way to demonstrate to investors that governments are reliable and have control over public expenditures (Moore and Robinson 1994).

Therefore, according to the value system underlying the current approach, social-policy reform rests on three related conditions: that the state does not interfere in the allocation and management of resources for social spending; that it spends its resources effectively and efficiently; and that various of society's organizations are given opportunities to act and participate. If these conditions are met, then it is believed that the problems of social and human development would receive a better response than with older public-policy solutions. In practice, this social-engineering logic explains many reform attempts implemented in Asia, in Latin America, and, to a lesser extent, in Africa. Examples can be found of reforms involving the decentralization of educational spending and services. Some experiences with the process of decentralizing education from state to regional, provincial, or municipal governments in countries as distinct as Chile, Ghana, and the Philippines were driven by efficiency considerations but justified on the expectation that such moves would help to address the key problems of access to and quality of education. The assumption was that by having the main actors involved in the educational process — providers, users, and beneficiaries, including the private business sector — better arrangements would be found to cover existing demand, to monitor quality more closely, and to evaluate progress. In practice, however, evidence shows increasingly that this happens only rarely and that, to a large extent, it is because the capacity to undertake these tasks is not present (Samoff 1995). Attempts have also been made to privatize social-security systems (Guhan 1994; Paul and Paul 1995; Zhang and Zhang 1995; Mesa-Lago 1996). One of the underlying assumptions of neoliberal social-policy reform is that if pension funds are privatized, they will compete to give the best service, citizens will get directly involved in the administration of their own pension retirement plans — thus taking better care of their own future — and national systems will be determined independently of pressures from particular clients. However, experience in this area has been mixed, and in most cases it is still too early to assess the longer-term consequences of such changes.

However, this set of values, adopted by many governments, raises strong reactions among sectors of civil society, in particular the community of non-governmental organizations (NGOs), which holds that social justice should be the driving force behind government actions. These opposite views often present a serious dilemma in determining the rights and wrongs of today's public-policy changes. Although some voices argue that the collective values of social responsibility expressed in the welfare-state model should not be forgotten and that current social-policy reforms are producing more marginalization and exclusion (Lusting 1994; Stahl 1996), when it comes to balancing resources and demands, there are no clear-cut operational-policy options to be implemented at a national scale. A number of factors contribute to this dilemma. First, there is the power and influence of those promoting the market as a social-provision regulator. Second, it is so by default: none of the alternative proposals can fully satisfy the efficiency requirements proposed in the neoliberal development paradigm. Third, objective financial and political problems weigh against the viability of the welfare-state model in places where it has been operating. Fourth, the traditional alternative, the "real" socialist system, no longer appears to be an alternative.

Understanding the values shaping current social-policy reform also provides a useful framework to situate the role of the political and technocratic elites in international organizations and in governments promoting policy reforms, as well as the role of civil society. To a large extent, the largest part of the populations affected by such reforms is often marginal to the debate or to the actual choices made to address the problems in social services and social-security systems, except for standard electoral political participation. In most developing countries, the majority of the population remains marginal to the management and evaluation of the national social-service system. This is the case despite noticeable advances during the last three decades, including advances in educational coverage, community health services, and the expansion of social-security systems (UNDP 1996). At the same time, it is common to find more and more people depending heavily on informal safety nets, relying on themselves or on informal systems for social services (Campbell 1993). This is happening even more in countries where social protection is not fully developed and where large sectors are not involved at all in formally sharing social benefits. This is, in part, because these population sectors have never been covered under any kind of welfare system and, in part, because they continue to rely heavily on traditional social safety nets operating parallel to any public system.

Evidence shows that social-policy reform in the 1980s and 1990s has not directly involved the larger population sectors most affected by these policy changes. There are also indications that in many cases, processes of consultation have been primarily political exercises. Experiences to date show that the neoliberal values guiding the reform process are producing social exclusion at a time when the visibility of the poor, their political power at the ballots, and their capacity for social protest are greater than before (Bessis 1995). The political practices surrounding policy changes continue to be unaccountable; corruption in the public administration remains a persistent problem; and the dominant attitude of some elite groups toward the existing inequity is indifference.

As the debate regarding the value system behind social-policy reform is complex, one may prefer to look at the empirical dimensions of the processes of social-policy reform. Several questions can be raised. Should efficiency be the predominant goal of public-policy reforms? Are the market and competition improving the quality, quantity, and relevance of social services? Is the market capable of serving as a vehicle to respond to basic needs with less waste and greater effectiveness? Are the values of competition and self-reliance conducive to a citizen's ethos that is more sensitive to equity and sustainable development? Is it realistic to rely on individuals' and communities' capacities to improve social-service provision, even when resources are limited? Empirical studies to respond to these questions are difficult to find but may help in identifying policy options and analyzing the practical implications of the values underlying current social-policy reforms. From a research perspective, there is a need, for example, to follow up on the implementation of sector-specific reform processes and the extent to which they may be exacerbating existing contradictions between pervading poverty, calls for less public involvement in social-service provision, and the prevalence of political and economic practices insensitive to growing social needs.

## Social-policy reform as an ongoing process

Although social-policy reform is a fact in many countries, the adoption of this agenda is not an exclusive outcome of recent economic pressures to deal with decreasing fiscal resources, nor the sole outcome of growing basic-needs demands. The shifts in existing social-policy paradigms in most countries reflect a more complex combination of factors that has evolved over time. In addition to economic and social pressures, we are witnessing the combined effect of demographic, technological, cultural, and political changes that have radically transformed the context in which the welfare-state model emerged after World War II.

Changes in population growth in developing countries, in the age structure of their populations, and in their epidemiological profile, coupled with increasing urbanization, democratization, massive rural–urban migration, growing complexity of public bureaucracies, and persistent social and economic inequities, have all eroded the conditions permitting the existence of the welfare state. In developing regions with a relatively long state tradition, such as Latin America, the implementation of the welfare-state model advanced considerably in some countries. In Argentina, Chile, and Uruguay, for example, the model was implemented through particularistic mechanisms for the integration of social groups. In countries such as these, public officials, unions, selected artisanal groups, the military, or some sectors of the urban work force had social services available to them through different institutional regimes for public education, health care, social security, and pensions. Retirement and pension plans, for example, were different for workers and public servants. Today, however, this kind of "particularistic" approach is no longer feasible. Social structures have changed in spatial, sectoral, and occupational terms in the last 50 years, and there are competing demands for limited resources. This evolution of development in social-protection systems gives fertile ground for national and transnational pressures to reform public-policy systems. The need for reform, a product of the evolution of social-support mechanisms typical of postwar welfare systems, adds an important dimension to the assessment of the public-policy changes occurring in many countries today.

Within this perspective, social-policy reform results from a number of policy and program decisions involving various modalities of financing, managing, or delivering services in education, health, social infrastructure, shelter, social security, and welfare programs tailored to particular groups in need. In many cases, these changes are not introduced or debated in the framework of a formal approach to reform but are part of regular government operations or decisions made as a part of a larger public-policy package, with little public debate. In other cases, these types of change are debated and even decided by referendum but often taken in isolation from the broader public-policy realm. In yet other cases, these changes are not targeted directly but introduced as part and parcel of macroeconomic policy changes, such as in several countries in Africa during the last 20 years (Gruat 1990; Ponte 1994; Ardington and Lund 1995).

Experiences with decentralization of educational and health services, the privatization of social-security systems, and the targeting of antipoverty programs are as varied as the countries where these forms of social provision have been implemented. Chile, China, Ghana, and Viet Nam provide common as well as quite different lessons (IDRC 1996; Osteria 1996; Konate 1997). In countries where social-policy reform results from the evolution of existing social-protection systems, the social-policy agenda is driven by a broad combination of factors, including public demands, political expediency, internal pressures from interest groups, international loan conditions, or simply the need to update existing social-protection systems. Often, the evolutionary change of social-protection systems leads to changes that involve a range of programs at different stages of implementation. These changes are often mediated by the capacity of the civil society to move toward more advanced and mature stages of social-protection policy. Brazil, Chile, and Colombia and some of the "tigers" in Southeast Asia are examples of countries where this process has been fairly smooth. In Chile, though, many of the major changes to national social policies began under political dictatorship, with political parties, unions, and other popular organizations under government control, thus making civil-society dissent almost impossible. This casts doubt on the replicability of the "Chilean miracle." In some countries, however, the population resisted drastic changes in social-policy systems, even as part of a routine process of improving those that already existed. In Bolivia, Uruguay, and Venezuela, for example, the reform of the pension system was rejected or opposed by the population and the unions. Similar examples of this are found in Kenya and Zimbabwe.

Even if the natural evolution of social-policy systems is accepted as a dimension of public-policy reform, there is still a growing feeling that in today's global circumstances, we suffer a profound lack of knowledge about what is really going on. This is not only something felt in civil society. Development banks are inquiring about the real impacts of loans supporting the reform of social policies or the implementation of social programs following the new parameters, especially those for which one can cite no precedents or formal and representative assessments of success. Vast amounts of money are spent with uncertainty about the impacts of these investments. We have no clear response to questions such as the following: Who benefits and loses with these changes? What are the enduring measurable outcomes? What are and how can one address the expected and unexpected impacts? What is lacking is the systematic assessment of the expected and unexpected results of the new policy approaches in the short and long term. In other words, we lack extrinsic evaluations. At the same time, it is important to highlight that evaluations of social programs in terms of their objectives — intrinsic evaluations — are not scarce.

THE EFFICIENCY DIMENSION — Efficiency is a central goal of the neoliberal proposal for social-policy reform and an expression of the value system promoting it; this dimension requires special attention (Schelager 1995). The "efficiency dimension" in social-policy reform responds to an instrumental view of social policies vis-à-vis economic policies. Social-policy reform in this framework is a means to establishing a fiscally balanced, globally competitive economy with low inflation, low unemployment, and a minimum of well-functioning and cost-effective mechanisms for social protection. Accordingly, two criteria are used to assess social-policy performance: low cost and high potential for capital gains. If at any point the social-policy system contravenes these criteria, social policies need to be changed.

In this framework, social-policy reform is an instrument to reinject efficiency into the economy through a variety of mechanisms aimed to change the management and governance of social-sector systems and the services they provide. In industrialized countries, the argument is as follows (OECD 1997, p.6): existing social policies were designed for a period

> when there was full employment, when families were stable, and where the most pressing social concern was to ensure that the elderly could benefit from the fruits of economic growth by using taxes to transfer income to them from the working-age population.

This is no longer the case. The family and the labour market as a base for the welfare state have suffered drastic changes. The phenomenon of jobless growth is critical to any government's capacity to maintain systems of reasonable social protection while keeping costs low and capital accumulation high. The conclusion is that existing social policies are essentially inefficient: it costs too much to deliver them; they do not produce the quality of outcome required by the economy; they often involve waste as they are insufficiently fine-tuned to help those most in need; and in an environment driven by market mechanisms, social services should not be protected from the dynamic of supply and demand. Accordingly, steps must be taken to lower costs and increase efficiency.

In most attempts to reform social-policy systems, the efficiency dimension is a driving force. Among the telling examples are the reforms of pension systems in Latin America (Uthoff 1995; Mesa-Lago 1996; Siri 1996; Osorio and Ramirez 1997); the reform of the social-security system in China (Zhang and Zhang 1995); and the reforms of the health system and social safety net in South Africa (Gruat 1990; Bhorat 1995; Pillay and Bond 1995). A frequently encountered view is that economic efficiency and social welfare are somehow opposite forces. It has taken several years of attempting structural-adjustment measures with dubious outcomes for governments and for international financial institutions (IFIs) to realize that adding a "human face" to reform, making the reform processes more participatory, or strengthening social safety nets to enhance human capital are not detrimental to the capacity of economies to adjust or of societies to grow (Blank 1993). We have, however, still a long way to go. Governments and IFIs need to realize that making only their discourse more sensitive to social- and human-development goals is not enough; it is not enough if the policy measures implemented change only in the letter.

On the positive side, concern with the efficiency dimension has brought about new ways of looking at both the direction and the content of social policies, particularly in considering education, health, and social-security options. Pressure to make these systems more efficient has forced a range of actors from government and from civil society, particularly the private sector, to reconsider their roles in policy implementation and service delivery and define more focused expectations of these systems.

THE TECHNICAL DIMENSION — The "technical dimension" of public policy takes at times a central role in shaping both the "what" and the "how" of social-policy reform. Because of the sensitive nature of social policies, both politically and in terms of social justice, often attention is mainly directed to the policy process. This tends to focus the debate on the technical value of policy blueprints, modeling exercises, formal political proposals, and the mechanics for coordinating public consultations and identifying social demands.

When reform processes are approached from this angle, often concerns are focused on the most appropriate and technically efficient ways to provide education, basic health services, or social security; the most convenient mix of roles of individuals, institutions, communities, the market, and the state for the provision of these services; and the best models of programs to be replicated. This leads to a concentration on the technical management of proposals that range from state-dominant schemes to community-based arrangements, from highly regulated scenarios to free-market-oriented provision of services, or from social promotion to profit-oriented arrangements. Although voices of opposition may always exist, what predominates is the opinion and evidence of a technical elite, who recognize no clear articulation of alternative options other than what "has been proven" or what "is based on hard scientific evidence." This can give the impression that there is no technically suitable alternative to a given policy option.

Given the relatively elitist character of this dimension, the extent to which the affected populations are involved in the process of policy innovation and in the identification of concrete benefits of policy changes is a critical issue. The assumption is that some technical modalities affecting the management of policies or programs, or both, allow us to better address the issues of equity, equality, and social justice. Still, however, the degree to which the technical strength of policy proposals is decisive is unclear. Empirical evidence concerning the contribution of technical solutions to success is insufficient and highly debatable.

IN SUM — The efficiency and technical dimensions of social-policy reform are not mutually exclusive. They are present to some degree in any process of social-policy reform. As such, they affect policy proposals, processes of implementation, evaluations, and policy recommendations. The differential weight of these dimensions contributes to making the understanding of the concept and the practice of social-policy reform difficult. It also contributes to making the analysis and assessment of outcomes and impacts arduous. We have therefore still a long way to go in understanding the effects of policy reforms on social and human development. Further research is required to answer questions such as the following: What type of emphasis in the reform of social policies is most suitable for reaching higher social development? What are the alternatives to the predominant neoliberal approach to public-policy reform and the value system it entails? Can the current social-policy approaches create the capacities to learn and participate required for social and human development in the next century? Although it is difficult to find responses to these questions, they are urgently needed because long-term development possibilities continue to be compromised by ongoing policy changes affecting the provision of social services. A discussion of risks and opportunities brought about by the process of reform will further underline the need to assess the effects of these policy changes.

## Risks and opportunities

If in a globalized world, the longer-term development goals are higher levels of social and human development, social-policy reform is a critical public-policy issue. This requires giving up the view that development is mostly the result of financial resources, technical capacities, good intentions, and dynamic national or international engines of innovation and progress. Part of the yet-undefined "new development paradigm" (Broad and Foster 1992) that seems to underlie current-reform approaches implies not only giving, in principle, a human face to development but also making it, in practice, a process of building decision-making capacities that remain after the development agents move on.

Achieving this in a framework of social-policy reform implies weighing the risks and opportunities that reform processes entail. It means examining how and with what degree of success social-policy reforms promote new value systems, generate new and more effective institutional arrangements, and develop more effective means to enhancing social participation, particularly at local levels.

## Who wins and who loses with the new value orientations?

As argued throughout this book, the process of social-policy reform is an opportunity for carrying out more than just a series of technical changes of a given public-policy system. It is also an opportunity to change social-development values and perceptions, particularly in terms of the prevailing social ethos and people's individual values.

Approaches to social-policy reform today take neoliberal social values as given. This is evident in the case of Latin American countries after the period of military regimes. Although many of these countries went into a process of redemocratization and reform of their public-policy systems, including their social-sector policies, the predominant view of desirable change has been driven by neoliberal economic ideology (Petras 1997). Neoliberal values often represent different value options to those societies that have gone through a mix of collective, socialist, and traditional value systems as alternatives to the colonial or postwar liberalism in social-service provision. In such contexts, social-policy reform can become an opportunity to change the values orienting the social role of the state and the individual, promote new ways to distribute individual and public responsibilities, create new attitudes, including the view that market institutions and open competition are the most effective means to achieve greater private and public accountability. This includes reformed pension systems based on personal savings accounts and the creation of new attitudes in parents associations and consumer groups organized to monitor educational processes or the production of reliable goods and services. It is also important to recognize that such policy reforms exacerbate the unexpected consequences of neoliberal social values. These can translate into persistent conditions of poverty, a lack of commitment to the poor, financial speculation, proliferation of underground economies, and weakened traditional social safety nets. These traditional social safety nets become vulnerable to market fluctuations or to global trends and incertitude. How to take advantage of the opportunities and how to face these risks are questions yet to be addressed.

Experiences across regions show that social-policy reforms tend to rest on and promote at least three neoliberal values. First, they promote the value of individual decision-making, rather than reliance on collective decisions. A desirable individual feature vis-à-vis the provision of social services is thought to be one of an educated consumer. The assumption is that if people make the right individual decision in the social-goods market, a selection will be made of the services that are most cost-effective and of the best quality. However, experience with the privatization of higher education in Chile showed that such measures can reduce individual decision-making and lower the quality of service (Espinola 1991; Tedesco 1991). Experience indicates that individual selection processes are not necessarily smooth and that what is more likely to emerge is an array of poor-quality services to serve primarily the poorer sectors of the population. Second, these social-policy reforms promote personal–private, rather than state–public, responsibility, as the central motivation to organize and provide social services. Based on the principle that individual decision-making is key, personal responsibility is perceived to go hand in hand with the right to chose. Relying on the state for the provision of social services not only takes away from the individual the opportunity to choose but also removes from the social-services system itself the incentive to do better. Additionally, it is assumed that state provisioning of social services tends to build a fertile ground for abuse on the part of users and for poor quality on the part of providers.

Third, these social-policy reforms promote participation as a means to generate citizen involvement in the process of public-policy decision-making, implementation, and evaluation. At one end, this forces traditional decision-making centres to be open to public scrutiny. At the other end, it universalizes the perception that popular participation and public consultation are effective mechanisms for policy change, though in practice empirical evidence shows that this is the case in only very few social settings. More often government bureaucracies are incapable of managing the diversity of consultation processes, and information on success is anecdotal (Malloy 1991).

These value orientations, predominant in public policy-making today, are not new. In one form or another they have been at the core of Western development discourse since World War II, through the advocacy-for-democracy and the peace movements of the 1960s, the market-oriented economic development stream of the 1970s and 1980s, and the discourse of the 1990s on sustainable and human development. However, in at least two ways these value orientations show a novel twist. One is their predominance in the visions of a wide range of international organizations and conventions for which they have become part and parcel of the type of society they promote. The other is the strong reaction these values generate among a mix of groups, ranging from community-based organizations to religious and fundamentalist groups that are devoted to maintaining traditional structures and practices that may be incompatible with current social-policy reform. Although these influences can play determining roles in shaping social-policy reforms, it is unclear whether they can articulate social-policy models as true alternatives to the neoliberal social-policy reform. Global trends may prove stronger than expected in shaping social-policy reforms at national levels.

Values do not exist in a vacuum. They affect and are affected by the relations of correspondence and contradiction that at different times reflect particular forms of social ethos and social, economic, and political conditions determining the development of a given society. These are key factors in the implementation of the neoliberal agenda of individual decision-making, personal responsibility, and citizen participation in many developing countries. In many instances, the neoliberal agenda is based on values that make no sense or represent no advantage to those most affected by the policy changes — the poor. Persistent unemployment, lack of opportunity, financial mismanagement, and corruption of public administrations, among other factors, create environments that easily become obstacles to the development of individual initiative, citizens' commitment to finding solutions to local problems, and even their willingness to accept greater responsibility. Most eroding are factors of abject poverty, unemployment, inequity, and corruption of the institutional and legal systems, which contribute to an atmosphere of total absence of social cohesion (Bessis 1995). This raises several questions in the analysis of the values underlying social-policy reforms: What are the preconditions for the successful adoption of the values implicit in social-policy reforms? Who shares the new values promoted by these reforms? Who is in a position within the social structure to take advantage of them? How can policy changes incorporate these types of consideration?

Processes of reform go beyond particular technical considerations, specific sectors, or individual national or transnational pressures. Reforms need to be designed and planned in the context of broader goals for social development. Thus, for example, unless people make a major effort to change institutional practices — particularly in political and judicial circles — and introduce effective mechanisms for public accountability, the new values promoted by neoliberal reforms can easily degenerate into an opportunity for the privileged, rather than the poor. Experiences in this regard are multiple. Private financial groups, for example, have found the call for private-individual pension programs extremely encouraging, as they represent a highly profitable business. The opening up of the education market has brought about the proliferation of worthless education and training programs. And the privatization of health has institutionalized two-tier health-care systems. In most cases, these experiences show that individual decisions, personal responsibility, and citizen involvement make sense only if the process of policy change is open; the relevant information is available for decision-making; politicians and profit-oriented organizations are responsible and accountable; and space is given for people to have a say in public policy. Otherwise, the focus on reform becomes the cynical rhetoric of people and institutions with too much to win and too little to lose.

Practical questions need to be addressed. At one level, we need to know what other values can complement and balance the assumptions of the reform approach and what kind of institutional arrangements are needed to make the realization of these values feasible. At another level, a series of questions can be raised related to social cohesion, which is central to the success of any change in the public-policy system.

## Policy reforms: social cohesion or "equitable" exclusion?

Social cohesion is not just a value but a fact that is observable with social and economic indicators of equity and participation. In principle, social cohesion is the base of sustainable development. In practice, it is the glue keeping economically different sectors of society together in circumstances of rapid change. It is of great importance to understand the impacts on social cohesion of the new social-policy reforms. How, for example, can competition and individual decision-making strengthen or undermine social cohesion? Are societies traditionally oriented by values other than the neoliberal better able to maintain their mechanisms of social cohesion once reforms are introduced? How is social cohesion affected by neoliberal values at the level of individual behaviour, the family, and the community? Are these reforms building new forms of social cohesion?

Responses to these questions are difficult. However, current trends in social-policy reform seem to make one issue clear. In a global environment, it is no longer possible to idealize the type of social cohesion promoted by the welfare-state model in most developing countries or in traditional, non-Western societies. Evidence cannot be ignored that the welfare-state model has advanced in a fragmented way and that only upper- and middle-class and selected popular groups have enjoyed real benefits (Lynn 1992; Esping-Andersen 1994; Muller and Wright 1994). The welfare-state model matured only in a few developing societies, such as Argentina, Chile, and Uruguay. Most cases, however, show a series of common features: the rural and the poorest populations remained marginal in terms of access to key services provided by the welfare system; political expediency led to more attention being placed on coverage than on quality; the best services often went to the urban and most organized social groups; and systems were scarcely affordable. A typical outcome of these experiences in societies in which social policy was perceived to be a state responsibility was that individual and more collective social responsibilities were ignored. In many cases, statements like "it is not my responsibility, but the responsibility of the state" or "this is not my money but public resources" epitomize justifications for disregarding personal involvement in public or community issues or for demanding a more careful management of public funds. The advocates of neoliberal reforms argue that the new value orientations may correct this kind of reasoning and behaviour as they promote more reliance on a "responsible citizen and informed consumer."

Global economic trends, a widespread economic crisis, and the global restructuring of labour markets have blurred the boundaries between social classes at the middle level and have deepened the polarization at the extremes of the social spectrum. The division between those with and those without opportunities not only persists but is even more profound than before. This is evident among the youth of lower socioeconomic strata and in countries where the middle class was traditionally a driving economic force. One of the consequences of this phenomenon is a widespread decline in solidarity values as reflected in the crisis of key social institutions, including the traditional family. Rates of family breakdown, one-parent families, and abandoned children have increased in developed and developing countries, bringing additional pressures on social-protection systems where they exist. Demographically, the proportions of socially and economically excluded populations and, in some societies, the aging economically active populations are likely to increase the burden on social-security systems in the years to come, to the point that public-support systems in their current form will be unfeasible. To expect the political pressure of transnational social- and human-development agendas or the market to turn this around is unrealistic at best. Market mechanisms are led by profit maximization and not by solidarity or principles of social equity, and international-solidarity agendas are often without the resources to implement corrective measures.

A final critical implication of the current trends in social-policy reform and their values is in the area of social equity. Values implicit in the reforms encourage the marginal, the excluded, and the poor to take steps to mobilize their individual and community capacities to achieve greater equity. However, not much is said about the responsibility of the other sectors of society. There are few indications, for example, of the extent to which the new values are assumed by the members of the elites or the extent to which they inspire new actions from elites and privileged groups to promote more equity. Similarly, no clear cases with any significant results are to be found of reform processes in which local, dominant elites have demanded better income distribution or more affirmative action on social policies. Those few examples that can be found show quite the contrary. The latest figures for developing countries show that income distribution has improved very little in a few countries and that it has not improved at all or even worsened in the majority (World Bank 1995c, 1996).

The lack of positive results, however, is not simply an issue of values per se. The globalization of the economy and the processes of regional integration are forcing capital to go elsewhere for profit opportunities. In this context, the reform perspective may be seen as an attempt to counterbalance some of the effects of globalization, as it argues for making improvements in the quality of social services and for making labour costs more competitive. In fact, this is one of the reasons cited to reform retirement, social-security, and pension-plan systems in many countries. The assumption is that if this is done, developing countries will be in a better position to compete and less vulnerable to global fluctuations. And, it is premised that, from an equity standpoint, the new value orientations may help to promote new opportunities for employment, income, and equity. However, these new values also risk contributing even further to the disregard for equitable income distribution and mechanisms to create opportunities for social cohesion and solidarity, for example.

## Policy reforms: alleviating or hardening the poverty?

One of the most important implications of the new value orientation is a progressive reconceptualization of what is needed to alleviate poverty. In some cases, this has led to the design and implementation of poverty-alleviation programs as part and parcel of broader reform processes. However, the impact of these programs on poverty levels is unclear. In part, this could be the result of problems in the design and implementation of these programs. In part, it could be that the notion of programs targeted to alleviate poverty as a means to create social development is in itself flawed.

Experiences with poverty-alleviation programs based on a transfer-oriented approach, whereby the goods and services required for subsistence are delivered to the poor directly, show mixed results. Often, a direct-transfer approach becomes less effective over time, as the benefits tend to dissipate in higher prices paid for services. Maintaining such programs is often beyond the fiscal capacities of virtually any developing country. In part, this is because of limited resources; it is impossible to adopt more differentiated approaches to enable the poor to decide on their own consumption patterns, based on their priorities and defined by their own circumstances and cultures.

Although central to the neoliberal reform ideology, most direct-service delivery poverty-alleviation programs ignore a central and potentially sustainable asset of the poor, their personal capacities. This is only partially related to education in the formal sense. Trained or otherwise, the income of the poor often depends on the products of life learning and the value of the services they can sell in the market based on the assets they have. In this regard, poverty in a market-driven society is to an extent a problem of the low quality of assets the poor can sell in the job market, low volume of market sales of these assets, or of low market prices.

Experiences show that even within the context of neoliberal reforms, programs to alleviate poverty often fail to increase these assets. To do so, poverty-focused approaches to social-policy reform would need to include measures to reach one or more of the following targets:

- Increase the quality of assets of the poor, including but not limited to relevant education and training;

- Increase the volume of their market sales, by generating a meaningful range of employment opportunities, including those in the informal sector;

- Increase the prices of the services they sell, by increasing productivity through upgrading the quality of labour, expanding the range of complementary support services available to the poor and the community; and

- Introduce productivity-enhancing technical change (Adelman 1986).

Whether or not these are real options, the issue is that unless capacities are built among the poor and unless ethical and social practices are rooted in the local culture, attempts to change poverty and policy measures to alleviate poverty risk being ineffective.

Empirical findings on "hard" poverty in some Latin American countries, such as Chile, show that poverty persists despite assistance programs. To many, this is the manifestation of values and practices corresponding to a culture of poverty that is difficult to change. In this sense, it could be argued that the new value orientation promoted in neoliberal reforms is an opportunity to change negative values among the poor by promoting more initiative and less dependence. To many more, however, this evidence shows that the problems of poverty are deeper and that the new values promoted by reform are a perfect political justification to blame the poor for all that happens to them and introduce measures that favour a small proportion of the population.

## Policy reforms: "universal" coverage with "segmented" quality

Another implication of the values promoted in social-policy reforms is the issue of coverage and quality of social services. A key question is the extent to which greater reliance on individual choice and on market competition in practice improves coverage and quality of service.

Despite problems of accountability and quality in most developing countries, considerable progress has been made in social-service coverage, thanks to what was being done under the welfare-state model. However, reform trends rest heavily on the assumption that open competition can do better. It is assumed that competition on the supply side and freedom of choice on the demand side will improve these two key social-policy aspects. The example often used is the progress made in several countries in education and, in some cases, in health-care services (Emmerij 1993b; Dillinger 1994; Bardhan 1995). Introducing modalities of public–private competition for schools or hospitals is perceived as a social innovation that may bring better services and eradicate the clientelism that plagues traditional and welfare-state social-policy systems in most of the developing world. This is also proposed as an alternative in situations in which social policy and social-service systems have to be built from scratch.

However, competition positively affects coverage and quality only in selected cases. Coverage is improved, for example, only if more people have access to the market, which is not always the case for the poor. In societies in which conditions of inequity are deeply rooted, the benefit of expanded coverage to the poor through competition is often counterbalanced by a decrease in quality. In a competitive service market, the poor may in principle have greater access to services, but in practice this happens at the lower end of the quality spectrum. Among the most common challenges in monitoring this type of situation is the lack of information, whether about the performance of services (for example, schools, clinics, pension plans) or about differential benefits (for example, different medical-insurance plans, market value of diplomas or social-protection schemes). This affects not only the assessment of reforms in these aspects but also the capacity of consumers to chose the best options.

The underlying assumption of neoliberal social-policy reforms with regard to coverage and quality is that a service market is available with good choices and current information to allow the individual to make the right choice. However, countries where service provision has been liberalized show that market mechanisms may render good results in service provision only if at least three conditions are met: individuals can make informed choices; an ethos and regulatory system among producers exist to provide the best products and services; and institutional mechanisms are in place — including legal and administrative provisions — to ensure high quality and monitor the results. A critical question is whether these conditions exist in most developing countries. Because the answer is most likely to be no, the challenge is to develop them.

The idea of markets open to all social sectors implies many things. For markets to operate within an equitable framework, the first requirement is to have legal regulatory institutions and effective enforcement mechanisms supported by a judiciary with the material and qualified human resources to monitor quality and fair competition. In a globalized world economy, most developing countries find themselves at a disadvantage in this regard. Second, each population sector needs the conditions for and the capacity to access the market. In part, the idea of a global society suggests that this is a reality. In practice, however, large sectors of the population, particularly the poor, remain excluded. The third requirement is information about what the market offers and the comparative advantages of different goods and services. Although this is at the reach of most sectors of the population, the opening up of markets through information has not so far been accompanied by better income distribution or more productive employment; thus the illusion of a utopian society is created that in actual practice is out of the reach of the large majority.

It can be argued that the poorer the society, the more difficult it is to have effective market mechanisms. This is, in part, because information systems, democratic and participatory mechanisms, communication, and institutional and administrative procedures are also lacking. Competition for the provision of services, for example, can be promoted only on the assumption that a sufficient market capacity exists to offer a wide range of services and that some kind of system of rights for obtaining the benefits of such services is in place. This is not always the case in developing countries, where quality control of social services provided through market mechanisms is most probably highly speculative.

## New institutional arrangements: precipitated dismantling of the state?

The emphasis on reform is also changing the character of the institutional frameworks supporting social policies. New institutional arrangements result from the reduction of the state's role in social-service provision, decentralization of financial and administrative functions to local entities, and the move to greater reliance on the private sector, particularly the profit-making organizations and NGOs.

In many cases, these new arrangements overlap or enter into conflict with the institutional frameworks in place, which rest predominantly on the welfare-state model, such as in some countries in Latin America, or relying heavily on traditional structures at the community and family levels, such as in countries in Africa and in some countries in Asia. The new arrangements brought about by reforms appear in different contexts of state–civil-society relations and various degrees of maturity of market institutions. This makes the successful implementation of reforms more difficult. Thus, privatization of education and health care, for example, come to depend to a large extent on a capacity to develop a range of local-level institutions to provide the opportunities and a range of choices of good-quality education and health services accessible to those in need. Something similar happens with the establishment of new pension-plan systems that depend heavily on institutions to support and sustain them. Where this is not the case, the privatization of pension plans tend to put many people's life savings into the hands of private enterprise, without reliable mechanisms for control and for ensuring accountability.

Experiences with decentralization, privatization, and delegation of responsibilities for the delivery of key services to lower levels of government show that social-policy reforms are highly likely to render more positive results if at least some type of state institution remains in place, local-government institutions are strong, and market institutions dealing with social goods and services are regulated. However, this is more often the case in more developed societies, large urban areas, or sectors more integrated into the global economy than in developing countries.

A critical issue for assessment is the extent of the risks and opportunities across the whole spectrum of institutional situations accompanying social-policy reform. In terms of the impacts of reforms on the institutional arrangements supporting existing social-policy systems, for example, there is the risk of increasing the marginality and vulnerability of poorer sectors. Thus, given new pressures to reform, these processes may create conditions in which the poorest groups continue to exhibit little institutional capacity to have a say in the public-policy process. And, the reform processes may actually weaken the institutional structures in place for the poor. In some countries, this is the case with middle-class groups who have lost their political capacity to influence social demands. The reforms also risk promoting institutional arrangements that, in practice, increase the control of social assets by new local-level bureaucracies, making the services less accessible to those with less power. In such cases, the new policy-reform trends may decrease the vulnerability of the existing social-policy system to political clientelism, opportunism, or corruption but do so at the expense of excluding large sectors that could benefit from those services.

A key question is, therefore, about the type of mechanisms required to ensure that new institutional frameworks for social policies — decentralization and privatization, in particular — attain their objectives, with a clear understanding of who gains and who loses in the process. It is also important to understand better how policy-reform processes can ensure that stakeholders have the opportunity to assert their rights and that new institutional actors fulfill their responsibilities. To an important degree, addressing these issues needs to take into account the new ways resources are generated and allocated, the ways decisions are accounted for, and the ways local institutional capacities are developed to accomplish the objectives of reform.

The new institutional arrangements promoted by social-policy reform require new administrative procedures, financial modalities, information systems, mechanisms of accountability, and new forms of accessibility. How this happens and the outcomes depend to a large extent on the values guiding the reforms and on the range of new institutional procedures put in place to ensure the "success" of the new reform ideology. In this regard, it appears that the advocacy dimension of policy reform has until now led the discussion, with very little input from systematic evaluations of achievements and results.

However, if the institutional-arrangement side of reforms is neglected, there is the risk of frustrated expectations of decentralization and privatization.

Until now, there seemed to be considerable faith that key elements of the reform process would follow from the efficient market allocation of resources and a capacity to offer the best choice based on competition among providers. At the same time, however, very little attention is being given to the need to manage these new institutional arrangements. To many, the reliance on institutional market mechanisms to provide accessible and good-quality social services raises some major concerns. In some developing countries, the limited economic and administrative capacity of the state and the weak development of local governments make the regulation and monitoring of new institutional market mechanisms very difficult, particularly the monitoring of the intervening actors and the quality control. Even in a region with mature state structures, such as Latin America, experiments with decentralization and privatization are facing difficulties, such as the lack of institutional infrastructure to support the changes. One of the outcomes of this phenomenon is additional pressure on traditional organizations.

It helps to look at the pros and cons of centralized versus decentralized and profit- versus nonprofit-oriented social-service provision. These are two of the key modalities of social-service provision promoted in social-policy reforms that have direct institutional implications. To many, central-state management of social services was prematurely discarded. After the first push during the 1980s to find alternatives to state management of services, the incapacity of the state is becoming a self-fulfilling prophecy. After ongoing processes of reform, state agencies in many countries were dismantled because decentralization was advocated. State agencies suffered a devastating impact with the restructuring of public policies, in many cases losing their most valuable human resources and institutional and legal frameworks. There are several examples of this. A well-known case is the deterioration of public education in countries where delegation of responsibilities to municipalities and privatization were the norm. In some instances, these measures have created vicious circles for teachers who face decreasing salaries, increasing teaching hours, less attractive working conditions and protection, and a general degradation of the teaching profession. Ultimately, this impacts on the quality of education. The dismantling of educational systems by public policies directed to cut costs by reducing teachers' salaries and school resources and altering the institutional makeup of educational systems is beginning to provoke a serious crisis. If this happens, and the crisis takes root, it will take 20–30 years to find a solution (Rama 1993). In social policy, accumulation of gains and continuity of processes are essential. Periods of "no investment," when accumulation and continuity break down, are not as easy to recover from in social policy as in economic investment. Under these circumstances, little can be expected from decentralization if other public policies move in a different or opposite direction. Empirical evidence indicates that with very few exceptions, local entities are unprepared to carry out decentralized operations. This type of example is beginning to raise new questions about the need for central management to lead the processes of policy reform and ensure they are sustainable.

Something similar happens with privatization occurring without clear market rules. To operate efficiently, markets require mature regulatory institutions, which, especially in developing countries, do not emerge spontaneously. Several examples show that in the absence of an effective state and central government, privatization is unfeasible. This is partly attributable to private investors' need for guarantees over and above the power of peers, competitors, or community-based institutions, supports at the root of the principle of private enterprise and fair competition. Examples of developing countries that have achieved steady economic growth and social development show that central and strong government capacity to lead the reform process is essential. It is not by chance that some of the most successful examples of privatization in developing countries are in authoritarian states. This obviously raises a number of questions.

Even in an ideal situation, where the changes brought about by reform imply a move from state control to NGOs and traditional structures, the importance of centralized systems has not disappeared. The NGOs' record is in many respects good — on project administration, access to beneficiaries, development of innovative forms of program delivery, etc. — but there are also strong indications that NGOs depend very heavily on external sources of funding and are in most cases effective only at the microlevel. Traditional structures also have their difficulties. Although they may have a number of positive cultural, political, and economic characteristics at some levels, they are not always the ideal vehicle for providing social services. They are often subject to a variety of local pressures and discriminatory practices in terms of gender, race, ethnicity, and age.

If nothing else, this shows that the institutional frameworks of the new social-policy reforms carry several risks, including the unnecessary dismantling of central-state agencies, the precipitated endorsement of private-sector management, the questionable reliance on NGOs, and the involvement of traditional actors and structures with no major evaluation of their weaknesses and strengths. In this context, the major opportunities still appear to be in more effective, efficient, universal, and democratic mechanisms for social-service provision, with adequate mechanisms to assess their performance.

## Social participation: asking too much from people?

Current social-policy reforms promote institutional arrangements on the assumption that these new policy processes create the capacity among stakeholders to participate more directly in public policy and thereby enable people to have a greater say in decision-making. These new institutional settings are expected both to prevent clientelism and to overcome corporatism and thereby to better provide services and respond to broader demands. However, as an integral part of the political system or by default, in many developed and developing countries clientelism and corporatism are still the modalities by which the power structure — modern or traditional — responds to basic needs.

The corporatist approach to social participation is ultimately about the social division of interests among groups with differential power to decide who gets what and when (Saul 1995). In practice, this means that particular groups in society, owing to their position in the power structure and to the political mechanisms at their disposal, obtain greater benefits while others, at the bottom of the power scale, are more likely to face losses. By changing existing institutional arrangements, social-policy reforms are expected to provide alternatives and bring a balance that will improve coverage and access to social services through other mechanisms, including — at least, in principle — enhanced universal social participation in decentralized or privatized institutional delivery of social programs.

In the experience to date, a key question is how is this expectation being met? It is strongly indicated that in corporatist systems, people who are not integrated in some way or who are marginal to existing social safety nets are likely to continue having little institutional capacity to put pressure on new social-policy systems. At best, their success seems to be at the microlevel, with little or no chance of broader impact or replication. Examples are found in social safety nets and welfare programs tailored to women or youth groups or the extremely poor in traditional societies or those tailored to rural workers, the unemployed, or the elderly in modern systems. A risk often encountered by social-policy reforms is that of having effects opposite to any of those aimed for in principle. Rather than increasing access to and participation in services for the most vulnerable people, reform measures encapsulate and treat them as special cases and thereby enhance the power of groups already integrated into the social-protection system. Experiences so far in Latin America, at least, seem to show that this is what is happening (BID–PNUD 1993; IADB 1996). For example, a discussion is ongoing in some countries in that region about the fact that the leading "reformed" social-policy institutions (that is, private pension plans, decentralized private educational services, private health and insurance programs, etc.) may favour the participation of more, rather than fewer privileged groups. Seen in the broader social-development context of the region, this is not surprising. Traditionally, social innovations have followed the established allocation of privileges, benefits, and social assets. In that context, unless there are effective ways of monitoring by, for example, a central-state agency, it is highly probable that the well-to-do classes will be the winners with social innovations.

Another issue is the extent to which social participation in new institutional settings is an effective means for dealing with equity. This issue goes beyond the actual processes of reform and links with the value framework underlying the reform approach. The reform approach contains doses of unfounded expectations about the capacity of local institutions and social participation of popular, indigenous, or local groups in the design and implementation of public policies, particularly in corporatist societies (for the case of education, see Morales-Gomez and Torres 1990). What few proponents of the reform approach to public policies recognize directly is that participation is possible and effective only when knowledge is fully available about the problem to be solved, about alternative options and their risks, and about the decision-making and power mechanisms. This, however, is not always the case, particularly in corporatist societies, where by definition knowledge is an asset of the elite. In this context, quite often social participation turns out to be rhetorical and instrumental to the power structures, and in the end, the people expected to participate become apathetic.

Empirical evidence shows two kinds of apparently contradictory situations. On the one hand, open social protest has come to the surface with increasing frequency and unbelievable force. Recent events in Albania, Bolivia, Ecuador, Indonesia, Kenya, and Venezuela are telling examples. In Albania, people went into the streets to protest the massive bankruptcy of private pension plans. In Ecuador, people protested the macropolicies of structural adjustment. In Bolivia, Kenya, and Venezuela, public unrest was the combined effect of public-policy reforms, political corruption, and growing poverty. More recently, in Indonesia, as a result of structural-adjustment measures, food riots have begun to break out. News about all kinds of civic unrest resulting from privatization in countries around the world is not uncommon. On the other hand, people's participation in local activities remains elusive. People are not getting involved in the same dynamic way in the new policy consultations in some countries. The explanation for this could be negative past experiences, lack of opportunities, insufficient information, or simply the lack of political power and resources to make participation worthwhile. In practice, the reform approach has failed to encourage greater participation among those who are most likely to be excluded. Even in cases in which some degree of participation has been achieved, the issue remains one of making it effective. If there is one lesson learned, it is that the participation of target groups, beneficiaries, or users in a reform process does not by itself necessarily guarantee a solution to a social problem. An example is the participation of parents in schools boards. In well-educated sectors, the parents will doubtless be quite able to contribute, monitor, and evaluate the educational process. However, in the poorest neighbourhoods, the results may be nil, unless the process includes ways to help the parents with professional orientation and information. This type of example multiplies across social sectors and geographic areas (Bray 1996). The opportunity to have a say in public policy is valuable only if one is in a position to identify needs and articulate demands.

Without doubt, the modalities of participation brought about by the institutional arrangements of social-policy reform also risk strengthening the negative aspects of traditional power structures. Under certain circumstances, these same structures can become vehicles to create effective social safety nets, for example, if former social policies had limited significance or the state still has limited capacity. However, in such contexts, the new balance of power has to come from the involvement of new stakeholders and traditional leaders.

## Looking ahead

One of the points made in this book is that social-policy reform is in various ways an ongoing process in many societies. This reform movement has transnational features and tends to be based on the assumption that the reform of public policies is a feasible way to overcome the limitations of available financial, institutional, and human resources to deal with social development and the problems with the welfare-state model.

The social-policy reform processes taking place today in most developing countries, with support from IFIs and other international organizations, represent a major shift in the current value orientations and in the existing institutional frameworks through which basic human needs are addressed in most countries. This book has argued that in the context of these trends, it should not be blindly assumed that the social-policy reforms have been a success, as much of the current development discourse seems to claim. We have still to cover considerable unknown territory.

The process of policy reform in the social sector has just started. There is no reliable evidence based on systematic research to prove that efforts have been successful or to show that they are sustainable. To declare with confidence that the policy-reform approach to improving social-sector policies is effective would take years. This is partly because of the time required to monitor, assess, and obtain meaningful results and partly because local capacities to assess the policy-reform processes do not exist in most countries where these changes are taking place.

An important consideration to keep in mind in examining current trends in social-policy reform, from both an international and comparative-development perspective, is that the policy-reform approach is currently predominant in many countries because, despite the many risks, it presents opportunities. In social- and human-development terms, most countries find themselves at the end of the 20th century without alternative meaningful policy options to deal with basic needs, global poverty, and growing social exclusion. At least in principle, the policy-reform approach offers an avenue to address these problems. Thus, to many, social-policy reform is not a matter of ideology but of pragmatism.

However, even if this is the case, a question central to this book is whether this type of proposal has any real prospect for success in a global environment. There is little doubt that this question needs further debate. Existing evidence is insufficient to make a final judgement. At one level, the discussion has until now focused excessively on the perceived material benefits of social-policy reforms in terms of eradicating extreme poverty, upgrading human resources, improving competitiveness, and increasing productivity. Over time, research will probably show that some social-policy reforms have been a mix of success and failure, with more collateral effects than originally expected. If this is true, then we urgently need to develop ways to monitor and assess ongoing processes of reform to draw knowledge, lessons to be learned, and recommendations to help introduce the mechanisms needed to make corrections.

Even if this is done, it is critical, however, in the overall assessment of these processes, not to lose sight of the fact that the policy-reform approach is by design or by default a proposal for achieving social development with its own internal ethos. We therefore urgently need to understand the directions of current transnational models of social and human development for recipient societies; the potential of market mechanisms to promote social and human development in the context of public-policy reforms; and the new mechanisms needed to guide the design, implementation, and evaluation of reform processes in societies redefining their roles in the global scenario. These are key questions to which answers are not yet available.

The reform approach to social policy is a call to build social institutions and develop individual practices based at least on three conditions: the capacity to make independent and informed individual decisions; personal responsibility, as opposed to corporate responsibility; and the significant involvement of citizens. From another perspective, the reform approach also raises issues of social cohesion, new approaches to defining poverty, and alternative ways of dealing with issues of efficient coverage, quality of social service, and social equity. How effective these will be is still unknown.

At the end of the day, the success or failure of social-policy reforms will depend most on how much the actors involved in the process are ethically committed to human development. This involves not only policymakers but also teachers in the classrooms, physicians and nurses in hospitals, public officials on ministerial committees and in the public bureaucracy, politicians in cabinets or on parliamentary committees, mayors in municipal offices, and citizens in general. This is more important than more financial resources, more technocratic solutions, and more adjustments to formal policies. No doubt, all the elements of the standard adjustment approach are necessary, but it is not the first time that they have proven insufficient.

The experience of the last three decades with public-policy reforms and changes in political democracy shows that top-down reforms can do little with a lack of participation and commitment, indifference of elites, and political and economic opportunism. Without question, the population at large and stakeholders need to be involved in policy processes. Participation in public policy-making by itself, however, is not enough. The less privileged cannot, by this means alone, overcome their lack of resources and access to power, which are intrinsic to their poverty. To be successful, the reform approach to social policies must go hand in hand with the examination of risks and opportunities presented by policy reforms from a social-development perspective.

In the current global environment, policymakers will continue to propose and implement structural-adjustment policies and reformed social policies on the assumption that they are the best ways to deal with the challenges of sustainable development, given that the world's population will reach 10 billion by 2050, with a social and natural environment even more degraded than now. Economic policies will continue to play a critical role in providing the increasing numbers of accessible employment opportunities and material goods required to ensure social welfare. From a human-development perspective, social-policy reform for the promotion of social development is expected to produce "more human value" in terms of learning capacities, better ethical practice, and stronger and longer lasting social commitment. The capacity to produce human value is the final criterion for assessing the effectiveness and efficiency of social policies and, by extension, of other development actions, including economic development. Economic development provides the material instruments and opportunities for growth and progress, but social policies produce the intrinsic social forces allowing growth and progress to equitably benefit people.

Still, the reform approach to social policies raises many questions and doubts. An empirical response to these issues requires research and evaluation. Research is needed to know about what is going on and with what results, in terms of both achievements and gaps. Evaluation is needed to assess expected and unexpected results and is the only way to introduce timely corrections and design alternative policy options as these are required. From an immediate, pragmatic point of view, it is almost irrelevant in the context of current global trends to ask whether or not to implement policy reforms. The issue, now, is *how* to do this.

# Appendix I

# Contributing Authors

**Tade Akin Aina** studied sociology at the University of Lagos, Nigeria, the London School of Economics, and the University of Sussex. He was a full professor in the Department of Sociology at the University of Lagos. He is currently the Deputy Executive Secretary (Publications) at the Council for the Development of Social Science Research in Africa, Dakar, Senegal. His publications include *Health, Habitat and Underdevelopment, The Challenge of Sustainable Development in Nigeria* (coedited with Ademola T. Salau), *Child Development and Nutrition in Nigeria* (coedited with M.F. Zeitlin and F.E. Etta), *The Experience of Migration in Africa* (coedited with Jonathan Baker), and *Globalization and Social Policy in Africa: Research Directions and Issues.*

**Arnon Bar-On** is a senior lecturer of social work at the University of Botswana, specializing in social policy and community work. He previously taught at The Hebrew University, in Jerusalem, Haifa University, and the University of Hong Kong. His research and publications include critiques of the Northern practice of social work and social work in Africa, social-service provision for ethnic minorities, street children, and the social integration of the physically disabled.

**Daniel A. Morales-Gómez** is a senior scientist in social policy and team leader of the Assessment of Social Policy Reform Program Initiative at the International Development Research Centre in Canada. He earned his PhD in educational planning from the University of Toronto, studied philosophy at the Catholic University of Valparaíso, Chile, and received a masters degree in international comparative education from Stanford University. Morales-Gómez's experience includes teaching, research, and management in higher education and international development. He was academic dean of the School of

Education at the Catholic University Valparaíso and taught at the Ibero-American University in Mexico and the University of Alberta, in Canada. He has published on international comparative education, adult education, research ethics, social policy, and international aid. He was author or editor of *Educación y Desarrrollo Dependiente en América Latina* (education and dependent development in Latin America); *The State, Corporatist Politics and Educational Policy Making in Mexico; Education, Policy and Social Change: Experiences from Latin America*; and *Social Policy in a Global Society: Parallels and Lessons from the Canada–Latin America Experience*.

**Kwaku Osei-Hwedie** is a professor and chair in the Department of Social Work at the University of Botwana. He earned his PhD in social welfare from Brandeis University, in the United States, and a postgraduate diploma in international law from the University of Zambia. He has taught at Brandeis University, Virginia State University, and St. Paul's College, in Lawrenceville, United States, and has been visiting lecturer at Makarere University, in Uganda. Osei-Hwedie has coedited or written some 16 books and has written several articles in areas related to youth development, planning for the social services, social policy, and the indigenization of the education and practice of social work in Africa.

**Trinidad S. Osteria** is the director of the Social Development Research Center at De La Salle University, in the Philippines. She earned her PhD from Johns Hopkins University. Osteria has been a visiting research fellow at the Institute of Developing Economies, in Japan, fellow and research coordinator on Asian–Pacific Urban and Women's Health projects at the Institute of Southeast Asian Studies, in Singapore, visiting scientist with the Harvard–MIT International Nutrition Planning Program, project expert for the United Nations Economic and Social Commission for Asia and the Pacific, Population Division, in Bangkok, Thailand, and research demographer for the International Center for Diarrheal Diseases Research, in Bangladesh. Her research includes evaluation of family planning and health programs, community participation, empowerment of women, female-labour migration, and decentralization of social policy.

**Andrés Pérez Baltodano** is an associate professor of political science at the University of Western Ontario, in Canada. He is a former director of the Nicaraguan Institute of Public Administration. Between 1983 and 1988, he worked with the International Development Research Centre, where he organized a multinational research program on public policy and participation. Pérez recently edited the book *Globalización, Ciudadanía y Política Social en América Latina: Tensiones y Contradicciones* (globalization, citizenship, and social politics in Latin America: tensions and contradictions). He has published extensively in the areas of public administration and comparative politics.

**Jeffry M. Puryear** is a senior fellow at the Inter-American Dialogue (IAD) in Washington DC and directs the IAD Partnership for Educational Revitalization in the Americas. He served as head of the Ford Foundation's regional office for the Andes and the Southern Cone and as a research scholar at State University of New York. He earned his PhD in comparative education from the University of Chicago. Puryear has written various articles on inter-American affairs. His book on intellectuals and democracy in Chile was published in 1994 by the Johns Hopkins University Press.

**Luis Ratinoff** is chief of the Strategic Studies Office at the Inter-American Development Bank in Washington, DC. He has taught at the University of Chile, the School of Advanced International Studies at Johns Hopkins University, and in the Latin American Program at Georgetown University. He has published extensively on issues related to educational development and democratization; basic- and primary-education reform; economic adjustments and poverty; the culture of globalization; urbanization and crime; and the new Latin American elites.

**Mario Torres A.** is a senior program officer in social policy at the International Development Research Centre regional office for Latin America and the Caribbean, in Montevideo, Uruguay. He earned his PhD in sociology and social demography from the university of Texas at Austin. He was a professor at the Catholic University of Peru, director of research for the Central American Postgraduate Program in Economic and Development Planning, researcher for the Executive Secretariat of the Latin American Program of Social Research on Population, and director of research for the National Population Council of Peru. His areas of interest include methodology of social research, population, and social policies.

# Appendix II

# Acronyms and Abbreviations

ASEAN       Association of Southeast Asian Nations

DAI       development-assistance institution
DONGO       donor agency-induced or donor agency-controlled NGO

ECLAC       Economic Commission for Latin America and the Caribbean

GDP       gross domestic product
GNP       gross national product
GONGO       government-induced or government-controlled NGO

IADB       Inter-American Development Bank
IFI       international financial institutions
ILO       International Labour Organization
IMF       International Monetary Fund

LGU       local-government units

MNC       multinational corporations

NGO       nongovernmental organization

ODA       overseas development assistance
OECD       Organisation for Economic Co-operation and Development

PREAL       Partnership for Educational Revitalization in the Americas

| RTI | reduced teaching intensity |
|---|---|
| SAcP | social-action program |
| SAP | structural-adjustment program |
| SDA | social dimensions of adjustment |
| SF | social funds |
| UNESCO | United Nations Educational, Scientific and Cultural Organization |
| VDC | Village Development Committee |
| WSSD | World Summit for Social Development |

# BIBLIOGRAPHY

ADB (Asian Development Bank). 1996. Outlook: key indicators of development in Asian and Pacific countries. Oxford University Press, Hong Kong, China.

Adelman, I. 1986. A poverty-focussed approach to development policy, In Lewis, J.P.; Kallab, V., ed., Development strategies reconsidered. Transaction Books, New Brunswick, NJ, USA. pp. 49-66.

Adepoju, A., ed. 1993. The impact of structural adjustment on the population of Africa: the implications for education, health and employment. London: United Nations Fund for Population Activities; James Currey, London, UK.

————— 1996. Population, poverty, structural adjustment programmes and quality of life in sub- Saharan Africa. PHRDA Research, Dakar, Senegal. IDEP Paper No. 1.

Aina, T.A. 1989. The Nigerian crisis and the middle class. Vierteljahresberikhte [Problems of international co-operation]. Journal of the Friedrich-Ebert-Stiftung, 116(Jun), 173–180.

————— 1992 Health, habitat and underdevelopment in Nigeria. Human Settlements Programme. International Institute for Environment and Development, London, UK.

————— 1993. Empowering environmental NGOs: the experience of the Nigerian Environmental Study Action Team. In Sandbrook, R.; Halfani, M., ed., Empowering people: building community, civic associations and legality in Africa. Centre for Urban and Community Studies, University of Toronto, Toronto, ON, Canada.

————— 1997a. Globalization and social policy in Africa: issues and research directions. Council for the Development of Economic and Social Research in Africa, Dakar, Senegal. Working Paper No. 6/96.

————— 1997b. The state and civil society: politics, government and social organization in African cities. In Rakodi, C., ed., The urban challenge in Africa: growth and management of its large cities. United Nations University Press, Tokyo, Japan.

Altimir, O. 1997. Desigualdad, empleo y pobreza en América Latina: efectos del ajuste y del Cambio en el Estilo de desarrollo. Desarrollo Económico, Revista de Ciencias Sociales, 37(145), 3–30.

Álvarez, B.; Ruiz-Casares, M., ed. 1997. Paths of change: education reforms underway in Latin America and the Caribbean. United States Agency for International Development, Washington, DC, USA.

Amin, S. 1972. Underdevelopment and dependence in Black Africa: origins and contemporary forms. Journal of Modern African Studies, 10(4), 503–524.

———— 1990. Maldevelopment: anatomy of a global failure. United Nations University Press, Tokyo, Japan.

———— 1992. The empire of chaos. Monthly Review Press, New York, NY, USA.

Ananta, A.; Nurvidya Arifin, E. 1991. Projection of Indonesian population: 1990–2020. Demographic Institute, University of Indonesia, Jakarta, Indonesia.

Anderson, B. 1991. Imagined communities: reflections on the origin and spread of nationalism. Verso, London, UK.

Anderson, P. 1974. Lineages of the absolutist state. NLB, London, UK.

Ardington, E.; Lund, F. 1995. Pension and development: social security as complementary to programmes of reconstruction and development. Development Southern Africa, 12(4), 557–577.

Ardrey, R. 1966. The territorial imperative: a personal inquiry into the animal origins of property and nations. Delra, New York, NY, USA.

Bahmueller, C.F. 1981. The National Charity Company: Jeremy Bentham's silent revolution. University of California Press, Berkeley, CA, USA.

Baker, R. 1995. Sweeping changes shape a new Pacific Asia. Asia Pacific Issues, 24, 1–8.

Bakker, I. 1994. Introduction: Engendering macro-economic policy reform in the era of global restructuring and adjustment. In Bakker, I., ed., The strategic silence: gender and economic policy. Zed Books, London, UK.

Barber, B. 1992. Jihad vs. McWorld. Atlantic Monthly, Mar, 53–65.

Bardhan, P. 1995. Research on poverty and development twenty years after redistribution with growth. Annual Conference on Development Economics, 1–2 May 1995, Washington, DC, USA. World Bank, Washington, DC, USA.

Barro, R. 1991. Economic growth in a cross-section of countries. Quarterly Journal of Economics, 106(2), 407–443.

Barry, A.; Osborne, T.; Rose, N., ed. 1996. Foucault and political reason: liberalism, neo-liberalism and rationalities of government. University of Chicago Press, Chicago, IL, USA.

Bathily, A. 1994. The West African state in historical perspective. In Osaghae, E., ed., Between state and civil society in Africa. Council for the Development of Economic and Social Research in Africa, Dakar, Senegal.

Becker, G. 1964. Human capital: a theoretical and empirical analysis. Princeton University Press, Princeton, NJ, USA.

Behrman, J. 1993. Investing in human resources. In Inter-American Development Bank, ed., Economic and social progress in Latin America: 1993 report. Inter-American Development Bank, Washington, DC, USA. pp. 202–210.

Beneria, L.; Mendoza, B. 1995. Structural adjustment and social emergency funds: the cases of Honduras, Mexico and Nicaragua. European Journal of Development Research, 7(1), 53–76.

Bessis, S. 1995. From social exclusion to social cohesion: a policy agenda. The Roskilde Symposium, 1995. Management of Social Transformations, Paris, France. MOST Policy Paper No. 2.

Bhorat, H. 1995. The South African social safety net: past, present and future. Development Southern Africa, 12(4), 595–604.

Blank, R. 1993. Does a larger safety net mean less economic flexibility? In Freeman, R., ed., Working under different rules. Russell Sage, New York, NY, USA.

Bonvin, J. 1997. Globalization and linkages: challenges for development policy. Development, 49(2), 39–42.

Booth, A. 1995. Southeast Asian economic growth: can the momentum be maintained? Southeast Asian Affairs, 1995 (Yearbook), 28–43.

Boothroyd, P. 1995. Policy assessment. In Vanclay, F.; Bronstein, D.A., ed., Environmental and social impact assessment. John Wiley & Sons Ltd, New York, NY, USA. pp. 83–126.

Bourguignon, F.; de Melo, J.; Morrisson, C. 1991. Poverty and income distribution during adjustment: issues and evidence from the OECD project. World Development, 19, 1485–1508.

Bourne, R. 1946. Herd impulses and the stare. In Browne, W.R., ed., Leviathan in crisis. Viking Press, New York, NY, USA.

Boyden, J. 1990. Childhood and the policy-makers: a comparative perspective on the global-ization of childhood. In James, A.; Prout, A., ed., Constructing and reconstructing child-hood: contemporary issues in the sociological study of childhood. Falmer Press, London, UK.

Bradford, C. 1993. El dinamismo del crecimiento y la reforma. In Inter-American Development Bank–United Nations Development Programme (IDB–UNDP), ed., Reforma social y probreza. IDB, Washington, DC, USA; UNDP, New York, NY, USA.

Bray, M. 1996. Counting the full cost: parental and community financing of education in East Asia. World Bank; United Nations Children's Fund, Washington, DC, USA.

Broad, D.; Foster, L., ed. 1992. The New World Order and the Third World. Black Rose Books, Montréal, PQ, Canada.

Brooks, E.; Nyireade, V. 1987. Social welfare in Zambia. In Dixon, J., ed., Social welfare in Africa. Croom Helm, Bakenham, UK.

Brunei Darussalam. n.d. Demographic situation and population projections, 1991–2011. Statistics Division, Economic Planning Unit, Brunei Darussalam.

Bui, Gia Thinh. 1996. Vietnam: decentralization through people's committee. In Osteria, T., ed., Social sector decentralization: lessons from the Asian experience. La Salle University Press–Assessment of Social Policy Reform Program Initiative, Manila, Philippines; International Development Research Centre, Ottawa, ON, Canada. pp. 160–211.

Bukharin, N. 1973 [1929]. Imperialism and world economy. Monthly Review Press, New York, NY, USA.

Burdette, M.M. 1988. Zambia: between two worlds. Western Press, Boulder, CO, USA.

Burdge, R.J.; Vanclay, F. 1995. Social impact assessment. In Vanclay, F.; Bronstein, D.A., ed., Environmental and social impact assessment. John Wiley & Sons Ltd, New York, NY, USA. pp. 31–65.

Calderon, F.; Dos Santos, M.R., ed. 1991. Hacia un nuevo orden estatal en América Latina: veinte tesis sociopolíticas y un corolario. Fondo de Cultura Económica, Santiago, Chile.

Camilleri, J.A.; Falk, J. 1992. The end of sovereignty: the politics of a shrinking and fragmenting world. Edward Elgar, London, UK.

Campbell, D. 1993. The voluntary non-profit sector: an alternative. School of Policy Studies, Queen's University, Kingston, ON, Canada. Discussion Paper No. 93-13.

CEA (Confederación de Educadores Americanos). 1997. La responsibilidad social de los sindicatos ante la educación y el desarrollo democrático. CEA, D.F. Cuadernos de Trabajo 9, Mexico. 55 pp.

CELADE (Centro Latinoamericano de Demografia). 1996. Impacto de las tendencias demográficas sobre los sectores sociales en América Latina. Centro Latinoamericano de Demografía, Santiago, Chile.

CGG (Commission on Global Governance). 1995. Our global neighbourhood. Oxford University Press, Oxford, UK.

Chambers, R. 1994. Poverty and livelihoods: whose reality counts? An overview prepared for the Stockholm Roundtable on Global Change, 1994. Institute of Development Studies, Sussex, UK.

Chikulo, B.C. 1985. Decentralization in centralism: an analysis of the Zambian experience (1964–1981). In Osei-Hwedie, K.; Ndulo, M., ed., Issues in Zambian development. Omenana, Nyangwe, Zaire.

Chole, E. 1991. Introduction: What is social development? In Mohammed, D., ed., Social development in Africa: strategies, policies and programmes after the Lagos Plan. Hans Zell Publisher, London, UK. ACARTSOD Monograph Series.

Choo, K.K. 1989. Modernization and social development in Malaysia. Regional Development Dialogue, 10, 38–60.

CIDA (Canadian International Development Agency). 1987. Sharing our future. Supply and Services Canada, Hull, PQ, Canada.

Clarke, I.M. 1985. The spatial organization of multinational corporations. Croom Helm, London, UK.

Commonwealth Secretariat. 1989. Engendering adjustment for the 1990s. Commonwealth Expert Group on Women and Structural Adjustment, Commonwealth Secretariat, London, UK.

Cornia, G.A.; Jolly, R.; Stewart, F., ed. 1987. Adjustment with a human face, vols. I and II. Clarendon Press, Oxford, UK.

Coser, L.A. 1956. The functions of social conflict. Free Press, New York, NY, USA.

Crowder, M. 1968. West Africa under colonial rule. Hutchinson, London, UK.

Culpeper, R. 1987. Forced adjustment: the export collapse in sub-Saharan Africa. North–South Institute, Ottawa, ON, Canada.

Dahlman, C.H. 1989. Impact of technological change on industrial prospects for the LDCs. World Bank, Washington, DC, USA. Industry Series, Industry and Energy Department Working Paper No. 12.

————— 1991. The role of government: education policy, technical change, R&D, and competitive advantage. In Haque, I., ed., International competitiveness: interaction of the public and the private sectors. Economic Development Institute of the World Bank, Washington, DC, USA.

Daniel, R. 1985. Zambia's structural adjustment or downward spiral? IDS Bulletin, 16(3).

Deacon, B. 1995. The Globalization of social policy and the socialization of global politics. Social Policy Review, 7, 55–76.

De Dios, E. 1995. The Philippine economy: what's right, what's wrong. Southeast Asian Affairs, 1995 (Yearbook), 274–288.

Demery, L.; Squire, L. 1996. Macroeconomic adjustment and poverty in Africa: an emerging picture. World Bank Research Chronicle, 11(1), 39–59.

de Swaan, A. 1992. Perspectives for transnational social policy. Government and Opposition, 27(1), 33–51.

Dillinger, W. 1994. Decentralization and its implications for service delivery. Urban Management and Municipal Finance, World Bank, Washington, DC, USA. Urban Management Programme, No. 16.

Dillon, M. 1995. Security, philosophy and politics. In Featherstone, M.; Lash, S.; Robertson, R., ed., Global modernities. Sage, London, UK.

Dowling, J.M.; Castillo, C.N. 1996. Recent economic developments in Southeast Asia. Southeast Asian Affairs, 1996 (Yearbook).

Drucker, P. 1989. The new realities. Harper & Row, New York, NY, USA.

Drysdale, P.; Elek, A. 1995. Community-building in East Asia and the Pacific. Paper presented at a seminar, 20–22 Sep 1995, Tokyo, Japan. Australian National University, Canberra, Australia. 28 pp.

[was Le Van Duy] Duy, L.V. 1994. The population of Vietnam by the year 2014. In Population Documentation and Information Centre, Hanoi, Viet Nam.

ECLAC (Economic Commission for Latin America and the Caribbean). 1990. Transformacion productiva con equidad. ECLAC, Santiago, Chile.

————— 1995. Social panorama of Latin America, 1995. ECLAC, Santiago, Chile.

————— 1997. Social panorama of Latin America, 1996. ECLAC, Santiago, Chile.

ECLAC; OREALC (Economic Commission for Latin America and the Caribbean; UNESCO Office for Latin America and the Caribbean). 1992. Educational situation of Latin America and the Caribbean, 1980–1989. ECLAC, Santiago, Chile.

Elias, N. 1992. Time: an essay [trans., E. Jephcott]. Blackwell, Oxford, UK.

Emmerij, L. 1993a. Ejes estrategicos para la reforma social. *In* Inter-American Development Bank–United Nations Development Programme (IDB–UNDP), ed., Reforma social y probreza. IDB, Washington, DC, USA; UNDP, New York, NY, USA.

——— 1993b. The World Bank's approach to social sector lending and poverty alleviation. Paper prepared for the Group of 24, Jun 1993, Paris, France. World Bank, Washington, DC, USA.

Endanda, K. 1993. Education and society. *In* Mbaya, K., ed., Zaire: what destiny? Council for the Development of Economic and Social Research in Africa, Dakar, Senegal.

Esping-Andersen, G. 1990. The three worlds of welfare capitalism. Polity Press, Cambridge, MA, USA.

——— 1994. After the Golden Age: the future of the welfare state in the New Global Order. World Summit for Social Development, United Nations Research Institute for Social Development, Geneva, Switzerland. Occasional Paper No. 7.

Espinola, V. 1991. Descentralizacion del sistema escolar en Chile. Comparative and International Development Education, Santiago, Chile.

Etta, F.E. 1994. Gender issues in contemporary African education. Africa Development, 19(4), 57–84.

Fadayomi, T.O. 1991. The history of social development in Gambia, Ghana, Nigeria. *In* Mohammed, D., ed., Social development in Africa: strategies, policies and programmes after the Lagos Plan. Hans Zell Publisher, London, UK. ACARTSOD Monograph Series.

Faist, T. 1995. Boundaries of welfare states: immigrants and social rights on the national and supranational level. *In* Miles, R.; Thränhardt, D., ed., Migration and European integration. Farleigh Dickinson University Press, Madison, NJ, USA.

Falk, R. 1993. Democratising, internationalising and globalising: a collage of images. Third World Quarterly, 13.

Faria, V.; Guimaraes Castro, M.H. 1990. Social policy and democratic consolidation in Brazil. *In* Graham, L.S.; Wilson, R.H., ed., The political economy of Brazil. University of Texas Press, Austin, TX, USA.

Farnsworth, C.H. 1990. Report by World Bank sees poverty lessening by 2000 except in Africa. The New York Times, 16 Jul, A3.

Founou-Tchuigoua, B. 1996. Africa confronted with the ravages of neo-liberalism. Africa Development, 21(2–3), 5–24.

Fowler, A. 1992. Distant obligations: speculations on NGO funding and the global market. Review of African Political Economy, 5, 9–29.

——— 1995. NGOs and the globalization of social welfare: perspectives from East Africa. *In* Semboja, J.; Therkildsen, O., ed., Service provision under stress in East Africa. Copenhagen Centre for Development Research, Copenhagen, Denmark.

Fraile, P. 1994. La voluntad de ordenar: la ciencia de policía Española. Suplementos: La Geografía Hoy, 43 (Apr).

Freeman, N. 1996. Vietnam: better managing reform. Southeast Asian Affairs, 1996 (Yearbook), 385–402.

Fyle, M.C., ed. 1993. The state and the provision of social services in Sierra Leone since independence, 1961–1991. Council for the Development of Economic and Social Research in Africa, Dakar, Senegal.

Gayi, S.K. 1995. Adjusting to the social costs of adjustment in Ghana: problems and prospects. European Journal of Development Research, 7(1), 77–99.

Gibbon, P., ed. 1995. Towards a political economy of the World Bank, 1970–90. In Mkandawire, T.; Olukoshi, A., ed., Between liberalization and oppression: the politics of structural adjustment in Africa. Council for the Development of Economic and Social Research in Africa, Dakar, Senegal.

Gibbon, P.; Olukoshi, A.O. 1996. Structural adjustment and socioeconomic change in sub-Saharan Africa: some conceptual, methodological and research issues. Nordiska Afrikainstitutet, Uppsala, Sweden. Research Report No. 102.

Giddens, A. 1990. The consequences of modernity. Stanford University Press, Stanford, CA, USA.

————— 1991. Modernity and self-identity. Stanford University Press, Stanford, CA, USA.

————— 1995. Affluence, poverty and the idea of a post-scarcity society. United Nations Research Institute for Social Development, Geneva, Switzerland. Discussion Paper No. DP 63.

GOB (Government of Botswana). 1995. Proposals for a community based programme strategy for rural development. Ministry of Finance and Development Planning, Gaborone, Botswana.

GOC (Government of Canada). 1995. Canada in the world: government statement. Canada Communication Group, Ottawa, ON, Canada. E2-147/1995.

Goliber, T.J. 1989. Africa's expanding population: old problems, new policies. Population Bulletin, 44(3).

Gottmann, J. 1973. The significance of territory. University Press of Virginia, Charlottesville, VA, USA.

Gruat, J.-V. 1990. Social security schemes in Africa: current trends and problems. International Labour Review, 129(4), 405–421.

Guerreiro-Ramos, A. 1970. Modernization towards a possibility model. In Berlin, W.A.; Totten, S.O., ed., Developing nations: quest for a model. van Nortrand Reinhold, New York, NY, USA.

Guhan, S. 1994. Social security option for developing countries. International Labour Review, 133(1), 35–53.

Hausman, R. 1994. What role for social policy? In Bradford, C., ed., Redefining the state in Latin America. Organization for Economic Co-operation and Development, Paris, France. pp. 173–193.

Heilbroner, R. 1992. Twenty-first century capitalism. House of Anansis Press Limited, Concord, ON, Canada.

————— 1995. Visions of the future: the distant past, yesterday, today, and tomorrow. Oxford University Press, New York, NY, USA.

Held, D. 1991. Democracy, the nation-state and the global system. In Held, D., ed., Political theory today. Stanford University Press, Stanford, CA, USA.

Helwege, A. 1995. Poverty in Latin America: back to the abyss? Journal of Inter-American Studies and World Affairs, 37(3), 99–123.

Herbold Green, R. 1996. Not farewell but fare forward voyagers: Africa into the 21st century. In Onimode, B.; Synge, R., ed., Issues in African development: essays in honour of Adebeyano Adedeji at 65. Heinemann Educational Books, Lagos, Nigeria. pp. 265–303.

Hernández Mella, R. 1997. The perspective of the reformers. In Álvarez, B.; Ruiz-Casares, M., ed., Paths of change: education reforms underway in Latin America and the Caribbean. United States Agency for International Development, Washington, DC, USA. pp. 44–46.

Hill, M.; Bramley, E. 1986. Analysing social policy. Blackwell, Oxford, UK.

Hintze, O. 1975. The historical essays of Otto Hintze [ed., intro., F. Gilbert]. Oxford University Press, New York, NY, USA.

Hope, K.R., ed. 1997. Structural adjustment, reconstruction and development in Africa. Avebury, London, UK.

Hughes, H. 1994. Development in Asia: a 50 years policy perspective. Asia Pacific Development Journal, 1, 1–25.

Hume, L.J. 1981. Bentham and bureaucracy. Cambridge University Press, Cambridge, UK.

Hunsley, T.M., ed. 1992. Social policy in the global economy. School of Policy Studies, Queen's University, Kingston, ON, Canada.

Hutchful, E. 1994. Smokes and mirrors: the World Bank's Social Dimensions of Adjustment (SDA) Programme. Review of African Political Economy, 21(62), 569–584.

Huysmans, J. 1995. Migrants as a security problem: dangers of "securitizing" societal issues. In Miles, R.; Thränhardt, D., ed., Migration and European integration. Farleigh Dickinson University Press, Madison, NJ, USA.

Hyden, G. 1980. Beyond Ujamaa in Tanzania. University of California Press, Berkeley, CA, USA.

IDB (Inter-American Development Bank). 1996. Economic and social progress in Latin America: 1996 report. Johns Hopkins University Press, Baltimore, MD, USA.

IDB; UNDP (Inter-American Development Bank; United Nations Development Programme). 1993. Social reform and poverty: towards an integrated development agenda. IDB, Washington, DC, USA; UNDP, New York, NY, USA.

IDRC (International Development Research Centre). 1996. Social development in the developing world: the challenge of policy performance. Report of the Social Development and Public Policies seminar, 30–31 May 1996, Hull, PQ, Canada. Canadian International Development Agency, Ottawa, ON, Canada.

Iglesias, E. 1993. Reforma económica y reforma social: visión integral. In Inter-American Development Bank–United Nations Development Programme (IDB–UNDP), ed., Reforma social y probreza. IDB, Washington, DC, USA; UNDP, New York, NY, USA.

Jinadu, G. 1980. Social development in Africa: a proposed change model. Journal of Business and Social Studies, 4(1), 57–71.

JMF (Japan, Ministry of Finance). 1994. Overseas development assistance. JMF, Tokyo, Japan.

JMTI (Japan, Ministry of Trade and Industry). 1994. Japanese overseas development assistance. JMTI, Tokyo, Japan.

Johnson, A.F. 1977. Strengthening society. III: Social security. In Johnson, A.F.; Stritch, A.J., ed., Canadian public policy: globalization and political parties. Copp Clark Ltd, Toronto, ON, Canada.

Jordan, B. 1996. A theory of poverty and social exclusion. Polity Press, Cambridge, MA, USA.

Kaplan, R.D. 1994. The coming anarchy. Atlantic Monthly, Feb., 44–76.

Kaseke, E. 1994. A situation analysis of the Social Development Fund. School of Social Work, Harare, Zimbabwe. Occasional Paper Series, No. 2.

———— 1995. Interpretations of society and social policy. Journal of Social Development in Africa, 1995.

Kennedy, P. 1993. Preparing for the 21st century: winners and losers. The New York Review of Books, 11 Feb, 32–44.

Khumalo, T.F. 1992. Swaziland. In Hall, N., ed., The social implications of structural adjustment programmes in Africa. School of Social Work, Harare, Zimbabwe.

Kibuka, E.P. 1990. The African social situation: major elements. In African Centre for Applied Research and Training in Social Development (ACARTSOD), ed., The African social situation: crucial factors of development and transformation. Hans Zell Publisher, London, UK.

Konate, H. 1997. Politique sociale en Afrique de L'Ouest et du Centre. International Development Research Centre, Ottawa, ON, Canada.

Koselleck, R. 1985. Futures past: on the semantics of historical times [trans., K. Tribe]. MIT Press, Cambridge, MA.

———— 1988. Critique and crisis: enlightenment and pathogenesis of modern society. Berg, Oxford, UK.

La Prensa. 1996. Pintan negro panorama de América Latina y el Caribe. La Prensa, Managua, Domingo, 7 Jul, p. 15.

Laakso, L.; Olukoshi, A.O. 1996. The crisis of the post-colonial nation-state project in Africa. In Olukoshi, A.O.; Laakso, L., ed. Challenges to the nation-state in Africa. Nordiska Afrikainstitutet, Uppsala, Sweden; Institute of Development Studies, University of Helsinki, Helsinki, Finland.

Laing, R.D. 1971. The divided self: an existential study in sanity and madness. Penguin, Middlesex, UK.

Lall, S. 1990. Building industrial competitiveness in developing countries. Organization for Economic Co-operation and Development, Paris, France.

Lamont, J. 1996. Reality bites and Zambians go to the polls accepting that government no longer owes them a living. The Sunday Independent, 17 Nov, 12.

Lash, C. 1994. The revolt of the elites. Harper's, Nov.

Le Goff, J. 1988. Medieval civilization: 400–1500 [trans., J. Barrow]. Blackwell, Oxford, UK.

Lefebvre, H. 1991. The production of space [trans., D.N. Smith]. Blackwell, Oxford, UK.

Leoprapai, B. 1996. Thailand: translating policy into action. In Osteria, T., ed., Social sector decentralization: lessons from the Asian experience. La Salle University Press, Manila, Philippines. pp. 85–123.

Lockheed, M.; Jamison, D.; Lau, L. 1980. Farmer education and farmer efficiency: a survey. Economic Development and Cultural Change, 29(1), 37–76.

Lockheed, M.; Verspoor, A.M. 1991. Improving primary education in developing countries. Oxford University Press, New York, NY, USA.

Long, C.; Soeung, S.C.; Menkea, M.; Sprechmann, S.; Kerr, H. 1995. KAP survey on fertility and contraception in Cambodia. Cambodia Ministry of Health, Phnom Penh, Cambodia.

Long, D.C. 1977. Bentham on liberty: Jeremy Bentham's idea of liberty in relation to his utilitarianism. University of Toronto Press, Toronto, ON, Canada.

Luhmann, N. 1982. The differentiation of society. Columbia University Press, New York, NY, USA.

————— 1990. Essays on self-reference. Columbia University Press, New York, NY, USA.

————— 1993. Risk a sociological theory. A. de Gruyter, New York, NY, USA.

Luke, J.F. 1992. Managing interconnectedness: the new challenge for public administration. In Bailey, M.T.; Mayer, R.T., ed., Public management in an interconnected world. Greenwood Press, New York, NY, USA.

Lusting, N. 1994. Coping with austerity: poverty and inequality in Latin America. Paper presented at the 9th Session of the Inter-American Dialogue, 8–10 Apr 1994, Washington, DC, USA. Inter-American Dialogue, Washington, DC, USA.

Lynn, L.E. 1992. Welfare reform and the revival of ideology: an essay review. Social Service Review, 66(4), 643–654.

Mabogunje, A.L. 1968. Urbanization in Nigeria. Africana University Press, New York, NY, USA.

Mabote, T. 1996. Ministry supports safe water supply. Daily News, Gaborone, Botswana, 21 Nov (No. 221), 1.

MacIver, R.M. 1964. The modern state. Oxford University Press, Oxford, UK.

MacKintosh, M. 1995. Competition and contracting in selective social provisioning. European Journal of Development Research, 7(1), 26–52.

MacPherson, S. 1982. Social policy in the Third World. Wheatsheaf, Brighton, UK.

————— 1989. Social welfare delivery systems and receiving mechanisms at the local level. Regional Development Dialogue, 1, 67–77.

Magdoff, H. 1969. The age of imperialism. Modern Reader Paperbacks, New York, NY, USA.

Malloy, J.M. 1991. Statecraft, social policy, and governance in Latin America. University of Pittsburgh, Pittsburgh, PA, USA. Working Paper No. 151.

———— 1993. Statecraft, social policy, and governance in Latin America. Governance: An International Journal of Policy and Administration, 6(2), 220–274.

Malo, M. 1996. Indonesia: setting the stage for full regency autonomy by 1997. In Osteria, T., ed., Social sector decentralization: lessons from the Asian experience. La Salle University Press, Manila, Philippines. 124–159.

Manchester, W. 1993. A world lit only by fire: the medieval mind and the Renaissance. Little, Brown, Boston, MA, USA.

Manyire, H.; Asingwiire, N. 1996. The state and dynamics of social policy practice and research in Uganda. Makerere University, Kampala, Uganda. Research report prepared for the Regional Project for Social Policy Practice and Research in Eastern and Southern Africa. Mimeo.

Marc, A.; Graham, C.; Scharter, M.; Schmidt, M. 1995. Social action programs and social funds: a review of design and implementation in sub-Saharan Africa. World Bank, Washington, DC, USA. Africa Technical Department Series, Discussion Paper No. 274.

Marcum, J.A. 1988/89. Africa: a continent adrift. Foreign Affairs, 68(1), 159–179.

Marshall, R.; Tucker; M. 1992. Thinking for a living: education and the wealth of nations. Basis Books, New York, NY, USA.

Marshall, T.S. 1965. Citizenship and social class. Cambridge University Press, Cambridge, UK.

Mbaya, K. 1995. The economic crisis, adjustment and democracy in Africa. In Chole, E.; Ibrahim, J., ed., Democratization processes in Africa. Council for the Development of Economic and Social Research in Africa, Dakar, Senegal.

McMeekin, R. 1996. Coordination of external assistance in Latin America and the Caribbean. United Nations Children's Fund, Santiago, Chile.

Meier, G.M. 1993. The new political economy and policy reform. Journal of International Development, 5(4), 381–389.

Mesa-Lago, C. 1996. Las reformas de las pensiones en América Latina y la posición de los organismos internacionales. Revista de la CEPAL, 60 (Dec), 73–94.

Mhone, G.C.Z. 1995. The Social Dimensions of Adjustment (SDA) Programme in Zimbabwe; a critical review and assessment. European Journal of Development Research, 7(1), 101–123.

Middleton, J.; Ziderman, A.; Van Adams, A. 1993. Skills for productivity: vocational education and training in developing countries. Oxford University Press, New York, NY, USA.

Migdal, J.S. 1988. Strong societies and weak states: state society relations and state capabilities in the Third World. Princeton University Press, Princeton, NJ, USA.

Mishra, R. 1995. Social policy after socialism. Social Policy Review, 7, 37–54.

Mitchell, J. 1992. The nature and government of the global economy. In McGrew, A.G.; et al., ed., Global politics: globalization and the nation state. Polity Press, Cambridge, MA.

Mittelman, J.H. 1995. Rethinking the international division of labour in the context of globalization. Third World Quarterly, 16(2), 273–295.

Mkandawire, T. 1989. Structural adjustment and agrarian crisis in Africa. Council for the Development of Economic and Social Research in Africa, Dakar, Senegal. Working Paper No. 2/89.

———— 1995. Adjustment, political conditionality and democratization in Africa. In Chole, E.; Ibrahim, J., ed., Democratization processes in Africa. Council for the Development of Economic and Social Research in Africa, Dakar, Senegal.

Mkandawire, T.; Olukoshi, A. ed. 1995. Between liberalization and oppression: the politics of structural adjustment in Africa. Council for the Development of Economic and Social Research in Africa, Dakar, Senegal.

Mohammed, D., ed. 1991. Social development in Africa: strategies, policies and programmes after the Lagos Plan. Hans Zell Publisher, London, UK. ACARTSOD Monograph Series.

Montenegro, A. 1996. An incomplete educational reform: the case of Colombia. World Bank, Washington, DC, USA. Human Capital Development and Operation Policy Working Paper No. 60. 19 pp.

Moon, B.E.; Dixon, W.J. 1992. Basic needs and growth–welfare trade offs. International Studies Quarterly, 36, 191–212.

Moore, M.; Robinson, M. 1994. Can foreign aid be used to promote good governance in developing countries? Ethics and International Affairs, 8, 141–158.

Morales-Gómez, D.; Torres, M., ed. 1990. The state, corporatist politics, and educational policy making in Mexico. Praeger, New York, NY, USA.

———— ed. 1995. Social policy in a global society: parallels and lessons from the Canada–Latin America experience. International Development Research Centre, Ottawa, ON, Canada.

Morna, C.L. 1989. Beyond the drought. Africa Report, 1989, Nov–Dec, 30–33.

Morton, F.; Ramsay, J., ed. 1987. The birth of Botswana: a history of the Bechuanaland Protectorate from 1910 to 1966. Longman Botswana, Gaborone, Botswana.

Mosley, P. 1994. Decomposing the effects of structural adjustment: the case of sub-Saharan Africa. In van der Hoeven, R.; van der Kraaij, F., ed., Structural adjustment and beyond in sub-Saharan Africa. James Currey, London, UK.

Muller, W.C.; Wright, V., ed. 1994. The state in Western Europe: retreat or redefinition? Western European Politics, 17(3), Special Issue, 52–76.

Mutahaba, G. 1989. Reforming public administration for development: experiences from eastern Africa. Kumrian Press, Hartford, CT, USA.

Muzaale, P.J. 1988. The organizational delivery of social services to rural areas. Journal of Social Development in Africa, 3(2), 33–48.

Mwansa, L-K. 1995. Participation of non-governmental organizations in social development process in Africa: implications. Journal of Social Development in Africa, 10(1), 56–75.

NIS (National Institute of Statistics). 1996. Demographic survey of Cambodia. NIS, Cambodia Ministry of Planning, Phnom Penh, Cambodia.

NESDB (National Economic and Social Development Board). 1995. Population projections for Thailand, 1990–2020. NESDB, Bangkok, Thailand.

Nisbet, R.A. 1981. The quest for community. Oxford University Press, Oxford, UK.

Nkrumah, K. 1967. Axioms of Kwame Nkrumah. Freedom Fighters edition. International Publishers, New York, NY, USA.

O'Donnell, G. 1992. Transitions, continuities, and paradoxes. In Mainwaring, S.; O'Donnell, G.; Valenzuela, J.S., ed., Issues in democratic consolidation: the new South American democracies in comparative perspective. University of Notre Dame Press, Notre Dame, IN, USA. pp. 17–56.

OECD (Organization for Economic Co-operation and Development). 1995. Education at a glance. OECD, Paris, France.

————— 1996. Development co-operation: a report by James H. Michel. OECD, Paris, France.

————— 1997. 20 years of aid to the Sahel: past record and ideas for the next generation. OECD, Paris, France. SAH/D (97)463.

Oman, C.P. 1997. The policy challenges of globalization and regionalization. Development, 49(2), 43–53.

Onokerhoraye, A.G. 1984. Social services in Nigeria: an introduction. Routledge & Kegan Paul International, London, UK.

Osei-Hwedie, K. 1990. Social work and the question of social development in Africa. Journal of Social Development in Africa, 5(2), 87–99.

Osorio, S.; Ramirez, B. 1997. Seguridad o inseguridad social: los riesgos de la reforma. Triana Editores, Mexico City, Mexico.

Osteria, T., ed. 1996. Social sector decentralization: lessons from the Asian experience. La Salle University Press, Manila, Philippines.

Ouma, S. 1995. The role of social participation in the socioeconomic development of Uganda. Journal of Social Development in Africa, 10(2), 512.

Oxfam. 1993. Africa — make or break: action for recovery. Oxfam, Oxford, UK. Oxfam Report.

Patel, L. 1992. Restructuring social welfare: options for South Africa. Ravan Press, Johannesburg, South Africa.

Patom, M. 1978. Governing a metropolitan area in Thailand: a study of public policies in Bangkok Metropolis (revised). Syracuse University, Syracuse, NY, USA. PhD thesis.

Paul, S.S.; Paul, J.A. 1995. The World Bank, pensions and income (in)security in the global South. International Journal of Health Services, 25(4), 697–726.

Paye, J.-C. 1996. Strategies for a learning society. The OECD Observer, 119 (Apr–May), 4–5.

Petras, J. 1978. Critical perspectives on imperialism and social class in the Third World. Monthly Review Press, New York, NY, USA.

————— 1997. Alternatives to neoliberalism in Latin America. Latin American Perspectives, 24(1), Issue 92, 80–91.

Phongpaichit, P. 1996. The Thai economy in the mid 1990's. Southeast Asian Affairs, 1996 (Yearbook), 369–381.

Pillay, Y.G.; Bond, P. 1995. Health and social policies in the new South Africa. International Journal of Health Services, 25(4), 727–743.

Ponte, S. 1994. The World Bank and "adjustment in Africa." Review of African Political Economy, 66, 539–558.

Poulantzas, N. 1978. State, power, socialism. NLB, London, UK.

Preston, L.T. 1993. Putting people first: poverty reduction and social reform in Latin America and the Caribbean. Paper presented at the Inter-American Development Bank Conference on Social Reform and Poverty, Feb 1993. World Bank, Washington, DC, USA.

Prinsen, G.; et al. 1996. PRA: contract and commitment for village development. Report on the Ministry of Finance and Development Planning's Participatory Rural Appraisal (PRA) pilot project. Ministry of Finance and Development Planning; Department of Adult Education and Social Work, University of Botswana, Gaborone, Botswana.

Puryear, J. 1996. Partners for progress. Inter-American Dialogue, Washington, DC, USA.

————— 1997. Education in Latin America: problems and challenges. Program to Promote Educational Reform in Latin America and the Caribbean. Inter-American Dialogue, Washington, DC, USA. PREAL Occasional Paper No. 7.

Puryear, J.; Brunner, J. 1995. Educación, equidad, y competitividad económica en las americas. Organization of American States, Washington, DC, USA.

Rabb, T.K. 1975.The struggle for stability in early modern Europe. Oxford University Press, New York, NY, USA.

Rama, G. 1993. Los modelos y la experiencia latinoamericana. In Inter-American Development Bank–United Nations Development Programme (IDB–UNDP), ed., Reforma social y probreza. IDB, Washington, DC, USA; UNDP, New York, NY, USA.

Reich, R.B. 1991. The work of nations: preparing ourselves for 21st-century capitalism. Alfred Knopf, New York, NY, USA.

Reimers, F.; McGinn, N. 1977. Informed dialogue: using research to shape education policy around the world. Praeger, Westport, CT, USA.

Reinikka-Soininen, R. 1990. Theory and practice in structural adjustment: the case of Zambia. Helsingin Kauppakorkea–Koullin Julkaisuja, Helsinki, Finland.

Richmond, A.H. 1994. Global apartheid: refugees, racism, and the New World Order. Oxford University Press, Toronto, ON, Canada.

Riggs, F.W. 1995. Economic development and local administration: a study in circular causation. Philippine Journal of Public Administration, 3, 86–146.

Rodgers, G.; Gore, C.; Figueiredo, J.B. 1995. Social exclusion: rhetoric, reality, response. International Institute for Labour Studies, International Labour Organization, Geneva, Switzerland.

Rodriguez, N,P. 1995. The real "New World Order": the globalization of racial and ethnic relations in the late twentieth century. *In* Smith, M.P.; Feagin, J.R., ed., The bubbling cauldron: race, ethnicity and the urban crisis. University of Minnesota Press, Minneapolis, MN, USA.

Rose, N. 1996a. Governing "advanced" liberal democracies. *In* Barry, A.; Osborne, T.; Rose, N., ed., Foucault and political reason: liberalism, neo-liberalism and rationalities of government. University of Chicago Press, Chicago, IL, USA. pp. 37–64.

————— 1996b. The death of the social? Refiguring the territory of government. Economy and Society, 25(3), 372–354.

Rosenau, J.N. 1992. The relocation of authority in a shrinking world. Comparative Politics, 24(3), 253–272.

Rosenthal, G. 1990. Some thoughts on poverty and recession in Latin America. Journal of Inter-American Studies and World Affairs, 30, 63–73.

Ruland, J. 1990. Urban government and development in Asia. Weltforum, Munich, Germany. 205 pp.

Sack, R.D. 1986. Human territoriality: in theory and history. Cambridge University Press, Cambridge, UK.

Sahn, D.E., ed. 1994. Adjusting the policy failure in African economics. Cornell University Press, Ithaca, NY, USA.

Salole, G. 1991. Participatory development: the taxation of the beneficiary? Journal of Social Development in Africa, 6(2), 5–16.

Samoff, J. 1995. Which priorities and strategies for education? Paper presented at the Oxford International Conference on Education and Development: Globalization and Learning, 21–25 Sep 1995, New College Oxford, Oxford, UK. Oxford University, Oxford, UK.

Sanda, A.O. 1981. Critical policy issues for social development in Nigeria. Research for Development, 1(2), 119–144.

Sanders, D. 1992. Social aspects of structural adjustment: health. *In* Hall, N., ed., The social implications of structural adjustment programmes in Africa. School of Social Work, Harare, Zimbabwe.

Sartori, G. 1977. Concept misinformation in comparative politics. *In* Macridis, R.C.; Brown, B.E., ed., Comparative politics: notes and readings. Dorsey Press, Homewood, IL, USA.

————— 1984. Guidelines for concept analysis. *In* Sartori, G., ed., Social science concepts. Sage Publications, London, UK.

Saul, J.R. 1995. The unconscious civilization. House of Anansis Press Limited, Concord, ON, Canada. 205 pp.

Schamis, H.E. 1993. Economía política conservadora en América Latina y Europa Occidental: los orígenes políticos de la privatización. *In* Muñoz O., G., ed., Después de las privatizaciones: hacia el estado regulador. Corporación de Investigaciónes Económicas para Latinoamerica, Santiago, Chile. pp. 51–71.

Schelager, E. 1995. Policy-making and collective action: defining coalitions within the advocacy coalition framework. Policy Science, 28, 243–270.

Schemetzer, H.; Jacobson, B.; Duncan, T.; Sverrisson, A. 1992. Evaluation of self-help school-building programmes in Zimbabwe and Zambia. Swedish International Development Agency, Stockholm, Sweden.

Schiefelbein, E.; Corvalán, A.M.; Peruzzi, S.; Keikkinen, S.; Hausmann, I. 1995. Quality of education, development, equity and poverty in the region, 1980–1994. The Major Project of Education in Latin America and the Caribbean, 38, 3–49.

Schmidt, W.; McKnight, C.; Valverde, G.; Houang, R.; Wiley, D. 1996. many visions, many aims: a cross-national investigation of curricular intentions in school mathematics. Kluwer Academic Press, Dordrecht, Netherlands.

Schmitt, C. 1985. Political theology: four chapters on the concept of sovereignty [trans., G. Schwab]. MIT Press, Cambridge, MA.

Schmitter, P.C. 1974. Still the century of corporatism? Review of Politics, 36(1), 85–131.

Schultz, T. 1961. Investment in human capital. American Economic Review, 51 (Mar), 117.

SDS (Singapore, Department of Statistics). 1996. Data sheet.

Semboja, J.; Therkildsen, O., ed. 1995. Service provision under stress in East Africa. Copenhagen Centre for Development Research–EAEP, Copenhagen, Denmark.

Silitshena, R.M.K. 1989. Village level institutions and popular participation in Botswana. Review of Rural and Urban Planning South Africa, 1 (Nov).

Simeon, R. 1991. Globalization and the Canadian nation-state. In Doern, B.; Purchase, Bryne B., ed., Canada at risk: Canadian public policy in the 1990s. C.D. Howe Institute, Ottawa, ON, Canada.

Singer, M.; Wildavsky, A. 1993. The real World Order: zones of peace, zones of turmoil. Chatham Publishers, Chatham, NJ, USA.

Siri, G. 1996. Los fondos de inversión Social en América Latina. Revista de la CEPAL, 59 (Aug), 71–81.

Sow, F. 1993. Les initiatives féminines au Sénégal : une réponse à la crise? Africa Development, 17(3), 89–115.

SSW (School of Social Work). 1996. The state and dynamics of social policy practice and research in Zimbabwe. School of Social Work, Harare, Zimbabwe. Mimeo.

Stahl, K. 1996. Anti-poverty programs: making structural adjustment more palatable. NACLA Report on the Americas, 29(6), 32–36.

Sunkel, O.; Zuleta, G. 1990. Neo-structuralism versus neo-liberalism in the 1990s. CEPAL Review, 42, 35–51.

Tan, J.L.-H. 1994. Japan and the Asia Pacific. Asean Economic Bulletin, 11(1), 1–15.

Tanaguchi, M.; West, J. 1997. On the threshold of a global economy. The OECD Observer 230(207), 5–8.

Tarnas, R. 1991. The passion of the Western mind: understanding the ideas that have shaped our world view. Harmony Books, New York, NY, USA.

Taylor, C. 1983. Social theory and practice. Oxford University Press, New York, NY, USA.

————— 1991. The malaise of modernity. Anansi Press, Toronto, ON, Canada.

Taylor, C.N.; Goodrich, C.; Bryan, C.H. 1995. Issue-oriented approach to social assessment and project appraisal. Project Appraisal, 10(3), 142–154.

Taylor-Gooby, P. 1991. Social change, social welfare and social science. University of Toronto Press, Toronto, ON, Canada.

Tedesco, J.C. 1991. Algunos aspectos de la privatización educativa en América Latina. Instituto Fronesis, Quito, Ecuador. Colección Educación No. 1.

Tembo, R. 1995. Structural adjustment and personal social services in Zambia: the case of urban poverty. Social Development and Urban Poverty, 1995, 81–88.

Thurow, L.C. 1996. The future of capitalism: how today's economic forces shape tomorrow's world. William Morrow and Company, Inc., New York, NY, USA.

Torres, M.A. 1995. Conclusion: Social policy in a time of uncertainty. In Morales-Gomez, D.; Torres, M.A., ed. Social policy in a global society. International Development Research Centre, Ottawa, ON, Canada. pp. 205–221.

Tungaraza, F. 1990. The development of social policy in Tanzania. Journal of Social Development in Africa, 5(2), 61–71.

UNDESIPA (United Nations Department of Economic and Social Information and Policy Analysis). 1996. World population prospects: the 1996 revision. Population Division, UNDESIPA, New York, NY, USA.

UNDP (United Nations Development Programme). 1991. The social dimensions of the structural adjustment programme. UNDP, Harare, Zimbabwe.

————— 1992. Human Development Report. 1992. Oxford University Press, New York, NY, USA.

————— 1993. Human development report 1993. Oxford University Press, New York, NY, USA.

————— 1996. Human development report 1996. Oxford University Press, New York, NY, USA. 229 pp.

UNESCAP (United Nations Economic and Social Commission for Asia and the Pacific). 1990. Government–NGO cooperation in social development. Proceedings, Seminar on Cooperation Between Government Agencies and Non-Governmental Organizations in the Planning and Delivery of Social Services, 1990, Hong Kong. UNESCAP, Bangkok, Thailand. 449 pp.

————— 1991a. Enhancing the role of NGOs in the implementation of the Agenda for Action on Social Development in the ESCAP Region. United Nations, New York, NY, USA. 65 pp.

————— 1991b. Proceedings, 4th Asian and Pacific Ministerial Conference on Social Welfare and Social Development, 7–11 Oct. 1991. United Nations, New York, NY, USA. 298 pp.

————— 1992a. Social development strategy for the ESCAP Region towards the year 2000 and beyond. United Nations, New York, NY, USA. 44 pp.

————— 1992b. Towards a social development strategy for the ESCAP Region. United Nations, New York, NY, USA. 226 pp.

————— 1994. Social development agenda for the ESCAP Region in the twenty-first century. Meeting of Senior Officials, 12–15 Oct 1994, Manila, Philippines. UNESCAP, Bangkok, Thailand. 22 pp.

————— 1995. Manila Declaration on the Agenda for Action on Social Development in the ESCAP Region. United Nations, New York, NY, USA. 44 pp.

————— 1996. Steps taken in the implementation of the Agenda for Action on Social Development in the ESCAP Region. UNESCAP, Bangkok, Thailand. 49 pp.

————— 1997. Population and development indicators for Asia an the Pacific. United Nations, New York, NY, USA.

UNESCO (United Nations Educational, Scientific and Cultural Organization). 1995. Statistical yearbook. UNESCO, Paris, France; Bernan Press, Lanham, MD, USA.

UNHCR (United Nations High Commissioner for Refugees). 1993. The state of the world's refugees. Penguin Books, New York, NY, USA.

United Nations. 1994. World urbanization prospects: the 1994 revision. United Nations, New York, NY, USA. Document ST/ESA/SER.A/150.

————— 1995. The Copenhagen Declaration and Programme of Action. World Summit for Social Development, 6–15 Mar 1995. United Nations, New York, NY, USA.

————— 1996a. Levels and trends of contraceptive use as assessed in 1994. United Nations, New York, NY, USA. Document ST/ESA/SER.A/146.

————— 1996b. Population and vital statistics report. 1 Jul. United Nations, New York, NY, USA.

UNRISD (United Nations Research Institute for Social Development). 1995 Adjustment, globalization and social development. Report to the International Seminar on Economic Restructuring and Social Policy, 11–13 Jan 1995, New York, NY, USA. UNRISD–United Nations Development Programme. UNRISD, Geneva, Switzerland.

————— 1997. Globalization and citizenship. Report of the UNRISD International Conference on Globalization and Citizenship, 9–11 Dec 1997. UNRISD, Geneva, Switzerland.

Uthoff, A. 1995. Pension system reform in Latin America. CEPAL Review, 56 (Aug), 43–60.

Van den Ham, A. 1989. An analysis of a strategic development framework in Indonesia. Regional Development Dialogue, 10, 218–227.

Van Rooy, A. 1995. A partial promise? Canadian support to social development in the South. North–South Institute, Ottawa, ON, Canada.

Ventriss, C. 1989. The internationalization of public administration and public policy: implications for teaching. Policy Studies Review, 8.

Viet Nam. 1992. 7th National Party Congress document. SU THAT Publishing House, Hanoi, Viet Nam. 34 pp.

Vilas, C.M. 1996. Neoliberal social policy: managing poverty (somehow). NACLA Report on the Americas, 29(6), 16–25.

Visscher, C. de. 1957. Theory and reality in public international law. Princeton University Press, Princeton, NJ, USA.

Vivian, J. 1995. How safe are social safety nets? Adjustment and social sector restructuring in developing countries. European Journal of Development Research, 7(1), 1–25.

Wallerstein, I. 1995. After liberalism. New Press, New York, NY, USA.

Watkins, B. 1995. The Oxfam poverty report. Oxfam, Oxford, UK.

WCEFA (World Council on Education for All). 1990. Meeting basic learning needs: a vision for the 1990s. United Nations Children's Fund, New York, NY, USA. 164 pp.

Whitehead, A. 1925. Science and the modern world. Macmillan, New York, NY, USA.

WHO (World Health Organization). 1989. Global strategy for health for all by the year 2000. Second Report on Monitoring Progress in Implementing Strategies for Health For All. WHO, Geneva. Switzerland. A42/4.

WHO; UNICEF (World Health Organization; United Nations Children's Fund). 1996. Estimates of maternal mortality: a new approach by WHO and UNICEF. WHO, Geneva, Switzerland.

Williams, F. 1989. Social policy: a critical introduction. Polity Press, Cambridge, MA, USA.

Wolin, S.S. 1960. Politics and vision: continuity and innovation in Western political thought. Little, Brown, Boston, MA, USA.

World Bank. 1991. World development report 1991. Oxford University Press, Oxford, UK.

————— 1993a. The East Asian miracle. Oxford University Press, New York, NY, USA.

————— 1993b. The Social Dimensions of Adjustment program: a general assessment. Social Dimensions of Adjustment Steering Committee, Washington, DC, USA.

————— 1994. Adjustment in Africa: reform, results, and the road ahead. Oxford University Press, New York, NY, USA. World Bank Policy Research Report.

————— 1995a. Global economic prospects and the developing countries: 1995. World Bank, Washington, DC, USA.

————— 1995b. Priorities and strategies for education: a World Bank review. World Bank, Washington, DC, USA.

————— 1995c. World development report. Oxford University Press, Oxford, UK.

————— 1996. World development report. Oxford University Press, Oxford, UK.

Zaiter, J. 1997. Civil society and educational reform: the Dominican experience. In Álvarez, B.; Ruiz-Casares, M., ed., Paths of change: education reforms underway in Latin America and the Caribbean. United States Agency for International Development, Washington, DC, USA. pp. 23–44.

Zeleza, T. 1994. A modern economic history of Africa, vol. I: the nineteenth century. Council for the Development of Economic and Social Research in Africa, Dakar, Senegal.

Zhang, J.; Zhang, J. 1995. The effects of social security on population and output growth. Southern Economic Journal, 62(2), 440–450.